The Fundamentals of Sacred Theology

The Fundamentals of Sacred Theology

Campegius Vitringa Sr.

Translated by Levi Berntson

Reformation Heritage Books
Grand Rapids, Michigan

Reformation Heritage Books
3070 29th St. SE
Grand Rapids, MI 49512
616-977-0889
orders@heritagebooks.org
www.heritagebooks.org

Printed in the United States of America
24 25 26 27 28 29/10 9 8 7 6 5 4 3 2 1

Library of Congress Cataloging-in-Publication Data

Names: Vitringa, Campegius, 1659-1722, author. | Berntson, Levi, translator.
Title: The fundamentals of sacred theology / Campegius Vitringa Sr. ; translated by
    Levi Berntson.
Other titles: Aphorismi, quibus fundamenta santae theologiae comprehenduntur.
    English
Description: Grand Rapids, Michigan : Reformation Heritage Books, [2024] |
    Translation of: Aphorismi, quibus fundamenta santae theologiae comprehenduntur.
    Franeker : Johannes Gyelaar, 1688. | Includes bibliographical references.
Identifiers: LCCN 2024009870 (print) | LCCN 2024009871 (ebook) |
    ISBN 9798886861136 (paperback) | ISBN 9798886861143 (epub)
Subjects: LCSH: Theology, Doctrinal—Quotations, maxims, etc.—Early works to 1800.
Classification: LCC BT77.3 .V5813 2024 (print) | LCC BT77.3 (ebook) | DDC
    230/.42—dc23/eng/20240328
LC record available at https://lccn.loc.gov/2024009870
LC ebook record available at https://lccn.loc.gov/2024009871

To Jordan, my beloved wife,
and to Thea Felicity, my darling daughter

Contents

Translator's Preface
and Acknowledgments

During my second year at Reformed Theological Seminary (Jackson, Mississippi), I was on a mission. Like any good seminary student searching for a doctoral research topic, I was keenly aware of my need to find something on which to write when I finished my seminary education and moved on to doctoral studies. Naturally, important figures in the history of the church quickly came to mind, such as Martin Luther (1483–1546) and John Calvin (1509–1564). But, as one might expect, writing on such figures proves to be a very large task, and there are many other figures in history that are worthy of serious investigation and consideration. It was at this point in my initial inquiry that one of my professors, John Fesko, introduced me to this late seventeenth-century Dutch theologian.

My first exposure to Campegius Vitringa (1659–1722) was Charles Telfer's translation of Vitringa's *The Spiritual Life*.[1] This is a wonderful little work on Christian piety, which includes instructions on prayer, worship, singing, discipline, and other very practical considerations. The work also included a brief biography of Vitringa, and the impressive life of the man struck me. Shortly thereafter, I came upon a copy of Telfer's dissertation on Vitringa's exegetical methodology, and the content of this work also caught my attention.[2] I discovered that there

---

1. Campegius Vitringa, *The Spiritual Life*, trans. Charles K. Telfer (Grand Rapids: Reformation Heritage Books, 2018).

2. Charles K. Telfer, *Wrestling with Isaiah: The Exegetical Methodology of Campegius Vitringa (1659–1722)*, Reformed Historical Theology 38 (Göttingen: Vandenhoeck & Ruprecht, 2016).

was great overlap between the strengths and contributions of Vitringa and my own research interests. As will be observed below, Vitringa was a master of the biblical languages (Hebrew, Aramaic, and Greek), and I, too, have a profound interest in these studies. Vitringa also contributed greatly to the developing field of post-Reformation hermeneutics (biblical interpretation), which is also an interest of mine. But further, Vitringa has an impressive ability to move from exegesis to biblical and dogmatic theological concerns, and even to a seamless application of these truths to the Christian life. These characteristics of Vitringa's work will be explained in more detail below, but I note them here in passing because they have fueled my own appreciation for his work.

I originally began the translation of this work as the first step of my dissertation because, of all his works, Vitringa's *The Fundamentals of Sacred Theology* (1688) most summarily and succinctly articulates his views on theological topics.[3] This work was written only a few years after he took the position as theology professor at the University of Franeker. In this work, Vitringa includes no Scripture references, so when he quotes or alludes to a Scripture passage, I provide these references in the footnotes. For the sake of modern English readers, I have also moved the Hebrew and Greek to the footnotes and have provided translations or transliterations in the body of the text instead. Further, this 1688 edition of Vitringa's theology was eventually expanded into nine large, annotated volumes entitled, *The Doctrine of the Christian Religion*.[4] For this reason, I have added footnote references throughout this translation that direct the reader to Vitringa's later discussion in the larger work (footnotes labeled as *Doctrina*). Finally, I have included at the end of this volume a bibliography of primary and secondary sources for those readers who are interested in diving deeper into Vitringa in particular or this period of Dutch theology in general.

This project would not have been possible were it not for the gracious help of others. I would like to thank my undergraduate Latin

---

3. Campegius Vitringa, *Aphorismi, Quibus Fundamenta Santae Theologiae Comprehenduntur* (Franeker: Johannes Gyelaar, 1688).

4. Campegius Vitringa, *Doctrina Christianae Religionis: Per Aphorismos Summatim Descripta*, ed. Martin Vitringa, 6th ed., 9 vols. (Arnhem: Joannes Henricus Möelemann; Leiden: Joannes le Mair; 1761–1786).

instructor, Brett Saunders, who faithfully taught me Latin for two years during my time at John Witherspoon College (Rapid City, South Dakota), even though I was the only one in the class for most of my time under his language tutelage. I also desire to express gratitude to John Fesko for encouraging me to begin this work during my studies at RTS, and for directing me toward Vitringa as a dissertation subject. I am also deeply grateful to Reformation Heritage Books and everyone there for being willing to publish this title, and for offering their team and services to edit, format, and bring this work to the press. Additionally, I am thankful to Reformation Bible College (Sanford, Florida)—where I teach theology, philosophy, church history, and Latin—for allowing me the time to work on this project. I am very appreciative to one of my students at RBC, Meredith Grouse, for her exceptional artistic abilities in gifting to me a drawing of Vitringa (included below). But most of all, I would like to thank my dear wife, Jordan, and my daughter, Thea Felicity, for putting up with my long hours translating, researching, and editing. Without their support, this work would not have come to fruition, and so it is to Jordan and Thea that I dedicate this work.

Levi Berntson
November 2022

Campegius Vitringa Sr. (1659–1722)

Drawing by Meredith Grouse (August 2022).
Used by permission.

Introduction to
Campegius Vitringa Sr. (1659–1722)

One curiosity of history is the way in which certain figures are remembered and others are forgotten. For example, many consider John Calvin (1509–1564) to be one of the most important Reformed theologians in the Reformation era. But Calvin was not the only Reformed thinker, nor is he the only figure of his age worthy of study. There were others like Ulrich Zwingli (1484–1531), Heinrich Bullinger (1504–1575), and Peter Martyr Vermigli (1499–1562), to name a few.[1] On the other hand, there are other Reformed thinkers who were also incredibly influential in their own day, whose names were forgotten as the centuries passed. One such thinker is the Dutch theologian Campegius Vitringa Sr. (1659–1722).

Shortly after Vitringa's death, Theodor Hase (1682–1731), professor of theology at Bremen, wrote a short biography of Vitringa's life, and he penned this poem about Vitringa's death:

> O sober men, has Campegius Vitringa come to life,
>> a delight for good men,
>> a torch of the learned
>> and the head of a chorus?
> Not here, O Frisians, is he hidden from us, O Athenians,[2]
>> as anguish weakens your glorious walls.

---

1. For more on this point, see Richard A. Muller, *After Calvin: Studies in the Development of a Theological Tradition*, Oxford Studies in Historical Theology (Oxford: Oxford University Press, 2003).

2. It was not uncommon during this period for the Dutch to refer to the Netherlands in general, or Franeker in particular, as an "Athens," warring over the intellectual battles of

Where there is reward for the studious,
 where there are lovers of piety,
  a public anguish resounds in this vast sphere.
Immense defeat, and irreparable loss has come,
  After which the days are not shortly redeemed.
Yet, although Campegius Vitringa has passed this world,
  I know that Campegius Vitringa lives.[3]

Anton Friedrich Büsching (1724–1793), a German translator of Vitringa's works, states that Vitringa's writings "have been useful both to the church and to the scholarly world, and their great worth will continue to be appreciated in the ages to come."[4]

Given such testimonies from his contemporaries, his modern obscurity remains somewhat curious. There are perhaps at least two reasons why Vitringa has been less than well-known as an influential Reformed theologian of the post-Reformation era. First, Vitringa was a professor at the University of Franeker in Friesland (Netherlands). In Vitringa's day, Franeker was one of the most prestigious universities in the Dutch world, with students flocking into Vitringa's classroom from all over Europe, including England. But Franeker was also a place where the new philosophy of the Frenchman René Descartes (1596–1650) gripped most of the theology faculty. Descartes's thinking emphasized the role of reason and certainty, and subsequently philosophy and theology began to attribute a much higher status to reason. Many theologians who were skeptical of this new philosophy were quickly swept under the rug of irrelevance. Vitringa was one who pushed against some of the new philosophy, and this might have invited his obsolescence. Alternatively, Vitringa may have been viewed with suspicion by others outside Franeker because of his own association with the university and its bent toward Cartesianism.[5]

---

the time. See Jonathan Israel, *Radical Enlightenment: Philosophy and the Making of Modernity, 1650–1750* (Oxford: Oxford University Press, 2001), 3.

3. In Vitringa, preface to *Doctrina Christianae Religionis*, vol. 1. Translation mine. This last line is either a subtle reference to Campegius Vitringa Jr., (1693–1723), or to Vitringa Sr.'s presence in heaven.

4. Translated and quoted in Telfer, *Wrestling with Isaiah*, 11.

5. For more on the theology and philosophy of Franeker University, see Johannes van den Berg, "Theology in Franeker and Leiden in the Eighteenth Century," in *Religious*

Another possible reason for history's neglect of Vitringa is that his works, especially his major works, have not been translated. There are a few short works in English which will appear below, but modern readers find his works hidden beyond a seemingly impenetrable wall of solid Latin. He wrote widely, including commentaries on biblical books like Isaiah and Revelation, dogmatic works like the present one, historical works, exegetical tool books, practical handbooks, and many other volumes. All of these are extremely helpful resources, but they have yet to be translated into English.[6] As such, the present work takes a step toward remedying this situation for English readers.

This introduction to Vitringa will provide a brief biography of his life, followed by several lessons for scholars, pastors, and all Christians today, as well as a brief historical survey of the present work.

A Brief Biography

Campegius Vitringa was born on May 16, 1659, in Leeuwarden, Friesland.[7] His father, Horatius, was a high-ranking city official with a deep love for the Protestant faith. As he grew, Vitringa exemplified a deep and skilled intellect, he was quickly recognized as a brilliant young man, and he thoroughly impressed his teachers. He so mastered both Latin and Greek, reading through the New Testament four times in his middle school years, that his teacher added Hebrew to his studies, and he excelled in this as well. It was at this time that Vitringa was exposed to the teaching of Herman Witsius (1636–1708), who was preaching regularly at a church in Leeuwarden. Later in his life, Vitringa would offer an oration so moving that it brought Witsius to

---

Currents and Cross-Currents: Essays on Early Modern Protestantism and the Protestant Enlightenment, Studies in the History of Christian Thought 45, ed. Heiko A. Oberman (Leiden: Brill, 1999), 253–67; W. B. S. Boeles, *Frieslands Hoogeschool en het Rijks Athenaeum te Franeker*, 2 vols. (Leeuwarden: H. Kuipers, 1878); Jacob van Sluis, *The Library of Franeker University in Context, 1585–1843*, Library of the Written Word 81 (Leiden: Brill, 2020).

6. A few of these works were translated into other languages, especially Dutch.

7. Much of this brief biography of Vitringa comes from Telfer, *Wrestling with Isaiah*, 23–41; Anton Friedrich Büsching, "The Life and Work of Campegius Vitringa Sr. 1659–1722," in *The Spiritual Life*, xxiii–xli; J. J. van der Sleen, "Johannes Coccejus en Campegius Vitringa: Een Vergelijking van hun Theologie op Hoofdpunten" (University of Utrecht, Thesis, 2001), 5–9; and Willem Frederik Caspar Johannes van Heel, "Campegius Vitringa Sr. als Godgeleerde beschouwd" (PhD Diss., 1865), 26–34.

tears. Vitringa recalled that he had many fond memories of Witsius's theological instruction, and that Witsius had gone above and beyond the call of duty to make sure that his pupils understood the basic doctrines of the Christian faith. Vitringa joked, however, that Witsius's lectures were occasionally conducive less toward piety than toward indigestion![8] But he deeply appreciated Witsius's instruction, which continued after he left Leeuwarden when Witsius took up a professorship at the University of Franeker.

The University of Franker was an important institution in Friesland. Founded in 1585, this university boasted a theological and classical liberal arts education, drawing many students, especially in light of the various theological debates like the Arminian controversy at the beginning of the seventeenth century.[9] Vitringa studied at Franeker beginning in 1675, which was the same year that Witsius began teaching theology there. Vitringa continued his education at Franeker for three years, focusing on the subjects of Hebrew and theology. After this, he went on to the University of Leiden, where he had to wade through various philosophical and theological controversies, such as the views of Descartes and Johannes Cocceius (1603–1669, discussed below).

After he finished his studies at Leiden, Vitringa immediately began his service to the church and then to the academy. He was first received as a candidate for pastoral ministry and began preaching for several months in his hometown of Leeuwarden. News of his eloquence and brilliance soon earned him a call as professor of Hebrew and Oriental languages at the University of Franeker on August 19, 1680, the same year that Witsius left Franeker to take a place on the theology faculty at Utrecht. Only a couple of years later, Vitringa was also called to become professor of theology at Franeker, finding himself with two professorships while still in his twenties. Nearly a decade later, he was offered a third professorship in Sacred History.

As Vitringa's fame spread, the University of Utrecht attempted to recruit him to join their faculty, but a series of political events thwarted

---

8. Vitringa, preface to *Doctrina Christianae Religionis*, vol. 1.

9. H. J. Selderhuis, ed., *Handbook of Dutch Church History* (Göttingen: Vandenhoeck & Ruprecht, 2014), 230.

their efforts. When Utrecht tried again, Vitringa decided to stay at Franeker, even though he was offered a more handsome salary. Ultimately, he stayed at Franeker for his entire teaching career—a sum of forty-one years. By all accounts, his students were quite fond of him, and they highly valued the opportunity to study under him.[10]

Aside from Vitringa's mastery of theology and church history, his supreme expertise in the biblical languages was one of his greatest strengths. He firmly grasped not only Latin and Greek, but also Hebrew and Aramaic, both biblical and rabbinic. On occasion, he would even create brand-new Latin words to catch the potency of the Hebrew or Greek terms in Scripture more forcefully. Vitringa was also a true advocate of liberal and classical education. Against those who argued for a shorter theological education for ministers, he maintained that it ought to be rigorous and intense, encompassing a wide range of subjects which included the liberal arts.

Yet with all Vitringa's academic achievements, his heart was not detached from his head. By all accounts, Vitringa was a deeply pious man. He believed that right doctrine leads to right practice. His exegesis of the Scriptures was meant to instill a life of godliness, which he exemplified in his work. In his debates with Herman Alexander Röell (1653–1718), whom he thought put too much emphasis on reason in theology, Vitringa distinguished himself as one who never lost his temper, always conducting himself with charity. Likewise, during the debates between the Cocceians and the Voetians, Vitringa was able to navigate the tumultuous waters with smooth and levelheaded sails.

With regard to his personal life, Vitringa had a happy marriage to a minister's daughter, Wilhelmina (1660–1728), and the two had five children together: Simon, Horatius, Hortatius (so-named because his older brother died at a young age), Campegius Jr., and Joanna Margeretha. Campegius Jr. (1693–1723) was a very bright young man who eventually earned his own professorship alongside his father at Franeker (1715–1723), a professorship which lasted until a deadly illness took his life only one year after the death of his father.

---

10. For accounts from Vitringa's students, see Ferenc Postma, "Campegius Vitringa Professzor," *Könyv és Könyvtár* 20 (1998): 151–61.

Throughout his life, Vitringa suffered with his health. According to Büsching, "Vitringa's body was weak and frail, but God furnished him with many gifts."[11] His biographers attribute his poor health to his habit of overworking and studying at night. His eyes became weak with excessive reading, and over the years he developed a stoop in his back from copious writing. He also had a nasty ear infection that rendered his auditory functions largely incapacitated, and eventually he suffered a stroke that brought about his death on March 21, 1722.

Commenting summarily on the life of this man, Büsching writes:

> Vitringa is indisputably considered one of the greats. He gained respect and a lasting name not only for his sincere godliness but also for his broad and deep scholarship and his great service to the church. I hope that distant posterity learns about his life and background, his excellent writings, and his commendable character qualities.[12]

The kind of hope expressed in this sentiment is the ground for this present volume which seeks to appreciate Vitringa's work in general and his *The Fundamentals of Sacred Theology* in particular. Having briefly treated his life, the next section turns to Vitringa's example for the modern Christian in both doctrine and practice.

Vitringa's Biblical, Theological, and Pastoral Example

One of the wonderful blessings of studying history is the great plethora of Christian examples which one may discover. Vitringa is no exception, for his strengths are remarkably applicable for the imitation of all modern Christians—whether scholars, pastors, or laypeople. This section seeks to capture several ways in which Vitringa serves as a commendable example for readers today.

A Sage of the Biblical Languages

Anyone who reads but one of Vitringa's works will inevitably become aware of his imminent mastery of the biblical languages. Those who have poured themselves over his literary corpus—especially his exegetical works—have certainly given testimony to this fact. Albert

---

11. Büsching, "Life and Work," xxxvi.

12. Büsching, "Life and Work," xxiii.

Schultens (1686–1750), a student of Vitringa's who became one of the most important Dutch philologists of the eighteenth century, exclaims: "The public acclaims you, Campegius Vitringa, as one of the greatest examples of interpreters."[13] Another important philologist, Wilhelm Gesenius (1786–1842), expressed his great appreciation for Vitringa's mastery of the languages.[14] Even the Princeton philologist Joseph Addison Alexander (1809–1860) summarizes his own admiration of Vitringa's philology in its time:

> So complete is Vitringa's exposition [of Isaiah] even now, that nothing more would be required to supply the public want but the additional results of more profound and extensive philological investigation during the last century.[15]

Vitringa's love for the original languages of God's Word stems directly from his high view of Scripture. He explains that Scripture is of divine origin, and its authority is not based on any man or church, but solely based on God's own authority (§21–23). In his view, therefore, when the biblical author speaks, it is the Holy Spirit who speaks (§953–54), and so when any Scripture speaks, the Holy Spirit speaks (§980). While traditions and ecclesiastical gatherings are helpful, all matters of doctrine and practice must rest on the authority of Scripture alone (§23, 978). Because Vitringa has such a high regard for every word of Holy Scripture, he believes that understanding those words as deeply as possible is critical for biblical exposition. For him, knowledge of Hebrew and Greek is one of the most important tools that a Christian pastor and scholar can possess. Of course, translating Scripture into the language of every Christian is a necessary endeavor for those who do not have the ability to learn the original languages, but this does not dampen Vitringa's enthusiasm.

Vitringa manifests this love for the biblical languages on almost every page of *The Fundamentals of Sacred Theology*. When he enters into a new theological subject, he follows the standard scholastic method

---

13. Quoted in Büsching, "Life and Work," xxxv.

14. Wilhelm Gesenius, *Commentar über Jesaia* (Leipzig: F. C. W. Vogel, 1821), 1:132–33.

15. Joseph A. Alexander, *The Prophecies of Isaiah*, New and Revised, 2 vols. (New York: Charles Scribner & Co., 1870), 1:38.

of carefully defining the terms of the discussion, and so he consistently lists the various Hebrew and Greek words related to a doctrine. It is this careful analysis of each biblical word that sets the tone for his theological reflection. For example, when discussing the subject of sin, Vitringa explains that the Hebrew words behind the concept of *sin* describe it as a *debt* before God (§701). This sets the stage for his discussion of justification as a *forensic* or *legal* concept of a substitution which pays the debt of sin (§752, 768), laying the groundwork for the doctrine of double imputation: Christ receives the believer's sin, and the believer receives Christ's righteousness. This kind of careful examination of the biblical vocabulary was a key part of the Reformed polemic against Rome in Vitringa's day. Roman Catholic theologians were doing everything they could do to defend the doctrine of justification proposed at the Council of Trent, which denied double imputation. Vitringa's argument rests primarily on a careful treatment of the Hebrew and Greek terms, grounding his theology in careful exegesis of the original languages. Vitringa understood, as Martin Luther (1483–1546) did before him, that the Protestant doctrine of justification rests on the original languages. It cannot be defended without them.

Another example of Vitringa's expertise in the languages is found in his doctrine of the covenants. In one place, he offers an argument for what he calls the *testament* of the Father and the Son, or what is more generally known as the covenant of redemption. This covenant is a covenant between the members of the Trinity, and it provides the foundation for the covenant of grace. While arguing for the covenant of redemption, Vitringa makes his case based on his careful reading of the New Testament in Greek by pointing to Luke 22:29, which states that Jesus "appoints" a kingdom to the disciples just as the Father "appointed" Him a kingdom. Vitringa explains that the word *appoint* in the Greek is simply the verbal form of the word for *covenant*.[16] So, the text literally says that the Father "covenanted" a kingdom to the Son. For Vitringa, this is clear proof that there is a covenant between the members of the Trinity (§384).

---

16. διατίθημι.

A Model for Faithful Exegesis

In addition to his careful study and diligent reliance on the biblical languages, Vitringa worked tirelessly to develop and employ a precise exegetical method for interpreting Scripture. His main focus was on the interpretation of biblical prophecy, especially in Isaiah, and his method won him the praise of many other commentators in subsequent centuries. Büsching provides a series of glowing testimonies from Vitringa's contemporaries about his Isaiah commentary, including Johann Joachim Lange (1670–1744), who states, "In terms of exegetical method, exposition and laying the foundations for a proper understanding of…Isaiah, the best and most excellent commentary of the famous Dutch theologian Campegius Vitringa stands out," and Johann Franz Buddeus (1667–1729) who calls it a "model of a perfect commentary in every respect."[17] Ernst Friedrich Karl Rosenmüller (1768–1835), the great German orientalist at Leipzig, frequently interacts with Vitringa's work.[18] In the English-speaking world, John Gill (1697–1771), a particular Baptist in England, explicitly expresses his own reliance on Vitringa's work in his Isaiah commentary,[19] the Princetonian Alexander interacts with Vitringa on almost every verse of Isaiah,[20] and Vitringa's commentary is even esteemed by contemporary interpreters.[21]

In Vitringa's day, one of the biggest debates surrounding biblical exegesis was the interpretation of fulfilled biblical prophecies. One popular exegete who took an extreme position on prophetic fulfillment was Hugo Grotius (1583–1645), who emphasized the literal context of the Old Testament prophecies such that he almost completely

---

17. Büsching, "Life and Work," xxxv.

18. Ernst Friedrich Karl Rosenmüller, *Scholia in Vetus Testamentum*, 16 vols. (Leipzig: Joh. Ambros. Barthius, 1808–1830). His exposition of Isaiah is in vols. 1–3.

19. John Gill, *An Exposition of the Old Testament*, 4 vols. (London: W. Clowes, 1810); Raymond C. Ortlund Jr., "John Gill as Interpreter of the Old Testament," in *The Life and Thought of John Gill (1697–1771): A Tercentennial Appreciation*, ed. Michael A. G. Haykin, Studies in the History of Christian Thought 77 (Leiden: Brill, 1997), 111.

20. Alexander, *The Prophecies of Isaiah*.

21. Carl Friedrich Keil and Franz Delitzsch, *Isaiah*, Biblical Commentary on the Old Testament 26 (London: T&T Clark, 1892); Brevard S. Childs, "Hermeneutical Reflections on Campegius Vitringa, Eighteenth-Century Interpreter of Isaiah," in *In Search of True Wisdom: Essays in Old Testament Interpretation in Honour of Ronald E. Clements*, ed. Edward Ball (U.K.: Sheffield Academic Press, 1999), 89–98.

removed Christ from the Old Testament. For him, prophetic fulfillment should be related almost exclusively to historical Israel. On the other side of the debate was Reformed theologian Johannes Cocceius, who saw Christ in so many places in the Old Testament that his exegesis received sharp critique from some Reformed commentators. It is said that "Cocceius found Christ everywhere in the Bible, and Grotius found him nowhere."[22]

In the preface to his Isaiah commentary, Vitringa makes it clear that both Cocceius and Grotius have helpful insights for hermeneutics, but he thought that Cocceius often violated the prophetic author's original intent and Grotius ignored the New Testament authors.[23] Vitringa consistently opposed both extremes. He believed that it is necessary to understand the prophecies of Isaiah as being fulfilled in Christ, because the New Testament says that this is the case. In this, he maintains the analogy of Scripture (namely, that Scripture interprets Scripture) and therefore finds much merit in Cocceius's exegesis. But Vitringa also insisted that this interpretation of the prophecies must be consistent with the intentions of Isaiah himself, the human author of the prophecies. If it were not, then it would be irrational, because the New Testament authors would be taking the prophecies out of context and adding new meaning to them. This then becomes Vitringa's thesis for his magisterial commentary on Isaiah: Christ as the fulfillment of Isaiah's prophecies is both *biblical* (it fits the analogy of Scripture) and *rational* (it fits the original author's intent).

One of the reasons why Vitringa argues that prophetic interpretation should fit both the analogy of Scripture and the original author's intent is because he thinks that it is crucial for defense of the Christian religion against the Jews. He explains,

> We Christians are miserable if, after we have labored and toiled to understand and interpret the Scriptures…the cause of the gospel of Christ has finally been driven back such that *no demonstration* of

---

22. For background, see Ernestine van der Wall, "Between Grotius and Cocceius: The 'Theologia Prophetica' of Campegius Vitringa (1659–1722)," in *Hugo Grotius, Theologian*, ed. G. H. M. Meyjes, Henk J. M. Nellen, and Edwin Rabbie (Leiden: Brill, 1994), 198.

23. Wall thinks that this was due to Witsius's influence on Vitringa. See Wall, "Between Grotius and Cocceius," 202.

the truth of our faith and religion is able to be offered against the Jews from the prophetic Scriptures. *No demonstration*, I say!…For if rational demonstration for the truth of the gospel hangs upon the prophetic writings of the old economy, then it ought to be founded on principles of reason which all mortals have in common among themselves and even the Jews with us. But if here you have recourse to the inspiration and authority of the apostles (whom the Jews not only call into doubt but fiercely deny and reject) then it is plainly absurd and alien to reason that they would be willing to be convinced by any such principle of the truth of our religion which is repugnant to them.[24]

In other words, when arguing with the Jews, Christians cannot merely appeal to the New Testament when interpreting Isaiah, because the Jews do not accept the New Testament as authoritative. Instead, Vitringa's burden is to show that Isaiah's intent as the original author is to point forward to Christ, the Messiah, and that the New Testament authors do not invent but rather confirm this interpretation of Isaiah. This is, for Vitringa, rational interpretation, which the Jews can understand even if they do not accept the authority of the New Testament.

In another work, *Type of Prophetic Doctrine*, Vitringa provides nineteen exegetical principles (or canons) to guide himself and others in this kind of interpretation of prophetic passages.[25] He writes that much like Jesus's parables, the intent of prophecy is both to *conceal* and to *reveal*. Prophecy conceals primarily because it makes copious use of symbolism, which can be frustrating to modern readers, so Vitringa wrote a work (published posthumously) on the interpretation of biblical imagery which is quite helpful even today.[26] But since prophecy also reveals, Vitringa thought that a careful reading of the way that Jesus and the apostles used the Old Testament yields at least nineteen

---

24. Campegius Vitringa, preface to *Commentarius in Jesaiam, Quo Sensus Orationis ejus sedulo Investigatur; in Veras Visorum Interpretandorum Hypotheses Inquiritur, & ex iisdem Facta Interpretatio Antiquae Historiae Monumentis Confirmatur atque Illustratur: Cum Prolegomenis*, Editio Nova (Basel: Joann Rodolph, 1732), 1:12.

25. Campegius Vitringa, *Typus Doctrinae Propheticae* (Bovardia: Joh. Bernhard. Hartung., 1722).

26. Campegius Vitringa, *De Theologia Symbolica Liber Posthumus: Accedit Index Omnium Lacorum S. Scripturae, Quae in Hoc Opusculo Explicantur* (Guilielmus Croon., 1726).

canons for right interpretation which serve to reveal prophetic meaning more clearly.

Vitringa's canons can be divided into four categories. The first category deals with the grammatical-historical context of the prophecy.[27]

1. Good interpreters of prophecy must consider the subject of the prophecy. For example, as the Ethiopian eunuch asked the apostle Philip: Is the prophet speaking about himself or someone else?

2. What are the attributes and characteristics of the subject? Mark them down, take notes, and organize them.

3. A good interpreter must never reject or overshadow the literal (or historical) meaning of the prophecy. Whatever one believes the fulfillment of the prophecy to be, one cannot disregard the historical context and original author's intent.

The second group of canons deals with a possible greater fulfillment of the prophecy that extends beyond the age (and perhaps the knowledge) of the original audience.

4. If the attributes of the subject in canon 2 do not seem to fit any referent in the historical context, then the interpreter must search for a greater subject, or an antitype (1 Peter 3:21).[28]

5. Sometimes, the subject of a prophecy is a mixed subject. One need not necessarily reduce the subject to a single referent, since the subject may be pointing to multiple fulfillments, perhaps one literal and the other figurative. For example, Edom in the prophecy of Obadiah certainly has the historical nation of the Edomites in view, but it also has a final future judgment on all the nations in view as well. Vitringa remarks that this is probably the most important of his canons: "For many years have I spoken highly of this Canon as being of the greatest service in interpreting prophecy."[29] In this way, prophecies with a mixed subject are fulfilled in stages of growing importance: Edom is judged first, and then the nations are judged in the end.

---

27. For an English translation of these canons, see Campegius Vitringa, "On the Interpretation of Prophecy," *The Interpreter* 4 (1835): 153–76.

28. According to Vitringa, 1 Peter 3:21 refers to baptism as an "antitype" (ἀντίτυπον) of the Noahic flood.

29. Vitringa, "On the Interpretation of Prophecy," 158.

The third group of Vitringa's canons helps the interpreter to understand and approach the confusing structure of the prophecies.

6. One must take note of the beginning and the end of prophecies and of prophetic scenes or segments.

7. Biblical prophecies are almost always focused on the beginning and the end of Christ's kingdom, since often these two extremes are placed right alongside each other.

8. It is quite common for prophecies to repeat themselves, or to tell the same event multiple times from different perspectives.

9. The prophets often bounce between subjects without warning, so the reader must remain vigilant for sudden subject changes.

Finally, the last category of canons speaks to the nature of biblical prophecy as ultimately coming from the mouth of God.

10. God is the author of Scripture.

11. The "infallible key"[30] to the interpretation of prophecy is the spiritual nature of the kingdom of Christ—namely, that His kingdom is not of this world.

12. The Old Testament is about Christ.

13. The Old Testament is about the church.

14. The book of Revelation is the key to understanding Old Testament prophecy. Vitringa wrote a massive commentary on Revelation to prove this point, which stretches over one thousand large pages of Latin text.[31]

15. If a prophecy attributes a superlative quality to its subject, then it ultimately refers to the Messiah.

16. Prophecies about the kingdom should be interpreted spiritually.

17. Prophecies are often nonchronological.

18. The apostles may lump multiple prophetic texts together and cite only one author to show the unity of the prophetic message.

---

30. Vitringa, "On the Interpretation of Prophecy," 163.

31. See Campegius Vitringa, *Anakrisis Apocalypsios Joannis Apostoli* (Franeker: Henricus Strickius, 1719).

19. Good interpreters should always be wary of idle curiosity because the prophets do not answer every question that one might have about the future.[32]

Regardless of whether one agrees with each of these canons as he defines them, it is certain that Vitringa put careful and attentive thought to his exegetical methodology. For him, one may not approach Scripture haphazardly, relying merely on intuition. Instead, Vitringa sought to articulate and deploy a method of interpretation that he thought is most faithful to both the analogy of Scripture and the original author's intent.

A Master of Biblical and Dogmatic Theology

As explained above, Vitringa always strove to ground his theological dogmatics in the careful exegesis of Hebrew and Greek Scripture, which not only included careful attention to grammar and syntax, but it also meant that Vitringa was tuned-in to the big picture, with respect to both biblical and dogmatic theology.

With respect to biblical theology, or the study of the covenantal biblical narrative, one writer calls him a "master of biblical theology."[33] Much like his synthesis between Grotius and Cocceius on biblical interpretation, Vitringa's biblical theology is often the result of a careful synthesis between Cocceius and Witsius.

Cocceius was less concerned with dogmatic and philosophical categories, and more with redemptive history as the foundation for his dogmatics. This does not mean that Cocceius ignored philosophy, but he did place a great deal of emphasis on the importance of progressive revelation for doing theology. For example, Cocceius, along with his own mentor, Johannes Cloppenburg (1592–1652), argued that believers in the Old Testament did not have their sins forgiven, but instead

---

32. For more extended discussion of these nineteen canons, see Telfer, *Wrestling with Isaiah*, 99–108; "Campegius Vitringa, Sr. Praefatio ad Lectorem and De Interpretatione Prophetiarum," in *Handbuch der Bibelhermeneutiken* (Boston: Walter de Gruyter, 2016), 433–48.

33. Antonie Vos, "Reformed Orthodoxy in the Netherlands," in *A Companion to Reformed Orthodoxy*, ed. Herman J. Selderhuis, Brill's Companions to the Christian Tradition 40 (Leiden: Brill, 2013), 130.

their sins were "passed over"[34] until Christ came and sin was finally "forgiven."[35] Other theologians like the followers of Gisbertus Voetius (1589–1676) believed that this was an unnecessary distinction because Cocceius was too strongly dividing the Old and New Testaments. For the Voetians, both Old and New Testament saints have full forgiveness of sins. Cocceius, however, believed that he was maintaining the progressive nature of Scripture and salvation history,[36] which earned him the sharp criticism of Herman Bavinck (1854–1921), who chastises Cocceius for prioritizing the covenants at the expense of the divine decree.[37]

Vitringa's tutor, Witsius, took something of a middle ground between the Cocceian and Voetian parties, since he recognized the strengths and excess of both, and he wanted to help solve the dilemma.[38] Vitringa largely followed this example, applying Witsius's mediating tendency even to the disagreements between Cocceius and Witsius. While Cocceius spoke of the "condition" of the covenant of grace as faith, Witsius sided with Voetius, Cloppenburg, and Francis Junius (1545–1602), who argued that there is no condition in this covenant. Grace is unconditional by definition. In turn, Vitringa positions himself between Cocceius and Witsius when he writes of a "quasi-condition," and explains that faith is the condition of the covenant of grace *in a sense*, but one must recognize that God Himself

---

34. πάρεσις.

35. ἄφεσις.

36. Johannes Cocceius, *The Doctrine of the Covenant and Testament of God*, trans. Casey Carmichael, Classic Reformed Theology 3 (Grand Rapids: Reformation Heritage Books, 2016), §339. For more on this controversy, see Brian J. Lee, "The Covenant Terminology of Johannes Cocceius: The Use of Foedus, Pactum, and Testamentum in a Mature Federal Theologian," *Mid-America Journal of Theology* 14 (2003): 11–36; Bruce P. Baugus, "Covenant Theology in the Dutch Reformed Tradition," in *Covenant Theology: Biblical, Theological, and Historical Perspectives*, eds., Guy Prentiss Waters, J. Nicholas Reid, and John R. Muether, (Wheaton, IL: Crossway, 2020), 392–95. For Cloppenburg, see Stephen Strehle, *Calvinism, Federalism, and Scholasticism: A Study of the Reformed Doctrine of Covenant* (Bern: P. Lang, 1988), 215–22.

37. Herman Bavinck, *Reformed Dogmatics*, ed. John Bolt, trans. John Vriend (Grand Rapids: Baker Academic, 2003), 1:185–86.

38. Strehle, *Calvinism, Federalism, and Scholasticism*, 286.

through the effectual grace of the Holy Spirit completely supplies this condition (§431).[39]

With respect to dogmatic theology, not only did Vitringa write his own dogmatics text, *The Fundamentals of Sacred Theology*, but Telfer explains that Vitringa, while commenting on Scripture, engages in brief but frequent theological excurses just as Calvin did in his commentaries. Telfer shows that in his commentary on Isaiah, Vitringa addresses the subjects of theology proper (divine aseity, impassibility, justice, power), anthropology (human depravity), Christology (divinity of Christ, Christ as hermeneutical center of Isaiah, substance of God's promises), soteriology (divine grace necessary for salvation, faith, law, and gospel), worship (idolatry, anti-Rome polemic, Sabbath observance), eschatology (last judgment, eternal punishment, millennium), and ecclesiology (God's people throughout history, two kingdoms).[40]

When controversy arose at Franeker during the late 1680s, Vitringa found himself as the lead defender of orthodox Trinitarian theology in Friesland. At this point in his teaching career, he entered into a series of debates with Röell, who was professor of theology and philosophy at Franeker from 1685 to 1704. Based on a strongly Cartesian doctrine of reason and its application to theology, Röell argued that the second person of the Trinity was true and eternal God, but he was critical of the *eternal generation* of the Son. For Röell, the innate idea of God as the most perfect being (*ens perfectissimum*) functions as the foundation for his doctrines of God and the Trinity. According to this innate idea of God, whatever is divine must be utterly independent since God does not depend on anything else. So, if one divine person is dependent on another divine person for His deity, then this contradicts the independence of God. For this reason, if someone claims that the Son is dependent upon the Father in any way, then this contradicts the clear and distinct notion of God as independent.[41] On this basis, Röell

---

39. Herman Witsius, *The Economy of the Covenants between God and Man*, trans. William Crookshank, 2 vols. (Edinburgh: Thomas Turnbull, 1803; Grand Rapids: Reformation Heritage Books, 2010), 3.1.8–18.

40. Telfer, *Wrestling with Isaiah*, 185–96.

41. Herman Alexander Röell, *Dissertatio Theologica de Generatione Filii, et Morte Fidelium Temporali, qua Suas de iis Theses Plenius Explicat, & contra Clarissimi Viri Campegii Vitringa Objectiones Defendit* (Franeker: Johannes Gyselaar, 1689), 14–15; Röell, *Dissertatio*

argued that there are no eternal processions which distinguish the divine persons, and therefore he also denied that there is any natural order of the three persons in the Godhead.[42] According to him, if one is to speak of the generation of the Son at all, then it only refers to the Son being manifested in the flesh.[43]

Vitringa wrote voluminously against Röell's doctrine, for Vitringa was well-prepared to address this topic from a scriptural perspective, since his doctoral work at Leiden was on the exegetical foundation of the eternal generation of the Son in Psalm 2.[44] In his works, he explicitly identified the generation of the Son and the procession of the Holy Spirit as the *personal properties* of the second and third persons of the triune God, and he rejected any attempt to remove these properties (§126–27). If one removes the personal properties, then the persons are necessarily removed, and therefore there is no Trinity. In his *Standards of Elenctic Theology* (his brief treatment of important polemical issues in theology), Vitringa states that the Father, Son, and Holy Spirit all subsist in one divine essence and unity.[45] But Vitringa also affirms that the second person of the Trinity, the Son, proceeds from the Father from all eternity. This is necessary, it is of the Son's nature, and is what is meant by the term *generation*. He further denies that this generation of the Son in any way necessitates the idea of a created Son of God or implies any less divinity, since the eternally generated Son

---

Theologica Altera de Generatione Filii, et Morte Fidelium Temporali, Opposita Epilogo Clarissimi Viri Campegii Vitringa (Franeker: Johannes Gyselaar, 1690), 33–36, 77–78.

42. Herman Alexander Röell, *Explicatio Catecheseos Heidelbergensis: Opus Postumum*, 4th ed. (Utrecht: Gysbertus van Paddenburg, 1728), 259–69.

43. Röell, *Dissertatio Theologica*, 36–37, 67–69. For more on Röell's theology and the surrounding controversy, see H. J. E. van Hoorn, *Disquisitio Historico-Dogmatica exponens Röelli Litem de Aeterna Generatione Filii Dei a Patre* (Utrecht: Uiterweer & Soc., 1856); Jacob van Sluis, *Herman Alexander Röell* (Leeuwarden: Fryske Akad., 1988), 86–98; Selderhuis, *Handbook*, 375–76; Brannon Ellis, *Calvin, Classical Trinitarianism, and the Aseity of the Son* (Oxford: Oxford University Press, 2012), 127–35.

44. Campegius Vitringa, *Disputatio Theologica Inauguralis de Genuino Sensus Versu VII Psalmi Secundi* (Leiden: Johannes Elsevirius, 1679); Campegius Vitringa, *Disputatio Theologica de Argumento Psalmi Secundi, Secunda* (Leiden: Johannes Elsevirius, 1679).

45. Campegius Vitringa, *Hypotyposis Theologiae Elencticae, Graviores Exhibens Controversias, Quae super Christianae Religionis Doctrina Ecclesiae Reformatae cum Diversis ejusdem Sectis Intercedunt* (Franeker: Franciscus Halama, 1702), 3.1.

is not dependent on anything outside of God Himself.[46] In another work, Vitringa addresses Röell head-on, and goes to great exegetical lengths to debunk Röell's rationalist arguments.[47] In this instance, Vitringa makes himself a commendable example of defending Christian orthodoxy against serious objections.

A Lover of History

Not only did Vitringa hold chairs in Hebrew, Oriental Languages, and Theology at Franeker, but eventually he also became professor of sacred history. Vitringa loved history deeply, because he believed that a knowledge of the past was absolutely critical for all Christians, especially pastors and scholars. He lived this conviction by example in his writings and his exegesis by producing many historical essays and works for the aid of the church, and these collected works appeared in six substantial volumes entitled *Sacred Observations*.[48] He also wrote a history of the ancient world, which covers history from creation to the first-century Christian church. In this work, he explains that all history is sacred history because all of history is centered around God's purpose for His people.[49]

But Vitringa's most important historical-theological work is undoubtedly his massive treatise, *On the Ancient Synagogue*.[50] This work was part of an ongoing debate among Christian churches about

---

46. Vitringa, *Hypotyposis Theologiae Elencticae*, 3.5; Vitringa, *Doctrina Christianae Religionis*, 4.96. For secondary account, see Klaas Marten Witteveen, "Campegius Vitringa und Die Prophetische Theologie," *Zwingliana* 19.2 (1993): 343.

47. Campegius Vitringa, *Epilogus Disputationis, Non Ita Pridem a Se Habitae, De Generatione Filii, et Morte Fidelium Temporali; In Quo Fidem Ecclesiae de His Articulis Porro Adstruit ex Verbo Dei, eandemque Tuetur contra Dissertationem, Illi Novissime Oppositam* (Franeker: Johannes Gyselaar, 1689).

48. Campegius Vitringa, *Sacrarum Observationum*, 6 vols. (Franeker: Johannes Gyselaar; Wibius Bleck, 1689–1708).

49. Campegius Vitringa, *Hypotyposis Historiae et Chronologiae Sacrae* (Bovardia: Joh. Bernhard. Hartung., 1722), 7.

50. Campegius Vitringa, *De Synagoga Vetere Libri Tres: Quibus tum De Nominibus, Structura, Origine, Praefectis, Ministris, & Sacris Synagogarum, Agitur; tum Praecipue, Formam Regiminis & Ministerii earum in Ecclesiam Christianam Translatam esse, Demonstratur: Cum Prolegomenis* (Franeker: Johannes Gyzelaar, 1696). For an English translation and abridgment, see Campegius Vitringa, *The Synagogue and the Church, Being an Attempt to Show, That the Government, Ministers, and Services of the Church, Were Derived from Those of*

church structure and worship practices. After the Reformation, because Protestants had sharply separated from the ecclesiastical structure of Rome, they quickly became interested in discussions about church structure and worship. Roman Catholics and Anglicans like James Ussher (1581–1656) were arguing that the early church derived its structure and worship from Jewish temple worship, and so this is why these traditions were maintaining the customs of priests, altars, and other such practices.[51]

In contrast, Vitringa's *On the Ancient Synagogue* argued that early Christian church structure and worship came directly from the Jewish synagogue, not the temple. Regarding church structure, Vitringa's burden is to show that the early Christian church derived its form of government from the Jewish synagogue structure. Vitringa argues that the church's structure of elders, presiding elders (or pastors), and deacons comes directly from the first-century Jewish synagogue, which was ruled by a council of elders, and each council had a presiding elder who led the rest. Like the church, elders were chosen by the people in the synagogue, and they were ordained by the laying on of hands, signifying the communication of authority indicated in Numbers 27:18. The elders could exercise synagogue discipline and excommunicate unrepentant members by means of a process nearly identical to that found in Matthew 18:15–17. Regarding church worship, every synagogue also had at least one *Chazzan*, or deacon, who was appointed by the elders to oversee the public reading of Scripture. The reading of Scripture followed by expositions of passages was essential to synagogue worship life, along with prayer and public eulogies—all of which were repeated by early Christians in their worship. In this work, one clearly observes Vitringa's careful attention to history's usefulness for exegesis and theology. *On the Ancient Synagogue* quickly became the gold standard on the subject for centuries, and even Princeton theologians cited it.[52]

---

the Synagogue, Condensed from the Original Latin Work of Vitringa, trans. Joshua L. Bernard (London: B. Fellowes, 1842).

51. For background on church government during this period, see Ian Hazlett, "Church and Church/State Relations in the Post-Reformation Reformed Tradition," in *The Oxford Handbook of Early Modern Theology, 1600–1800*, ed. Ulrich L. Lehner, Richard A. Muller, and A. C. Roeber (New York: Oxford University Press, 2016), 242–58.

52. Telfer, *Wrestling with Isaiah*, 29–30.

An Example of Warm and Rich Piety

With all this careful scholarship in the biblical languages, exegesis, theology, and history, one might expect that it would be easy for Vitringa to fall prey to a cold, heartless intellectualism. But Vitringa was no ivory-tower theologian. While he was still a young man, Vitringa experienced the unfortunate fall of one of his tutors, Johannes Wübbena (d. 1681). Wübbena was a gifted philosopher, dubbed the "Foremost Professor of the Philosophy Faculty" at the university of Franeker. Though he was brilliant, he eventually lost his professorship due to frequent absences, poor demeanor, lack of financial management, and promiscuous activity with women. He was arrested, and he died in 1681 while waiting for his trial.[53]

It was experiences like this that had a profound impact on Vitringa's doctrine of Christian piety. Vitringa always strove to make sure that his students understood not only the intellectual duties of theological study but also the duties of piety. In the preface to his *Doctrine of the Christian Religion*, he writes to his students:

> Have you considered whether there is any knowledge in the universe that is more excellent, noble, profitable, and worthy of industry, labor, and energy of the intelligent creature than God Himself, the most noble and most excellent Being, and also the cause of all other things and of us, and of His works? Or what is more beautiful, harmonious, or delightful for man to set forth than to discuss, meditate, understand, and interpret those most pure Words by which God has deemed worthy to deliver His will to mankind? Has there ever been a study of the arts or sciences with which the excellence of this study can be compared? What can be more worthy to consider than *how to be wise*—that is, how to understand most excellent things in the order in which God Himself understands them, whose knowledge and wisdom all mortals admire? And so, in His own Word, God has declared to the church those things in which the most excellent part of divine knowledge are found. And that Word is very *near to us*[54] in our mouths and hearts (Deut. 30:14).[55]

---

53. Harro Buß, "Johannes Wübbena," in *Biographisches Lexikon für Ostfriesland*, ed. Martin Tielke (Aurich: Ostfriesische Landschaft, 2001), 3:441–43.

54. ‫היא לא רהוקה‬.

55. Vitringa, preface to *Doctrina Christianae Religionis*, vol. 1.

In order to do theology, one must become like a child, and trust the sacred Scriptures above all else. Further, the student of God must rely on the Holy Spirit and pursue Christ with faithfulness. Perhaps Vitringa was thinking of his former tutor, Wübbena, when he says,

> But unfortunately, if anything else, many devotees of theology are disgraced here [in their piety], and they disgrace those studies which they have chosen by their morals. They approach these sacred things with unwashed hands, and they do not properly esteem the price of these divine truths. They have a soul which has turned away from God. His virtues and works they hear preached daily. His laws they read and meditate upon. What does it mean to honor God with friendly discourse, and to taste of the heavenly gift of divine grace and the powers of the age to come,[56] to be led, guided, and live by the Holy Spirit, to be sealed by that same Spirit unto a better and eternal life; and then to be humiliated and afflicted because of sins and various infirmities before God? These things and other similar things which they do and absolve to do in the life of the Christian man, they become unwilling to do just as those most ignorant. They strive to separate piety from truth, which Paul teaches are most closely linked together. And since they, being excited to another kind of life by their own precepts or example or exhortations, are often most strongly persuaded that they are walking in pleasure and covenant with God, yet they retain themselves as Augustine says *trifles upon trifles* and *vanities upon vanities* so that they do not give themselves to God and to communion with and the glory of Him *fully* and *wholly*. It is for this reason that they coldly and sluggishly receive theological instruction, but they have no attention or understanding to think about the more difficult things. The precepts pass through their memory after a few hours like a loose strain. And so they both delude the wishes of their parents and friends, and frustrate the expectation of the church.

One can feel Vitringa's passionate plea, for he deeply desires his students to truly understand, embrace, and live the theology that they claim to believe. They must approach the sacred letters with *humility* and *diligence*, and if they do not, then they will not only pollute

---

56. Cf. Hebrews 6:4–6.

themselves, but they will do great damage to their families and to the church of Jesus Christ.

Because Vitringa had such a concern for both scholarship and piety, he wrote several works for both pastors and lay people to help them develop their Christian life. *The Spiritual Life* is a wonderful little handbook on Christian living, in which Vitringa delves into devotional practices for the Christian and explains how to best enrich the mind and soul in private reading of Scripture, prayer, dealing with sin, attending Christian worship, and much more. This work was recently translated into English and is blessing many Christians today. Another important work is his *Guidelines on the Method of Rightly Preparing Sermons for the Church*, which is divided into two parts.[57] The first part deals with the pastoral preparation of public prayers, stating the importance of the minister praying *as one of the people* of the congregation by taking on the persona of the people (specifically the elect). The minister must also offer praise to God for His divine attributes in public prayer—rather than rushing right into requests, he should begin with carefully and beautifully crafted praise. The second part covers guidelines for preparing the sermon itself, in that Vitringa provides instructions for exegeting the text, finding the main point of the text, how to preach dogmatic theology from the text, how to make proper applications from the text, and how to treat paradoxes or mysteries. He also includes chapters on major genres of Scripture such as parables, typology, and historical narrative. In praise of this work, one scholar comments,

> This was the swan song of a most faithful minister of Jesus Christ, whose permanent concern was not for the academy only, but indeed he expended himself for the protection of (and in watchful care for) the church universal. And he made the attempt as his final will, even as he had continually instilled such wise counsels and precepts and such practical discipline into his students, to press the concern on all their minds (even with his voice dying and his hand weak) that by dividing and dispensing the true, solid, vital, living, spiritual, and

---

57. Campegius Vitringa, *Animadversiones ad Methodum Holiliarum Ecclesiasticarum rite Instituendarm* (Franeker: Henricus Halma, 1721).

fully rational word of God in preaching, they were to feed the Lord's flock and to lead them to the springs of living water.[58]

Vitringa won the respect not only of his Reformed brothers, but also of those outside the Reformed faith through his pious life. While treating the doctrine of the Roman Catholic Mass, Vitringa mentions that many of the arguments against that doctrine also apply to the Lutherans and their view of the local presence of Christ in the Lord's Supper. But even while offering this critique, he writes that this disagreement between the Reformed and Lutherans was the "first fruit of strife" among "brothers." And in a statement of theological regret, he wrote, "If only it had never been raised!" (§927). This reveals a love for his Christian brothers that often does not surface in such theological battles. It is perhaps sentiments like these that won Vitringa the praise of Büsching, one of his biographers, who was himself a Lutheran. At the end of Vitringa's biography, Büsching concludes:

> This has been an incomplete description of the praiseworthy qualities of the blessed man. One category in a useful biography seems to be missing—an account of his accompanying faults. I honestly testify that I have not been silent when some of them were known to me, but rather I know none. That the remarkable and accomplished man should err a little in his views, feelings, or outward behavior is easy for anyone to believe. He was just a man. And as with all of us, the greatest prudence and wisdom does not always keep us from missteps. Even great souls err and may be oblivious to their own faults. That Vitringa had such faults I do not doubt. By the grace of God, however, his integrity and accomplishments so predominated when you consider his whole life that the failings are entirely lost from view.[59]

Vitringa continues to speak beyond the grave by the remarkable example which he provides for us. May we, too, live such warm and pious lives that our own theological opponents may say such things about us.

---

58. Büsching, "Life and Work," xxxiv.
59. Büsching, "Life and Work," xli.

This Work

We have titled this present work *The Fundamentals of Sacred Theology*. Vitringa's original title was *Aphorisms which Comprehend the Fundamentals of Sacred Theology*. The first edition of Vitringa's *Aphorisms* was published in 1688, not long after Vitringa's second appointment as professor of theology at Franeker. The *Aphorisms* was originally written for his theology students, serving as the textbook for his lectures in theological dogmatics. It consists of exactly one thousand statements (aphorisms) that summarize theology. It was first published in Latin, and one historian notes: "On the publication of his *Aphorismi* (1688), a work designed to appeal to a general audience…Vitringa became one of the best-known Cocceian theologians in the Republic."[60]

In his preface to the reader, Vitringa indicates that he intentionally tried to make this work as brief as possible. He states that in his day there were already larger and fuller treatments of theology that his students might consult, and that the purpose of this little work was simply for the brief comprehension of the most fundamental statements of the Reformed faith.[61] Vitringa was very clear that he did not want to see this work abused by his students who might be tempted to see it as an end in itself—rather, he wanted them to consult the larger dogmatic treatments available. Vitringa states that the *Aphorisms* is not

---

60. Jonathan I. Israel, *The Dutch Republic: Its Rise, Greatness, and Fall: 1477–1806*, The Oxford History of Early Modern Europe (Oxford: Clarendon Press, 1998), 899.

61. Vitringa never says explicitly what systems that he prefers, but it is possible that he is thinking of at least some of these influential works at Franeker: William Ames, *The Marrow of Theology: Translated from Latin with an Introduction by John Dykstra Eusden*, trans. John D. Eusden (Grand Rapids: Baker Books, 1997); Johannes Cloppenburg, *Exercitationes super Locos Communes Theologicos: Quibus Praecipui Religionis Christianae Articuli Lucide Explicantur, ac ab Adversariorum Corruptelis Nervose Vindicantur* (Franeker: Idzardus Balck, 1563); Johannes Maccovius, *Loci Communes Theologici* (Franeker: Johannes Archerius, 1650); Johannes Marckius, *Compendium Theologiae Christianae Didactico Elencticum: Immixtis Problematibus Plurimis & Quaestionibus Recentioribus Adauctum* (Amsterdam: Borstius, 1690); Johannes Cocceius, *Summa Theologiae ex Scripturis Repetita* (Amsterdam: Joannes Ravesteinius, 1665). Vitringa also mentions his love for the works of Witsius. He may be thinking of Witsius, *De Oeconomia Foederum Dei cum Hominibus Libri Quatuor* (Leeuwarden: Jacob Hagenaar, 1677); Witsius, *Exercitationes Sacrae in Symbolum Quod Apostolorum Dicitur*, 3rd ed. (Amsterdam: Joannes Wolters, 1697). For English translations, see Witsius, *Economy of the Covenants*; Witsius, *Sacred Dissertations: On What Is Commonly Called the Apostles' Creed*, trans. Donald Fraser, 2 vols. (Edinburgh: A. Fullerton, 1823).

a complete system for two reasons. First, he says that his statements lack necessary explanation, since he used the *Aphorisms* as the outline for his theological lectures, and so perhaps he would read each aphorism to his class and then explain it more extemporaneously. Indeed, he expresses that in his lectures he would forget major points in his arguments or omit important terms and concepts without the aid of these aphorisms. In this way, Vitringa is careful to make sure that his readers understand that the *Aphorisms* is not a comprehensive compilation of theology but encompasses only the basics.[62]

Second, in this original edition, Vitringa included no Scripture references.[63] He explains that some of his colleagues advised him not to do this, and to make sure that he included proof texts. But Vitringa did not heed their counsel. The reason he excluded proof texts is because he did not want his students to be reliant on them, for he desired his students to read Scripture for themselves and to find the doctrines there. While one may or may not agree with his reasons, it demonstrates that Vitringa did not want his students to use proof texts as a crutch. Indeed, the purpose of the *Aphorisms* was simply to give a basic outline of the teachings of Scripture, to provide a kind of paradigm through which one may read Scripture. For this reason, Vitringa desired his students to move on from the *Aphorisms* and to plunge themselves into the depths of the Word of God, thereby knowing God's Word in its context by careful reading and not by a list of isolated selections. In later editions, however, Vitringa did add proof texts to his discussions, probably at the insistence of his students.

The 1688 edition of the *Aphorisms* was only the first of a total of five more Latin editions (1690, 1693, 1702, 1714, 1760) and four Dutch editions (1696, 1708, 1717, 1736). In each subsequent edition, Vitringa expanded his thoughts and included more material. Eventually, because the work grew so much, Vitringa decided to change the title to *The Doctrine of the Christian Religion* (*Doctrina Christianae Religionis*).

The final and definitive edition of Vitringa's *Doctrina* was published several decades after his death. In this sixth and final edition,

---

62. See Vitringa, "Greeting to His Readers" below, p. 9.

63. Throughout the translation below, whenever Vitringa quotes or alludes to a biblical passage, the Scripture reference is provided in the footnotes.

Vitringa's *Doctrina* was published in nine large volumes with much editorial material added, though it should still not be considered as a full system like that of Amandus Polanus (1561–1610) or Peter van Mastricht (1630–1706).[64] Vitringa's great-nephew, Martin Vitringa (n.d.), undertook the task of producing this new edition. In his preface to the new edition, Martin mentions that before he was inspired to begin this task, he had spent long hours burning midnight oil as he poured over Vitringa's commentary on Zechariah,[65] and he found abundant spiritual benefit in his great-uncle's work. He also recounts that as he browsed the local book shops, he was delighted to discover a copy of Vitringa's *Doctrina* on a shelf in the store. While conversing with the bookstore clerk, he discovered that the text was greatly desired in the academies of the day, and that the bookstores were unable to meet the demand for it. The bookstore clerk begged Martin to begin the task of producing a new edition of the work for a new generation of theology students. Thus, he felt a "duty" to again publish "this synopsis of celestial truth."[66]

Martin undertook the task, and the first of nine volumes appeared in 1761. In this new edition of Vitringa's *Doctrina*, Martin included a brand-new preface, prolegomena, analysis, and annotations throughout the work. In all subsequent volumes, large annotations continued to be appended to the original body of the text. These annotations were not original to Vitringa's own work but were written and added by Martin as supplemental aid for theology students. Martin explains in the preface that he spent long hours poring over theological libraries to provide the diligent reader with much information. The annotations were designed to expand whatever subject of theology that Vitringa himself treated in

---

64. See Amandus Polanus, *Syntagma Theologiae Christianae ab Amando Polano a Polandsdorf iuxta Leges Ordinis Methodici Conformatum atque in Libros Decem Tributum,* 10 vols. (Hanau: Johannes Aubrius, 1609); Petrus van Mastricht, *Theoretico-practica theologia: qua, per capita theologica, pars dogmatica, elenchtica et practica, perpetua sumbibasei conjugantur; præcedunt in usum operis, paraleipomena, seu sceleton de optima concionandi methodo,* 2 vols. (Amsterdam: Henricus et Vidua Theodorus Boom, 1682–87). For English translation, see Van Mastricht, *Theoretical-Practical Theology,* trans. Todd Rester, 4 vols. (Grand Rapids: Reformation Heritage Books, 2018–2023).

65. Vitringa's *Commentarii ad Librum Prophetiarum Zachariae* was published posthumously in 1734 by Herman Venema (1697–1787).

66. Martin Vitringa, preface to *Doctrina,* 1:2–4.

the body of the text. Martin's annotations essentially compare Vitringa's thought to a wide host of other theologians. The comparisons not only extend to the various branches of the Reformed tradition, but also helpfully summarize the views of Roman Catholics, Lutherans, Socinians, Anabaptists, and others. The final volume of the *Doctrina* appeared in 1786, and it included a large index for the whole set.[67]

Vitringa's *The Fundamentals of Sacred Theology* is humbly offered to the reader as a helpful summary of the Christian faith as expounded by the Reformed tradition. The present work is the first 1688 edition, which is smaller and simpler than the later and more robust editions. References to the larger *Doctrina* appear throughout this work which direct the reader to relevant sections. Readers will benefit greatly from Vitringa's expertise both in scholarship and in piety since each of the thousand aphorisms of this volume are worthy of attentive meditation and reflection. Explanatory footnotes have also been included throughout for names, groups, technical terms, and so forth. It is our prayer that the closing words of this volume be true for all Vitringa's readers: "By denying impiety and worldly lusts, let us live temperately, justly, and piously in the present age, expecting that blessed hope and that brilliant advent of the glory of our great God and Savior, Jesus Christ. To Him be the glory" (§1000).

---

67. Herman Bavinck made frequent use of Vitringa's *Doctrina* in his *Reformed Dogmatics*, especially in the fourth volume. See John Bolt, "The Bavinck Recipe for Theological Cake," *Calvin Theological Journal* 45.1 (2010): 11–17. It should be noted, however, that Bavinck is often particularly interested in Martin Vitringa's historical annotations.

The Fundamentals of
Sacred Theology

Vitringa's Dedication

To the respected and most learned men of the churches
which are found in Friesland, to the
Pastors, his brothers in Christ honoring the Lord,
Campegius Vitringa gives greetings.

When I committed these theses in writing, respected men, it came to mind that I gave testimony to you several years ago in a solemn inaugural oration that I would intend to continue steadily in our orthodox thoughts of religion.[1] For this was firmly established in my soul when the Lord Christ called me by his gracious dispensation to teach theology. Indeed, although I pledged to you at that time that in my opinion there is no cause for you to have reason for assuming some improper thing on my part, yet it must be examined because of the peculiar character of this time in which this duty is required of me.

For what pertains to me was certainly investigated by you, that having been born in Friesland and educated in theological knowledge I learned in the academy of this land[2] from many doctors, some of whom are still alive by the kindness of God, whose instruction was irreproachable.[3] Yet others have died, a most gracious memory to us all.[4] The name of Herman Witsius ought to be honored on his own

---

1. Campegius Vitringa, *Oratio de Amore Veritatis Dicta in Templo Academico* (Franeker: Johannes Gyselaar, 1683).

2. University of Franeker.

3. ἀνέγκλητος.

4. Vitringa here probably refers to Johannes Terentius (d. 1677) under whom he studied Hebrew at Franeker.

great merit in the church of this age. He led, instructed, and directed my youth with admonitions and precepts, for he knew each young boy in the church of Leeuwarden and taught them the first principles of the Word of God. Having moved to the cathedral of this place, he willingly pressed his own teaching, and above what the rule of his profession required, he helped and spurred them on toward greater things. But herein I conceal something which I have never revealed, which I have made a great part of my own personal delight. After some time in the academy (which was an intensely challenging and difficult time), I met this historian, who easily and precisely explained various wonderful things. And he instructed each of his hearers not less toward piety than toward a solid indigestion. This is my memory of the instruction of Witsius; beloved indeed, and it will never pass away.

But thereafter, when I went on to the school in Leiden, I worked solely so that I might finish, for I had a desire for knowledge. And indeed, at that time my progress increased such that I was beginning to realize what I did not know. Therefore, I was eager to fill this void in whatever way I was able by committing myself to our renowned professors as a student, though not by observing a two-faced life which clubs and passions had introduced in that place. For there is nothing whatsoever in this world, nor will there ever be, and whatever will be in the end, that I am able to ignore and set myself away from to be able to press on. Therefore, I had reason for rejoicing in returning to my homeland, because my furnishing was made more rich and ornate by a most helpful plundering at this place.[5] I knew that the opportunity for thinking was given to no one, and that I, having been founded as a kind of house which was raised up in that place, would be destroyed there.

Afterward, when I was called to the profession of the Hebrew language by divine providence, I discovered helpful things with this language because it has remained in the common works which have survived. And when the special opportunity for spending time on these things which pertain to theology presented itself, I worked tirelessly, not because I had a reason to earn the favor or friendship of various people, but chiefly because my soul desired understanding. This

---

5. I.e., Vitringa's "intellectual furniture" was well prepared at Leiden.

intellectual pursuit at that time certainly did not seem unpleasant to those who later turned it into a fault of mine. Nevertheless, my nature was formed, and I would never give up.

Now, since this rule in my life had become fixed, let it not be, most learned men, that by presenting this pledge of orthodoxy[6] to you I had tacitly suggested unjust presumptions about myself, unless the uniquely peculiar situation of this age demands it.[7] Indeed, the attempts of certain ministers of the divine Word to preserve orthodoxy (since they have certainly said amongst themselves that it has been destroyed by certain teachers) results in every household in our nation's church being thrown into confusion. But even if there are many good teachers and pious men who greatly disapprove of the order[8] observed by these teachers, yet they all seem to pay careful attention such that dear, dear truth might not take a bribe of defeat.

The source of these various suspicions was how one was heated by another, how brother was heated by brother, the worst heated by the best. For in that heat the matter was pushed such that any belief about something which also pertained to another discipline (even if it was far from common sense) was numbered among heresies. If anyone suggested that the new ideas, or that the *Sephiroth Kabballah*,[9] obscured the incarnation of Christ, the Mediator, he was worthy of being exposed to universal hatred. But though it began with seriousness, there was one cause why this business passed away in jest and joke. For whoever mixes his own affections with the cause of truth is inept for defending the truth and for undertaking the character of a defender. Indeed, at the time in which they chiefly engaged in these squabbles, the duty of professing theology came to certain doom. The desires that were held by all determined it. There were those who

---

6. ὀρθοδοξίας.

7. Because Vitringa was educated at Leiden, theologians who were committed to Reformed orthodoxy had reason to be suspicious of him. Leiden was a hot bed of philosophers and theologians that were sympathetic to Cartesianism, and the debate was also raging at Franeker. Even popular preachers such as Balthasar Bekker (1634–1698) were praising the new philosophy in Friesland at the time.

8. By "order" (*ordo*), Vitringa means a theological system.

9. *Sephiroth Kabballah* is a Jewish mystical doctrine which seeks to offer an explanation of the relationship between an infinite God and a finite creation.

wished to prescribe laws with special zeal and boldness to most wise noblemen, since they decreed that certain men ought to be entrusted publicly with those laws in the name of the church.

This was the state of things in which it pleased these illustrious nobles to allot for me this station. Therefore, because of our time—rather than my age and dignity—I sufficiently understand that I lack the weapons for defending myself against all suspicions which may come against me. But it was not with a hand that I was able more certainly and aptly to apply a remedy for this evil, than that I commit myself to you in public faith. Just as I was formerly most convinced of all the fundamentals of theology, so I will remain unmoved. And from this time, I begin to liberate the faith delivered, tested by God and conscience and even testimonies to your children whom you have entrusted to us in great number for education. For it is certain that I rejoice and give thanks that you sealed with pledges of this kind each day a favorable opinion of me, which you have from my work,[10] so that I may say, whatever the matter is, you have regarded me greater than before.

Certainly, respected brothers, even if our households tread on the outside, nevertheless know that nothing is more pleasing to me than that I can demonstrate and devote my progress and work to your people and mine, especially to the children. You have seen the fruit, which is not displeasing to you nor shameful to me, and you will see more of it if God wills. But if the liberating of the faith delivered has not yet been proved by me, I hand down to you by my hand these aphorisms, by which the heads of theology are comprehended. Read them, and reread them; know them, and receive them, for I speak and think the same as you.

If you desire another reason why I publish them, consider this. Over the years, I have practiced a certain method of teaching, so that I have discussed the *loci* of theology as they occur in a certain order in common systems, either by examinations or by bare explanations according to the desires of my hearers, which are certainly not bound to authority.

---

10. *institutione nostra.*

Meanwhile, I commended to students a certain system according to its skill, comprehension, and usefulness, which seemed to be most fitting for my teaching and method. In this vein, I remembered the work of Witsius at the time which I gave myself to his work. But this was set forth to the studious by custom, so that they believed that those things which were thus handed down were special precepts, and so they decided to select, describe, and guard those things with a stick, as if they were a precious object in its case. These attempts were not entirely problematic, though often greatly mangled, corrupted, and cracked, since in them was the proof of diligence. Just as no mortal who is now able to exercise the ability to walk did not frequently fall as an infant, and the man who has learned wisdom did frequently mock it as a boy, so one cannot become learned without learning to avoid error. Therefore, let our young ones fall. I imagine they will rise again with increased understanding. Let them wander and stagger in their walking. Further, let them learn to choose the right path, and to firmly tread it. Also, let them play, if they wish, and learn wisdom after.

Truly, when I reflect on these earlier times, I observe when I teach in this way, as I have said, that the same order is not preserved when I teach, and neither do I often say all those things which I had purposed to say. For it could often happen that one thing or another which was extremely necessary to say was accidently forgotten. Therefore, I took up this discussion concerning general aphorisms by which I might form for myself an explanation or presentation in a certain order, which would not be of great difficulty nor unfitting for our youth. Indeed, I have produced this most gladly, since the thoughts of my mind concerning the various heads of sacred theology which have been for a long time undecided (on which an understanding of Holy Scripture depends either more clearly or more obscurely) I now plainly regard as decided. For although what little there may be which I understand, I think that I understand it with a clear apprehension of the divine Word toward which every young person of ours is led. I am certainly unwilling to admit that I composed these aphorisms because I have a perfectly accurate grasp of them.

Additionally, I understand that outside this region there are very learned men who desire to know according to what order I arranged these things which pertain to the divine Testaments and covenants, which is the most common method for speaking and writing throughout the years of the church. I am certainly persuaded that, through the writings and discussions of most prudent men, and through industrious meditation and collection of spiritual matters, I have followed the order of these themes which the Holy Scriptures set forth. But the judgment is left to the reader. I welcome disagreements. Indeed, I am fond of disagreements, if the cause of disagreement is not an affection, nor true perceptions, nor founded upon mere opinion, but rather from the love of truth. For we are all men, in whom there is much imperfection.

Now I close my letter to you, respected brothers, because of what I regard as the weakness of my mind. Perhaps you are waiting for me to speak to you about what subjects I disagree with, which have exercised the printing presses of this place for a whole two years. And certainly, how many men have been revered who do not more carefully examine the appearance of present matters, who could become as those for whom I was not able to hold my tongue. Yet I was entirely silent in every case.

So, brothers, to see and to hear is a witness of all the things which have occurred among us. But I have been silent, since I have seen and now see that nothing is able to be said by me with fruit. This is prudent to concede at this time since we are not able to overcome this ill will. I have prepared to sustain injuries, insults, abuses, and accusations for the preserving of the truth, all of which I have not wholly been able to escape without a word, but only in a matter conducted to the extreme. For how long ought hope to prepare medicine amid judgment? But if we have been influenced everywhere by those who not long ago willed to allow that we be rudely insulted, this I easily overlook. Honest, learned, and Christian characteristics of men are kindness, modesty, and love. Whoever seeks certain praise among men walks forth in these footsteps. So, it has been determined by my soul that a good conscience preserves these things and denies the rest. You, most respected men, be strong, and labor with me diligently for the advancement of the kingdom of the Lord Christ.

Given in Franeker on July 4, 1688.

Vitringa's Preface

Greeting to His Readers

It is superfluous, most honored youth, to adorn such a brief writing with a double preface, except that I think it is entirely necessary to admonish you with certain principles. You think that you desire these theses on the whole of theology, but how do you wish to use them? Do you think that I have explained them for you to receive and to stamp on your memory, and after completing them, to leave other authors behind? I truly fear this. This is not my scope and intention, and this is why now from the beginning I have given this counsel to provide at least two rules.

First, I have set forth very brief theses which lack necessary explanation. Second, I have refrained from adding Scripture references which ought to be employed for confirming them. There were friends whose judgment I greatly trust who dissuaded me from both of these points. But I have most serious reasons why I did not comply with them. For if these theses were greatly lengthened, this book would grow into a system. But I determined in my soul that I would never write a full dogmatic work, since certain ones have been published by most learned men in this day and age which are quite to my taste. My burden is this, that if many felt the need to enrich the world with books of this kind, they would likewise understand that they lack instruction, prudence, and experience of various matters which are required for such a work. For it is not enough that someone merely does it, prevails to some extent, and learns the fundamentals of theology, but it is necessary that he have a soul with wide reading, wide proficiency of judgment, and also of age; not that he be learned only, but also prudent, and well-equipped, and meticulous. Who are the worthiest men now who arise before us in the church, who might be the cause of another who may prove his attempts anew in a work of this kind?

Let us therefore praise the work of our colleagues, who now for some years have begun to write after this harvest, and also to complete this, so that those things in the whole body of theology which were neglected or treated carelessly by others might be reread and rendered in an accurate order. And so, I did not have the full desire of composing a larger account than I did. But I did not wish to add Scripture references so that I would compel and persuade you against your will to consult other authors. For I know that no one is frightened by excessive brevity. Everyone who accepts us knows that my whole work[1] is scriptural. For I truly believe that the whole of theology is summed up by the questions which I have offered. Since it has been proved and accepted that the Scriptures are divine, nothing is asked except that it is comprehended in these lists. This is the sense of the words. This is the binding of the pen. This is the intention of the Holy Spirit.

Therefore, however well someone understands theology will determine how well he can prove that it is found in the Scriptures. Hold fast to this, most dear brothers, and also read and meditate on the Scriptures, so that in this way you may gather this treasure of good things. I know that it is very tiresome, that they are loaded with continuous work. But shake off idleness! The task cannot be completed in any other way. Consider this only, whether the work which I present before you has weight. For a long time, the ears are most incapable of bearing the load of listening to commands, and they lack sense, or are led in vain in a present matter. But rare is this experience among us, for we are accustomed to pick out these sayings, and so they are set forth.

What use do you say that this little book is for us? For this, listeners, first, that you may have a certain order by which I discuss the matters of theology, and second, that I may explain the collected fundamentals of these things clearly and truthfully. Thus, in this brief

---

1. *nostram institutionem.*

space of time, you would be able to repeat this sum of all truths as handed down to me and memorize them.

Initially, I had decided to add other theses by which elenctic theology[2] would be comprehended. But I changed the method when I put it together, for I saw nothing with which I disagreed among us and any adversaries which cannot be treated most conveniently in the explanation of our positions. Let us be accustomed to handle controversies with the same zeal by which we handle the pure dogmatics of theology, even if these two can hardly be separated from one another. Therefore, for what purpose shall we repeat this same thing twice?

You have known in addition to me, most ornate youth, in this age of the church it is more pleasing for some to impress bare dogmatics than to build up youth in the many mysteries for disputations. For a long time it was different, yet this is its fate at this time. But those who reject elenctic theology err from imprudence. A specific reason why I changed this method, is that for the last two years, each week I have devoted two days to public lectures, first against the Papists, and now disputing against the Socinians. I have done this for this reason, that many about whom the academy is concerned have deplored that elenctic theology is denied here.

Further, readers, what should I say? I have many thoughts which ought to be said, and many things that I wish to say, but I have spoken enough about this little book. I add this one thing: fear, cherish, and love God, and pray continually if you wish to prosper. He who approaches this holy task with an impure soul dreads the judgment of God. If you believe as I do that the Lord Christ sits at the right hand of His Father and that He reigns equally over all earthly things, then you are consecrated to His service, and at some point, you shall be rewarded according to your industrious work. Rejoice, if you do well, and be terrified if you do badly. Our Lord is at hand. He repays the one according to his works. Because this is evident, use our labors as far as it is pleasing to God, and await with me, by a certain hope, His

---

2. *Elenctic theology* is theology which is particularly interested in defeating opposing arguments through logical refutation. See Richard Muller, *Dictionary of Latin and Greek Theological Terms: Drawn Principally from Protestant Scholastic Theology*, 2nd ed. (Grand Rapids: Baker Academic, 2017), s. v. "elenchticus."

gracious mercy which is found in heaven.[3] Now I bid you farewell, my dearest ones, and let me go on to love the Lord.

---

3. Vitringa also makes the following corrections to the body of the work: "There are a few errors which ought to be noted in the text. In the annotations: §135 ἀϊδίον should be written as ἀΐδιον…; §137 For *quamque dirigendam* read *quaque dirigenda*; §174 For *damnandi* repeat *damnando*. The rest of these errors are rather trivial. There is no time for a revision of the writing." These corrections have been applied in the translation below.

CHAPTER 1

Definition of Theology

1. *Theology,*[1] according to the force of the term, is the discussion about God.[2]

2. Comprising this study are the loci of doctrine. These instruct us about God and the ways of God for sure comfort in this life and salvation in the next. Or, *for the faith of God's elect and the knowledge of the truth which is according to godliness.*[3]

3. By *God* we mean the all-sufficient Being. By *ways* we mean God's actions, counsels, and all His divine works, His setting all things in order by His miraculous ordering, and every command by His ordination to the glory of the divine name.

4. God knows Himself and His own ways most perfectly. Some often call this *archetypal theology.*[4]

---

1. Θεολογία.

2. τοῦ Θεολόγου. *Doctrina,* 1.1.

3. τή πίστιν ἐκλεκτῶν θεοῦ καὶ ἐπίγνωσιν ἀληθείας τῆς κατʼ εὐσέβειαν. Titus 1:1. *Doctrina,* 1.7–8. Unless otherwise noted, all Scripture translations mine.

4. *Doctrina,* 1.9. Vitringa's discussion of the various divisions of theology in §4–13 come from Franciscus Junius's *De Theologia Vera.* See esp. chs. 2–8; Junius, *A Treatise on True Theology: With the Life of Franciscus Junius,* trans. David C. Noe (Grand Rapids: Reformation Heritage Books, 2014), 91–139. See also Muller, *Post-Reformation Reformed Dogmatics: The Rise and Development of Reformed Orthodoxy, ca. 1520–1725,* 2nd ed. (Grand Rapids: Baker Academic, 2003), 1:222–69.

5. The learning of the ways of God which is in the creatures is often called *ectypal theology*, and it is less perfect.[5]

6. Among the creatures, no one has known God perfectly more than the human nature of Christ because of the closest union with His divine nature, which is often understood by the term *theology of union*.

7. The idea of the perfections of the divine Being which is among the angels and blessed spirits is called the *theology of vision*.

8. What is among men is called *revelation*.[6]

9. It has truly been revealed to the mind and conscience of man that God exists.[7] This is called *innate natural theology*.[8]

10. This same and particular [natural theology] exists in the one who understands,[9] both from his own self and from created things by contemplation and consideration. This is called *acquired theology*.

11. From this first principle of truth which is seated in his own mind, man is truly able to dig out many other visible truths both about God and about himself. Yet although he deduces without any difficulty that God wills good for mankind from the all-sufficiency of God and also from His preservation of all things, this knowledge of God is not able to lead him to a sure hope of salvation.[10]

12. Moreover, since the conscience damns him continually as a sinner and likewise instructs him that God is holy, it is therefore necessary that he continually fear the just penalty.[11]

---

5. *Doctrina*, 1.9.
6. Cf. *Doctrina*, 1.11.
7. *Deum esse*.
8. *theologia naturalis innata*. *Doctrina*, 1.1.22–26.
9. νοοῦντι.
10. *Doctrina*, 1.34–35.
11. Cf. *Doctrina*, 1.45.

13. This just fear of penalty in the human sinner who otherwise regards God with hate is the most potent cause of religion. We call this *natural religion.*[12]

14. Nevertheless, this does not please God, because it is not done out of love for Him, nor is it directed to His glory.

15. Therefore, it is obvious that that there must necessarily be some revelation besides the natural if God desires to be sought and glorified by sinful man.[13]

16. Since we know what the will of God is from so many signs of long-suffering and mercy which He demonstrates toward mankind, we conclude that it is probable that such revelation exists.

---

12. *Doctrina,* 1.46.
13. Cf. *Doctrina,* 1.47.

CHAPTER 2

Holy Scripture

17. Divine revelation of this kind, if it exists in the world, ought to be able to be demonstrated through certain proofs and such criteria[1] in the consciences of all men, and through this should be distinguished from other vain and fictitious revelations.[2]

18. We especially believe that these proofs and criteria can be discovered in the revelation of the ways of God, which for a long time had been frequented among the Jews, and which the prophets and apostles have embraced by a wholly common writing.[3]

19. These books are designated by the name *canonical*, so that they are distinguished from the *apocryphal* books which are not to be treated as equal to these writings.[4]

20. The criteria and signs of the divinity of Scripture are for this reason clear and evident, so that they are discerned by the right use of every conscience. However, since the constitution of man is so corrupt that he flees from God and wishes of his own will to be ignorant of Him (for God manifests Himself to his conscience), so man stands in need of the efficacious illumination by the Holy Spirit for the full and saving conviction

---

1. κριτήρια.
2. *Doctrina*, 2.1.
3. *Doctrina*, 2.2.
4. *Doctrina*, 2.10–16.

of the mind, which is called in the schools *the testimony of the Holy Spirit.*[5]

21. The church—that is, the doctors, ministers of the divine Word, and all the faithful having been well instructed (for these offices exist so that they may teach these arguments of divinity to any who are unskilled)—ought not to be understood in such a way that the divinity of Scripture (or the *authority of Scripture with respect to us*, as they call it) depends on these offices.[6]

22. These Scriptures, having been received by us as divine, compel our minds toward reverently and humbly receiving everything that they say. This is called the *authority of Scripture.*[7]

23. Likewise, it perfectly instructs us concerning the whole will and counsel of God for salvation. Therefore, the church of this time does not have need of other traditions outside of Scripture, whether true or fictitious.[8]

24. The *pure* Scripture from Moses, the prophets, apostles, and Evangelists has surely reached us today, and these works have never been corrupted by the Jews.[9]

25. The integrity has not been lost by the changes in the literature of the Samaritans[10] or by the addition of the vowel pointing among the Chaldeans, nor the variant readings placed in the margins of

---

5. Cf. *Doctrina*, 2.16–18, 32–35.

6. *Doctrina*, 2.32.

7. *Doctrina*, 2.36.

8. *Doctrina*, 2.45–46.

9. Cf. *Doctrina*, 2.48. The suspicion of Jews tampering with the Old Testament manuscripts was a debated issue in Vitringa's day.

10. Vitringa here is referring to the Samaritan Pentateuch, an ancient version of the books of Moses (Genesis–Deuteronomy) that was edited by the Samaritans.

the Hebrew and Greek text.[11] Rather these arguments confirm its integrity.[12]

26. The perfection of Holy Scripture also necessitates its *perspicuity*. By this we mean that the prophets and apostles through the singular leading of the Holy Spirit used such terms and phrases in their writing which were most fitting for the concepts themselves which they meant, and that those concepts are able to be perceived and understood adequately, clearly, and manifestly in the same manner by all who pay due attention and have a mind affected by that same Spirit.[13]

27. But we especially defend this perspicuity of sacred Scripture in those places which contain the fundamentals of religion. Without understanding these, no one safely escapes.

28. This Scripture has been clearly handed down by God to the church for no other end than that all those who make up the church might *read* and *understand* it.

29. Indeed, the whole of Scripture ought to be read, and the Old Testament ought not to be torn away from the New.[14]

30. Scripture is not able to be read by all who make up the church under the new covenant unless it is translated into the vernacular languages. Therefore, we judge these versions to be necessary in our time.[15]

31. Nevertheless, no versions ought to be equal to or more-or-less placed before the original text, no matter how ancient or

---

11. Ancient Hebrew copies of the Old Testament had only consonants, no vowels. The vowels were added later by a medieval group of Jewish scholars called the Masoretes who also added various symbols to the margins of the Hebrew text to indicate minor corruptions and to suggest corrections.

12. *Doctrina*, 2.48–51.

13. *Doctrina*, 2.52.

14. Cf. *Doctrina*, 2.53.

15. *Doctrina*, 2.54.

authoritative they might be in the church, as for example, the Septuagint[16] and the Latin Vulgate of the Papists.[17]

32. But it is most useful and necessary that the church should always remain free to judge the versions modestly with the original text, and to compare that knowledge for herself with the Hebrew and Greek languages with sound responsibility.[18]

33. That tireless study for Holy Scripture ought to render a right understanding and interpretation—that is, a true understanding of the *sense* of Scripture and exegesis from the text.[19]

34. By the *sense* of Holy Scripture, we mean the *thought* or *truth* which corresponds to the sacred terms in their true meaning and has been prudently judged in all circumstances. These terms speak properly, directly, and for their own sake.[20]

35. The sense of Scripture is only one—the literal—or what is intended by the terms and examination of the sacred text.[21]

36. Nevertheless, this sense can often be most plentiful, so much so that many singular truths concur toward one common and plentiful truth through those terms which are intended. So, if someone produces confusion in the interpretation of Scripture, it is rather the case that this shining argument may be from the wisdom of the Holy Spirit.[22]

---

16. τῶν ὁ. The Septuagint (LXX) is an ancient Greek translation of the Old Testament. The Latin Vulgate is Jerome's (ca. 347–420 AD) Latin translation of the Old and New Testaments, which is highly esteemed by Roman Catholics.

17. *Doctrina*, 2.55. At the Council of Trent (1545–1563), the Roman Catholic Church declared the Latin Vulgate as an authoritative translation of Scripture.

18. *Doctrina*, 2.56.

19. *Doctrina*, 2.57.

20. *Doctrina*, 2.58.

21. *Doctrina*, 2.59.

22. *Doctrina*, 2.60.

37. The sense can be so full that the concepts through the literal sense of meaning may be signs of many other illustrious things. This is called the *mystical sense* of Scripture,[23] and the Papists distinguish it as *allegorical, anagogical,* and *tropological.*[24]

38. The right of interpreting Scripture has been granted to all those who are to read Scripture—that is, to all the members of the church, and not just to those who are learned or others.[25]

39. Now that which interprets Scripture and judges from the interpretation of Scripture is the *mind* or *reason*, having been put in man by God.[26]

40. Many interpret reason wrongly and not in a healthy way, as if all concepts which are meant by the terms and phrases of Scripture ought to be examined by reason as to whether they are true or false, as if nothing of the true sense of Holy Scripture ought to be received if it is not able to be deduced from principles of reason. This we wholly reject.

---

23. *sensus mysticus.* For one scholar's analysis of Vitringa's *sensus mysticus,* see Ludwig Diestel, *Geschichte des Alten Testamentes in der christlichen Kirche* (Jena: Mauke, 1869), 375–533. Diestel understood Vitringa's *sensus mysticus* as a negative aspect of Vitringa's exegesis. Diestel viewed the *sensus mysticus* as a hangover from traditional interpretation that needed to be wrested away in order to establish a newer and more enlightened exegetical method. Although Vitringa believed that the sense of the text is singular (*unicus*) and literal (*literalis*), nonetheless from that one sense flows the mystical sense by the authorship of the Spirit. The literal pertains to the original audience, while the mystical looks to the future and presents types of Christ. Elsewhere, he cites Matthew 7:6 in support of the *sensus mysticus* (*Doctrina,* 1.2.41–42). See also Telfer, *Wrestling with Isaiah,* 46–51. Cocceius rejected the *sensus mysticus.* See Cocceius, *Praefatio ad Romanos,* thesis 41, cited in van Asselt, "Biographical and Historical Introduction" in *Doctrine of the Covenant,* xxiii. For a review of scholarship on Vitringa's exegetical methodology, see Telfer, *Wrestling with Isaiah,* 43–81.

24. *Doctrina,* 2.61. Interestingly, Vitringa removes the reference to the Papists in *Doctrina* and attributes this sense to the ancients (*Veteribus*) who divided this sense into *allegorical* (Gal. 4:24; 1 Peter 3:21), *anagogical* (Heb. 9:11), and *tropological* (Deut. 25:4; 1 Cor. 9:9–10).

25. *Doctrina,* 2.62.

26. *Doctrina,* 2.63.

41. Rather, reason may only judge whether one sense or another is properly intended by one term and phrase or another.

42. But if indeed reason shall judge that one sense or another lies hidden under the terms and phrases and likewise seizes them so that the sense itself contains such a thought which is not able to be deduced from the principles of reason, then we do not permit that the sense itself should be rejected on that account. Nor do we permit that another sense should be made subject to it which better agrees with the judgment of the flesh and is bent according to it, as the Socinians[27] have done. But nevertheless, we understand that common notions should never be cast away in the interpretation of the Scriptures.[28]

43. Rather, we accept every thought as most certain truth which the conscience may judge to lie hidden under the received terms and phrases of Holy Scripture in its proper meaning.

44. Even further, we perceive quite easily that God can reveal many truths to us even though we have no ideas of them; namely, the infinite perfections in God which exceed the common capacity of our minds.

45. In addition, we are not always certain concerning the *binding of the consequences*,[29] which we often wrongly bind by applying them and unsuccessfully seizing them from the principles of reason due to the stupor of our own minds. For in other respects, it stands that the truths of Scripture do not fight against deductions of sound reason.

46. But there is no doubt on this point that for the one who correctly plucks the sense of Scripture from the text and in this way understands Scripture, it is truly necessary that the efficacious

27. For note on the Socinians, see §355.
28. *Doctrina*, 2.64–66.
29. This phrase means "logical deductions."

help of the Holy Spirit, who leads the faithful in all truth, is required.[30]

47. Likewise, one must prudently use the various means of interpreting Scripture, such as the knowledge of the languages, the consideration of the scope of the context, the binding of the antecedents and the consequents, the knowledge of the history of the times and rituals, and a diligent and true comparison of other Scriptures.

48. The consequences which have been deduced by the instrument of reason have the same degree of certainty with those truths which are first made known to us by the sense of Scripture.

49. All the faithful, to whom the reading of Scripture has been granted, likewise have the faculty for judging theological controversies, since no infallible judge is given.

50. Nevertheless, it is very useful when a controversy arises that many brothers convene in one place, as we read was done in the early church. Not that they should decide from authority what ought to be believed or not, but that they should bring together those truths which they have learned from the Scriptures as one friend to another and confirm their own brothers with themselves in the same mutual truth by collected arguments.[31]

51. But the norm for judging controversies ought to be none other than Holy Scripture.[32]

---

30. *Doctrina*, 2.69.
31. *Doctrina*, 2.77.
32. *Doctrina*, 2.78.

CHAPTER 3

God

52. Scripture not only teaches that God exists, but that God is such that He is able to be sought by the sinner and to be *a rewarder for those who diligently seek Him.*[1]

53. So then it is clearly set forth that God is *being*, not only sufficient for His own existence and of the creatures outside of Himself, but sufficient also for the sinner unto salvation, which is the highest *power*[2] of God.[3]

54. For Scripture everywhere speaks about God as He wills to be known by the sinner, and it does not reveal perfections, powers, and works of God other than what pertains to His counsel, which God considers for the saving of the sinner.[4]

55. What God reveals about Himself in Scripture is summarized in one word: the name *Jehovah.* By this name we mean all that by which and through which God is known. For His names are both signs of things, and they imitate the perfection of things.[5]

---

1. μισθαποδότης τοῖς ἐκζητοῦσιν αὐτὸν. Hebrews 11:6. *Doctrina*, 3.3.
2. כה.
3. *Doctrina*, 3.4.
4. *Doctrina*, 3.5–6. There is an error in *Doctrina*, in which aphorism 5 is labeled as 6.
5. *Doctrina*, 3.7.

56. So those signs and titles by which the Fathers addressed God and all the perfections of God reveal His name. These signs He has plainly accomplished for the sinner by a work of grace.[6]

57. The whole name of God is summed up in that name which God first revealed to Moses: *I am who I am,*[7] or the same name *Jehovah.*[8]

58. God explains the meaning of this name in Exodus 34:9. Since this name does not apply to any creature, it is plainly foolish to think that any other can be addressed by this name than the God of Israel.[9]

59. Because of the superstition of the Jews, it came to pass that the true pronunciation of this name (Jehovah) was forgotten, and the foreign vowel pointing of this term was substituted with *Adonai.*[10]

60. Next, God addressed Abraham with the name *God Almighty.*[11] With regard to the name *Yah (God),*[12] we do not believe that it is of the same force as the name Jehovah, nor is it derived from it.[13]

61. The titles *Adonai*[14] and *Elohim*[15] have their own basic meanings. But as time went on, the ancients wished to express *deity* with

---

6. *Doctrina,* 3.8–10.

7. אהיה אשר אהיה.

8. יהוה. Exodus 3:14. *Doctrina,* 3.11–12.

9. *Doctrina,* 3.13.

10. אדני. *Doctrina,* 3.14. In the Masoretic text, the name "Jehovah" is a result of the Hebrew consonants for "Yahweh" (or "Jahveh") combined with the vowels for "Adonai."

11. אל שדי. Genesis 17:1.

12. יה.

13. *Doctrina,* 3.15. Some believe that "Yah" is a shortened form of the Hebrew word for the divine name, "Yahweh." Others, such as Vitringa, think differently.

14. אדני.

15. אלהים.

these names,[16] the essence or the divine nature. In other languages, these were expressed by other words like *Lord*[17] and *God*.[18]

62. The word *God* in Hebrew comes from *Elah*[19] which has the same meaning in Arabic. Like many, we are firmly unwilling to deny the *mystery*[20] of this name.[21]

63. The *perfections* which Scripture attributes to God speak of Him such that the name of God itself might be clearly revealed to man, and that the *nature* or *essence* of God might be more plainly understood.[22]

64. For although the perfections of God cannot truly be divided from the divine essence or from one another, they do exhibit the *divine nature itself,* which although it is infinite and thus cannot be comprehended by our minds, it becomes known to us through various contemplations of the divine power.[23]

65. Concerning the perfections of God, none of them are first grasped in our minds except those which are directly opposite as imperfections of which our minds are conscious. And for this reason, the opposite names are chosen for names which express the imperfections of the creatures. For example, man is *finite*, and God is *infinite*. Man is *mutable*, and God is *immutable*. Man is *dependent*, and God is *independent*.[24]

66. These perfections are usually called *perfections of essence*. The first kind are *incommunicable*, and they are called the *attributes of life*. The second kind are *communicable*. Nevertheless, there is

---

16. τὸ Θεῖον.
17. Κύριος.
18. Θεός, *Deus, Godt. Doctrina*, 3.16.
19. אלה.
20. μυστήριον.
21. *Doctrina*, 3.17–18.
22. *Doctrina*, 3.19–28.
23. *Doctrina*, 3.35.
24. *Doctrina*, 3.28.

still something ambiguous in the term *communicable*, even if it may be used in a suitable sense in the schools.

67. First among these perfections is *primacy* or *aseity*, by which we understand God as the most sufficient Spirit who has life in Himself, *the living Father*,[25] and who is the font of life for everything which is outside of Him. This is called the *independence of God*.[26]

68. There is no doubt that He is His own cause (insofar as we could say this about the sufficiency of God), for He imparts all His perfections to Himself in an infinite manner. Therefore, it follows that God, who exists of Himself, is *infinite*—that is, that none of His perfections reach an end.[27]

69. That infinity of God, as it is conceived in the human mind, is called *incomprehensible*.

70. To this infinity of God it pertains that all things both exist and are sustained in Him and through Him, and for this reason He is intimately present with all things. This is His *omnipresence*.

71. From the primacy of God also follows His *simplicity*. For every composite thing acknowledges collected parts which are prior and so are a collected cause.[28]

72. From the simplicity of God flows His *immutability*, by which it is received that He is the same at all times, with absolutely no variation from the things arising submissively outside of Himself.[29]

73. With the immutability of God closely coincides the *eternality of God*. By this we understand that God *is*, and for this reason that He is permanent and constant, so that not only can He not

---

25. ὁ ζῶν πατὴρ. John 6:57.
26. *Doctrina*, 3.29.
27. Cf. *Doctrina*, 3.33.
28. *Doctrina*, 1.3.34.
29. Cf. *Doctrina*, 3.33.

be circumscribed with a measure of time, but also, He cannot be examined or conceived of in any way with any account of time whatsoever.

74. It is also evident from the simplicity of God that God is a *spirit*, or a *spiritual essence* since we are only able to conceive of Him as a spiritual essence.

75. Hence it follows that God is *invisible, indescribable,* and *untouchable.*

76. From this, namely that God is a spirit, it is evident that God's nature is thus: that He lives, that is, that He has His active essence from Himself, and that He clearly thinks and wills what is the life and activity of His spirit. So those perfections which pertain to the intellect and the will of God are called *attributes of life.*

77. But God understands His own self necessarily, as well as His all-sufficiency and all His perfections. He understands this because (as we say) a being is not able to be conceived as *knowing* without having a conscience. And so, the schools call the intellect of God the *knowledge of a simple, natural, and necessary intellect.* This pertains to this nature of God, and for this reason is understood to be in God before any decree.[30]

78. Additionally, God understands all things outside of Himself, even the binding and sequencing of those things, as well as all those things which must follow His truth by Himself and from Himself. This is called the *free and visionary knowledge* which follows the *decree.*[31]

79. And indeed, although comprehension or intellect in man precedes the will since man is not the cause of things, yet in God, in whom all being and all truth is established, the intellect necessarily follows the will, since the knowledge of God is nothing

---

30. Cf. *Doctrina*, 3.41–44.
31. *Doctrina*, 3.47.

other than the consciousness of His own decrees concerning what He has willed.[32]

80. To this knowledge of God wholly pertains *foreknowledge of future contingencies.* Whoever denies this of God not only does injury to the prophets who argue for that same foreknowledge, but they also subvert the perfections of God and the rule of all theology.[33]

81. It is not satisfactory when some conceive of a *middle knowledge*[34] as an acceptable account. They obviously involve themselves in many more difficulties than those who simply ascribe to God foreknowledge of all future things.[35]

82. We ascribe to God a *will,* since we understand that God conducts Himself freely. In this sense, not only does the love of God pertain to His will, but also His precepts, ordinances, and decrees which appear most often in the Scriptures as *the will of God.*[36]

83. Since a will desires what is good as its object, it follows that God wills Himself since He is good.

84. Further, since God alone is good, it is therefore evident that God wills nothing outside of Himself, except whatever is from Himself and for Himself—namely, those things which can be for His own glory. For this reason, the will of God always terminates in God Himself.[37]

---

32. *Doctrina,* 3.48.

33. *Doctrina,* 3.50.

34. Middle knowledge (*scientia media*) is the proposition that God's knowledge is conditioned on future contingencies. In other words, God knows the future simply because He foresees what will happen. The term comes from the idea that middle knowledge sits between God's necessary knowledge (*scientia necessaria*) which He knows as God, and God's visionary knowledge (*scientia visionis*), which is His knowledge that flows from His decree of what will come to pass. See Muller, *Dictionary,* s.v. "scientia media." The Spanish Jesuit Luis de Molina (1535–1600) was one important thinker who popularized this doctrine.

35. *Doctrina,* 3.51.

36. Cf. *Doctrina,* 3.59.

37. *Doctrina,* 3.60.

85. If some object of the will appears to be beautiful or ornate (fitting for oneself) then the desire for that object is called *love*.

86. In God there is something most fitting to Him, and so beautiful and ornate, which in Scripture is called *the seemliness of Jehovah*[38] or the *glory* of Jehovah.[39] These are the pure perfections and virtues of God which exceedingly adorn God and harmoniously sound the ever-exhibited magnitude of God most intimately to us.

87. Since God loves those perfections (those beauties and ornaments, which are most harmonious with Himself), He is called *holy*, such that the holiness of God which Scripture expresses most significantly by the term *glory*[40] is properly His own love as such, or His most zealous and intense love for His own perfections. God surely conceives of His own perfections Himself.

88. *Holiness in man* is that constitution of the human will by which he is carried toward this seemly love for God with true and devout zeal; or all of God's perfections which the mind perceives to be most fitting for God and good to itself. For Paul, this is *the holiness of truth*,[41] or *glory*.[42]

89. God loves everything outside of Himself because it is for Himself insofar as His perfections are revealed in it. In this manner, the love of God always terminates in Himself.

90. But God most loves the creatures in which He can excite a love for His own perfections and in this way to unite them with Himself, and in whom He is able to show the riches of His own sufficiency—that is, rational creatures, and among them, men.

---

38. יהוה יה. E.g., Isaiah 12:2; 26:4. Vitringa, *Commentarius in Jesaiam*, 1:476.
39. כבד. Vitringa, *Commentarius in Jesaiam*, 1:168.
40. חסד.
41. ὁσιότης τῆς ἀληθείας. Ephesians 4:24.
42. חסד. *Doctrina*, 3.76.

91. *The love of God toward men*, which refers to the eternal will of God for the uniting of His creatures with Himself and for doing good to them, is called His love of *benevolence*. From this, indeed, God's love of *good pleasure* is understood as the zeal of God toward men whom He now unites with Himself, and in whom He excites His love, those certainly most pleasing to Himself.[43]

92. This love of God, which we understand as His will of mercifully (that is, *not by merit*) and graciously doing good to the sinner, is His patience and long-suffering.

93. It follows from this holiness and uprightness of the divine will that God prescribes precepts to rational creatures. In these precepts He naturally expresses His own self and His uprightness, and applies those things as the means of uniting men with Himself and restoring their likeness to Himself. For the highest of all precepts is this: *Be holy, as I am holy.*[44]

94. Likewise, it follows from God's holiness and uprightness that He is *truthful*, both in words and in deeds: that the creature who does His precepts is rewarded, and He punishes the one who neglects them. The will of God which steadily executes this is called the *justice of God*. For the justice of God is nothing other than the steadfast will of God for demonstrating His own holiness to the rational creature in the governance of him. Indeed, God manifests His own holiness to the creature (namely, that He loves Himself) since He does good to the rational creature who loves Him, and in turn He punishes the creature who rejects Him.

95. From this we may well understand that God necessarily punishes the sinful creature who rejects Him, since (it is of the highest right with liberty) He necessarily loves His own self and His glory (that is, He is holy), and since it is necessary that He

---

43. *Doctrina*, 3.102–6.
44. Leviticus 19:2; 20:7, 26; 21:8; 1 Peter 1:16; 1 Thessalonians 4:7. *Doctrina*, 3.78.

would demonstrate His own holiness in the governing of His creatures because He is holy.

96. Indeed, the governing of the rational creature not only includes that He prescribes holy laws to the creature and adds promises and threats to those laws, but also that in the execution of the law He manifests that it is not up to Him whether the creature observes the laws or not, or whether the creature may seek the glory of his God or not. For it is certain that if God in His execution as a just judge did not manifest that this is not up to Him, then we would not be able to deduce from the deeds of God that He is holy—that is, that He loves Himself.

97. The *vindicating justice of God* is the holiness of God demonstrated to the creature in the inflicting of a penalty for sin which is set up by the laws on account of the demerit of sin.

98. The *decree* is the freest will of God determined for the appointing of things outside of Himself. In the schools it is called the *hidden will* or the *will of good pleasure*.

99. The will of God in whatever way it is used—whether for the love of God toward Himself and His own perfections (or rather, for the holiness of God) or for the demonstration of the holiness of God in the governance of rational creatures, or for the decree of God—ought always to be conceived as eternal, immutable, and a most pure act, and for this reason is commonly called *volition*.

100. The *power of God* is the will which is considered as effective for His producing determined or appointed things. And it is according to this double *desire*[45] by which it appears to us as *absolute* or *ordained power*.[46]

---

45. χρέσει.

46. גבורה, כח, δύναμις. The *absolute* power of God is that power by which God could do something if He so desired. The *ordained* power of God is what God has decreed to do. *Doctrina*, 3.110.

101. The *power*[47] over the creatures is considered as the highest station of independence and liberty concerning any right or position.

102. The foundation of this power is nothing other than that all creatures *are, are created,* and *are preserved by God.*[48]

103. This power used to conduct existing things is expressed by the *dominion* and *reign of God.*[49] From this, the *majesty*[50] of God comes to mind and is the foundation of adoration.[51]

104. For adoration not only dictates that God should be venerated, since He is so great, but this also: that I should subject myself to Him as my God, and I should recognize Him to have the right of disposing of me for His own glory according to His own choice. This cannot occur without the highest submission of my soul.

105. Indeed, from this it arises that God is always most perfectly conscious of all His perfections. This is called the *beatitude of God.*[52]

---

47. ממשלת, ἐξουσία.
48. *Doctrina,* 3.117.
49. מלכות.
50. גדולה, הוד.
51. *Doctrina,* 3.120–22.
52. *Doctrina,* 3.113.

CHAPTER 4

❧

The Mystery of the One God:
Father, Son, and Holy Spirit

106. God, whom we have previously understood as a most simple essence, has revealed Himself in both the Old and New Testaments as *one Jehovah*.[1]

107. When expressing His sufficiency to the church for the saving of sinners, this one God has revealed Himself as *Father, Son,* and *Holy Spirit.* So indeed, the Father is not the Son, the Son is not the Father, the Father and the Son are not the Holy Spirit, and yet the Father is said to be *in the Son,* and the Son and Holy Spirit to be *in the Father.* Therefore, *these three are one.*[2]

108. We hold to this *mystery*[3] even if we are not able to understand it with our reason. It has been so evidently revealed in the Holy Scriptures that, unless someone has fixed his mind against the dictates of Scripture, he is not able to ignore it. Therefore also, we hold that no article of divine wisdom, as God has revealed to the sinner, is able to be rightly explained without the acknowledgment of this mystery.[4]

---

1. יהוה אחד. *Doctrina,* 4.1.

2. Cf. *Doctrina,* 4.3. Vitringa's language here reflects Augustine's teaching on the Trinity in *De Doctrina Christiana,* 1.5.

3. μυστήριον.

4. *Doctrina,* 4.4.

109. Nevertheless, we ought to perform most diligent work lest we speak about this mystery[5] either more or less than has been revealed in the Scriptures so that we might not stumble upon the two extreme rocks of Sabellianism[6] or Tritheism.[7]

110. Likewise, it ought to be considered how we may prudently proceed in disputing or discussing this mystery.[8] First, before rightly judging, let us lay out our reasons in order. Second, let us not summon any arguments selectively, but only valid ones. And third, let us argue not only from one place but from various places of Scripture by comparison and *logical*[9] arguments which certainly have the highest strength in the demonstration of truth to the conscience.

111. But it seems that the best procedure for our demonstration of this truth is that our soul should be prepared by the consideration of one or two firm truths before we set forth its full explanation.

112. Let us earnestly recall to mind that in the Scripture of the Old Testament God allowed Himself to be called by many various titles and *appellations*,[10] even if at that time God most willed to avoid them, lest His own people neglect the unity of God's self. Thus, He was called *holy*,[11] *creator*,[12] *husband*,[13] etc. Indeed, because the title *God*[14] was usurped for the *one* God, it was construed with the word and quality of the plural number, as for example, *the God who reveals Himself.*[15]

---

5. *arcano.*

6. Sabellianism is the heretical teaching that the one God exists in three different modes.

7. *Doctrina*, 4.5.

8. *mysterio.*

9. ἀλληλουχία.

10. ἐπίθετα.

11. קדושים.

12. בוראם.

13. בעלים.

14. אלהים.

15. אלהים נגלו. *Doctrina*, 4.27.

113. Our souls will be the best prepared if we contemplate and consider those things which are read from the Old Testament about the Angel of Jehovah in Exodus 3. Here there is mentioned, by some twofold division of the mind, *the Angel of Jehovah*[16] who is called in verse 4 *Jehovah*[17] and *God*[18] in verse 6, *the God of Abraham, of Isaac, and Jacob.*[19] That same term *God*[20] appears again in verse 7 as *Jehovah*[21] who promises that He will lead out the people from Egypt. In verse 14, He gives to Himself the name, I WILL BE WHO I WILL BE,[22] and in verse 15 He calls Himself *Jehovah, God of the Israelite fathers, the God of Abraham, Isaac, and Jacob*, and likewise He swears by Himself, that *His name is everlasting, and that it is a memory unto every generation.*[23]

114. Next, let us consider something concerning the Angel of Jehovah whom everyone understands as *Jehovah's messenger*. Everything written by Moses and the prophets reveals very clear testimonies. And let it be concluded through infallible *demonstration*[24] that in Jehovah, the one God of Israel, He both *sends* and *is sent*. By these testimonies *perhaps*[25] the titles *Jehovah*, and *God of Abraham, Isaac, and Jacob* are sufficient.[26]

115. Finally, let us set forth *in theory*[27] what Scripture says about the *pact, counsel, surety*,[28] and *contract* which has been enacted by those who are God, and its effects and the proceedings of the justification and sanctification of sinful men.[29] If we believe that

---

16. ‏מלאך יהוה‎.

17. ‏יהוה‎.

18. ‏אלהים‎.

19. ‏אלהי אברהם אלהי יצחק ואלהי יעקב‎.

20. ‏אלהים‎.

21. ‏יהוה‎.

22. ‏אהיה אשר אהיה‎.

23. *Doctrina*, 4.29.

24. ἐπίδειξιν.

25. ἴσως.

26. *Doctrina*, 4.30.

27. ὑπωθετικῶς.

28. *sponsione.*

29. Vitringa refers here to the covenant of redemption. See ch. 5.

Scripture teaches these things, then we are not able to understand them in any way without the recognition of plurality in God.[30]

116. Now in order to prepare our souls for this subject, the whole idea should be explained and sought from more clear places, first from the New Testament and then from the Old Testament, namely that there is *three in one God*—Father, Son, and Holy Spirit. I say of the New first because more clear testimonies certainly stand out in it and because it is held by all that the Old Testament ought to be explained by the New.[31]

117. Since we have come this far, it is necessary that we pursue a new way of arguing which is established on this *assertion*,[32] that on the one hand it is surely necessary that we be very careful lest we call something *God* which is not God, and on the other hand we cannot deny the name and honor of God to one whom Scripture attributes that name and divine perfections without total slander and injury.

118. This assertion is advanced by a most certain principle, that although God gives His glory to no other, it cannot be that someone is not also *true God* if the name, perfections, and works of God in which His glory is established are attributed to Him.

119. So, Scripture attributes to the Son the names, perfections, and all the divine works exclusive to the Father (which will be demonstrated from evident places). He wills also that the Son be honored *as* the Father. Therefore, we conclude that is it a great sin to deny any deity to the Son that is of the Father.[33]

120. Likewise, Scripture attributes to the Holy Spirit (being distinct from the Son) the same names, perfections, and especially the *works* which are nothing less than the highest and truest of God.

---

30. *Doctrina*, 4.31.
31. *Doctrina*, 4.32.
32. ὑπόθεσις.
33. Cf. *Doctrina*, 4.39.

The same Spirit is honored among all faithful souls as God. So again, we deduce that it is not permissible to deny to the Holy Spirit that deity which is of the Father and the Son.

121. But it warrants the highest attention in this *argument*[34] that Scripture refers to the *blasphemy of the Holy Spirit* as the most serious sin of all.[35]

122. We again confirm *undeniably*[36] from what we have already rightly said that there are three in God, or that the one God is three—Father, Son, and Holy Spirit.

123. Finally, it is also helpful at this point in the discussion that we should state those things which work toward the illuminating of this *mystery*.[37] Because we do not understand these things very well, we often observe that the things which are also advanced by nature and from the philosophy of both the Jews and the gentiles are more vain than the clear statements which are found in the Scriptures of the Old Testament. But the full force of these statements is not clear without this preconceived truth [of the Trinity]. And these things cannot be helpfully used as arguments or foundations for disputation. For example, God was often expressed by the patriarchs with a threefold name. This name in the public blessing appears to be the threefold repetition of the name of Jehovah. Other names do likewise.[38]

124. Therefore, according to this proof, we argue that this *Trinity* in God is not merely a variety or difference of names which are able to join into a unity of the person in its various operations, but that it requires a true distinction of *subsistence*[39] in

---

34. ἐπιδείξει.
35. *Doctrina*, 4.47, 49–51.
36. ἀναντιρρήτως.
37. μυστήριον.
38. *Doctrina*, 4.59.
39. ὑποστάσεων.

the divine essence. We argue from these very places of Scripture which have been treated in the first proof.

125. But this truth is most powerfully confirmed from the *personal properties* (as they are often called) which are attributed to the distinct subsistences of the one divine essence. These are *to generate*, and *to be generated*, *to spirate*, and *to be spirated*, *to work through another* or *by another*, *to send*, and *to be sent*.

126. Next, from these personal properties, the names of the distinct subsistences should be set forth, of the Father, Son, and Holy Spirit, and this *teaching*[40] about the mystery of the generation of the Son and the *procession*[41] of the Holy Spirit which is *emphatically*[42] found throughout all Scripture should bring it right before our eyes.

127. But the modes of distinction should not at all be reduced to the limits of distinction which the philosophers use in their discipline.

128. We also need to remember that you should not differ with the order which Scripture teaches us to observe in their works *ad extra*: Father, Son, and Holy Spirit. For when the Father is of Himself, thus He works of Himself. The Son, who is from the Father *according to subsistence*[43] works from the Father. The Holy Spirit works from the Father and the Son. And so the Father works through the Son and Holy Spirit.

129. Therefore, reason ought to seek why so often in the Scriptures the title of *God* is attributed to the Father *with emphasis*[44] just as the title *Lord* is to Christ, as in 1 Corinthians 8:6. So we must

---

40. ῥήσεις.
41. ἐκπορεύσεως.
42. ἐμφατικοτάτως.
43. κατ᾽ ὑπόστασιν.
44. κατ᾽ ἔμφασιν.

not subtract any of *the equality*[45] of the deity of Christ or of the Holy Spirit.

130. It is also useful from the Scriptures to observe differences *in time* by which the Father, Son, and Holy Spirit reveal themselves now to a greater extent than at other times in the church.

131. Indeed, because the doctrine of this mystery is spread widely throughout the whole of Scripture and nothing of the ways of God can be understood without this knowledge, it is absolutely certain that this investigation and knowledge is necessary for salvation. We are not rash in our definition of this rule of knowledge.

132. These things are absolutely essential for the true practice of piety since Christ not only displays to us the *unity* of Himself and of the Father by example, but also God would not be able to dwell rightly with His church at this time without this mysterious knowledge.

---

45. τῇ ἰσότητι.

CHAPTER 5

The Eternal Work and Decrees of God[1]

133. We chiefly understand the name and glory (or what I prefer to call the *perfections of the sufficiency and magnitude of God above all things*) from the works of God, by which He is pleased to make Himself known to us in time.[2]

134. For even if we perceive that God in His nature is *blessed*[3] in Himself and that He does not lack other things outside of Himself for the completion of His own blessedness, nevertheless we do understand that it is most sufficiently and aptly fitting for God that He give proofs of His own goodness and sufficiency *outside of Himself.*[4]

135. God is surely able to do this, since it has been said before that in Him is *eternal power.*[5] [His eternal power] is that conscience of His will by which He who is necessary understands that He can produce something which is not necessary.[6]

---

1. This chapter is entitled "On the Counsel of the Divine Will" in *Doctrina*, 5.
2. *Doctrina*, 5.1.
3. μακάριον.
4. *Doctrina*, 5.2.
5. ἀΐδιον δύναμιν. Romans 1:20.
6. *Doctrina*, 5.3.

136. Indeed, we know *a posteriori*[7] that God wills to produce things outside Himself and that He preserves those produced things by a certain ordination. For when we look at the world and the various things in the world it is clear to our consciences that nothing exists by itself, nor does anything exist necessarily.[8]

137. The *decree of God* is the divine will concerning all things appointed outside of Him, preserved by a certain ordination, directed to certain ends, and always directed to His *glory*.[9]

138. And so the divine decree consists in this: that there was an eternal *idea*[10] in God, or a *preformation and predeliniation*[11] which was wholly certain and determined by Him. God willed this to exist in time both in order and in manner so that it would exist for certain and determined ends. Scripture calls this the *predelineation of things*.[12]

139. And the ends to which God has determined future things are certainly varied according to each, but in the idea of God their one end is His glory—namely, the illumination of His various perfections.[13]

140. But this will of God receives various names which are necessarily predicated of it according to its various attributes.

141. If it is considered as the magnitude of the things decreed, Holy Scripture expresses that by the name *work*[14] or *works*.[15]

---

7. That is, an argument which moves from effect to cause—i.e., God is known as Creator by looking at the creation. See Muller, *Dictionary*, s.v. "a posteriori."

8. *Doctrina*, 5.4.

9. *Decretum Dei.*

10. *aeterna idea.*

11. *praeformatio & praedelineatio.*

12. *praedelineationem rerum.* In *Doctrina*, Vitringa relabels this idea as *praeformatio.* See Doctrina, 5.9. יצירה. Isaiah 37:26.

13. *Doctrina*, 5.16.

14. פעל.

15. מפעלים. Psalm 64:10; Proverbs 8:22. *Doctrina*, 5.18.

142. If one desires to put the wisdom of God before the eyes, which is apparent in the eternal decrees and ordinances of God, then one attributes *counsel*[16] to God.

143. Indeed, the *wisdom of the decrees* consists in this: that all means reach their ends in a singular and laudable order, and that those various ends have been established for the illuminating of divine glory.

144. When Scripture considers the discerning of the highest liberty in God, then we read of *the divine will of good pleasure*.[17]

145. By *liberty* we mean that God not only has formed the decrees with the highest of freedom (this liberty is called *good pleasure*[18]), but that He was able *not* to decree (which is liberty of *contradiction*) or to decree *otherwise* (which is liberty of *contrariety*), so that nothing at any time might be denied of His perfections.[19]

146. The liberty of the decrees depends on the fact that we clearly understand that outside the will of God there cannot be any truth, necessity, or order on those things. And indeed, there is nothing at all which can move God toward acting or determining otherwise.

147. It is surely necessary to attribute this liberty to God in the highest degree. For if we deny this we run hastily and necessarily toward fate, and therefore toward a denial of Him being most free.

148. This liberty does not contradict the *eternality* of the decrees. Eternality is actually vindicated by the divine decrees. Scripture calls it *foreknowledge*[20] and *predestination*.[21]

---

16. עצה, βουλήν. Isaiah 14:26; 46:10; Ephesians 1:11. *Doctrina*, 5.19.
17. חפץ, רצון, εὐδοκία. Ephesians 1:9. *Doctrina*, 5.21.
18. *complacentiae*.
19. *Doctrina*, 5.22.
20. πρόγνωσιν.
21. προορίσον.

149. For even if it is difficult to hold these two together since we cannot form an adequate concept of eternity with our reason, nevertheless our very reason teaches that it is not able to conceive of God in any other way.

150. The immutability of God leads to the eternality of the decrees. From this also the immutability of the decrees follows, which Scripture calls by the term *decree*[22] and *determination*.[23]

151. The magnitude of these decrees is such that it is not possible to remove the determining nor the circumstances of even the smallest things.

152. Now we surely understand that the divine decree circumscribes rational creatures, the beloved creation, and its government. And on the governing of the creatures, it prescribes the more important events of their lives such as the birth and death of families, changes of governments, allocations of any office and status, marriage, and the end of life. We do not remove any *free actions* here of whatever kind that they might be. The apostle speaks well: *He determined their allotted times, and the boundaries of their dwelling.*[24]

153. This is because rational creatures have been especially created for glorifying God. So, I say, it follows that it is necessary that in the decrees the God of everything especially proclaims the signs of His wisdom and demonstrates His independence to those who see them.

154. Since indeed the *wisdom of the decrees* means that all works decreed by God, being excellently bound up with one another, flow from God toward the highest glorious ends, it cannot be the case that God determines the order, conditions, actions,

---

22. גזרה, προθέσεως.

23. ὁρισμοῦ.

24. ὁρίσας προστεταγμένους καιροὺς καὶ τὰς ὁροθεσίας τῆς κατοικίας αὐτῶν. Acts 17:26.

habits, and births of rational creatures (I think specifically of men) unless He likewise determines the end of the actions of rational creatures. The eternal state of those same creatures must be included.

155. Indeed, if the divine decree is understood in this way (namely, with respect to the eternal state of rational creatures) it is called in the schools, *predestination*.[25]

156. Now the state of rational creatures is only of two eternal kinds. With respect to God, it is called *the manifestation of all-sufficiency of God* toward some, and *the righteousness of God* toward others. With respect to the creatures, *eternal life*[26] and *eternal destruction*.[27]

157. Here it is evident that in predestination we ought to conceive of two divine acts because of this twofold end. These are called *election* and *reprobation*.

158. Now, the term *predestination* in Scripture is never strictly used for the destining of the eternal state of reprobation. But it is used concerning their actions which have a certain binding with the end, and so the term is also rightly ascribed to *reprobation*. Phrases of greater *emphasis*[28] are also discovered concerning reprobation because it is included in predestination.[29]

159. The foundation of this predestination in God is the *power*[30] of God. For since all things are from Him, nothing is more fitting than that the God of all things should freely distribute His glory. The apostle expresses this *emphatically*[31] by *the power of God*.[32]

---

25. προορίσος.

26. ζωή αἰώνιος.

27. ὄλεθρος αἰώνιος.

28. ἐμφάσεως.

29. Vitringa cites Romans 9:22 and 1 Peter 2:8 in *Doctrina*, 5.37.

30. ἐξουσία.

31. ἐμφάτικοτατως.

32. τὸ δυνατὸν τοῦ θεοῦ. Cf. Romans 9:22; *Doctrina*, 5.45.

160. As men who contemplate this part of the divine decree, we need the highest humility. For every error which has been made against the concept of this subject throughout the ages has been born because man imagines in himself that he is *something,* although he is *nothing.*[33]

161. For nothing is more familiar to a man than to think that the will and pleasure of God, the salvation of the determining of the creature, terminates in the saving of that man himself, who in this way then judges himself to have been more deserving than others. Or for that reason, that his salvation has been seen by God. Or alternatively, that the will of God is the exercise of destining someone to His justice, as if God delights Himself in the misery of man. The first man who says this errs. The second *blasphemes.*[34] Certainly, God pursues and loves nothing but *His own glory.* He does not manifest in any creature His all-sufficiency except on account of Himself, not on account of the creature. Neither does He manifest His own righteousness except on account of Himself, not on account of the creature. *O the depth of the riches of the wisdom and knowledge of God!*[35]

162. From this same consideration of the primacy of God and the *nothingness of man*[36] it follows that the condition of predestination toward one end or the other can be no *impulsive cause,*[37] whether faith in election, or sin in reprobation. *Who gave a gift to Him, that it might be repaid to Him?*[38]

163. So again, it follows that in a true and proper conception of predestination all things decreed by Him which have been ordained

---

33. ἒιναι τί, μηδὲν ὄντα. *Doctrina,* 5.46.

34. βλασφημεῖ.

35. ῏Ω βάθος πλούτου καὶ σοφίας καὶ γνώσεως θεοῦ. Romans 11:33.

36. *nullitatis hominis.*

37. The *impulsive cause* refers to a cause which provides the occasion for the efficient cause.

38. τίς προέδωκεν αὐτῷ, καὶ ἀνταποδοθήσεται αὐτῷ. Romans 11:35.

by God for bringing about the ends of His creatures ought to be considered as *means*. These are *creation* and *permission of the fall* with regard to the elect and the reprobate in general. But in particular with regard to election, the *mission* of His Son into the world, the arousing of faith and love for Him. And with regard to reprobation, the abandoning and governing of the creature, and often hardening in sin. These ideas are called *supralapsarianism*.[39]

164. Indeed, these means which God has ordained for attaining the ends are glorious to Himself because they work so that the conscience of man gives testimony to God *that the ways of God are just*.[40] For God does not save any man in time unless he seeks Him in His Son. Neither does God damn any unless his conscience itself testifies that *they who do such things are worthy of death*.[41] And so no one who is saved can allege any other cause of his salvation than the infinite sufficiency of God, which is called His *love*[42] and *grace*.[43] No one who is damned can allege any cause other than sin, which he freely committed, and on account of this he has now been damned in his own conscience.

165. Therefore, in this withdrawal there is no *unrighteous*[44] place nor *partiality*[45] in God. Indeed, there is no *unrighteousness*,[46] since God unjustly damns no one. But *damnation* is specifically related to that virtue which is called *holiness* and *righteousness* in God.

---

39. *Supralapsarianism* is the idea that God's decree of redemption comes logically prior to His decree for the fall (i.e., God predestinates unfallen people). Supralapsarianism is contrasted with *infralapsarianism*, which suggests that the fall comes logically prior to redemption in the decree (i.e., God predestinates fallen people).

40. Cf. Deuteronomy 32:4.

41. Romans 1:32.

42. ἀγάπη.

43. χάρις.

44. ἀδικίαν.

45. προσωπολημψίαν. Romans 2:11; Ephesians 6:9.

46. ἀδικίαν.

166. Indeed, there is no partiality or *accepting of persons*[47] since God in predestination respects no *conditions*[48] (as they say) on account of which He presents better grace to one than to another. But with the highest liberty He ordains the means to the ends. I contend that predestination is an act of His power, but not of righteousness in which *partiality*[49] has a sole place.

167. Since it is evident from what was said before that predestination pertains to rational creatures and that those are either *angels* or *men*, it follows that predestination is of two kinds.

168. Likewise, since we know from the Scriptures that the eternal states of the angels are of a twofold kind, it stands also that there are two acts of election and reprobation which we have observed in predestination that ought to be observed with respect to the angels.

169. For eternal election is the free and immutable decree of God concerning the revealed glory of His grace and sufficiency in the eternal salvation of a certain group of men.[50]

170. Indeed, this decree of God is improperly called *election*[51] since this decree works itself out among men in time, *choosing* them out of the world and leading them to His glory.[52]

171. For *to elect*[53] properly means *to take up* and *to vindicate* in time some out of a multitude of others who are rejected. But since God does nothing in time except what He has now established to do from eternity, so in many places in sacred Scripture *election* is used for the eternal decree of *choosing* someone out of

---

47. προσωπολημψίαν.
48. *qualitates.*
49. προσωπολημψία.
50. *Doctrina,* 5.51.
51. ἐκλογή.
52. *Doctrina,* 5.55.
53. ἐκλέγεσθαι, חפלה.

the world through faith in Christ. It is plainly called *the purpose according to election.*[54]

172. In addition, it is evident by reason of this argument that by the term *election* we do not mean the whole decree of the predestination of created and fallen man toward the glory of God's all-sufficiency, but only part of this decree, which begins from *the fall* of man and terminates in the *salvation* of man. The whole act of predestination has the creation of man as the first means of execution and the glory of God for the final end.

173. The reason for this is that all the means have been ordered together, and so one is able to be considered with respect to another as an end.

174. The same ought to be observed in those places where Scripture speaks of reprobation, which is often repeatedly described as a counsel of *passing over* and abandonment of whatever sinners are in the state of sin and as a rock of damning because of sin. But in those same places it gives the occasion of knowing that reprobation is a negative action, although it is nevertheless truly positive.

175. Indeed, it ought to be remembered that Scripture in those places does not describe the whole counsel of reprobation and of revealed justice or exercised anger, but only part of it.

176. This sole reason ought to unite the varying thoughts of the *supralapsarians* and the *infralapsarians*, as they are called.[55]

177. Indeed, it was pleasing to the Holy Spirit in the Scriptures that He often place the whole predestination of man before our eyes under the terms *election* and *reprobation*, or *love* and *hate*, which make only part of the counsel of predestination, so that the power of grace and the justice of God clearly reveal themselves to our conscience.

---

54. ἡ πρόθεσις ἡ κατ᾽ ἐκλογὴν. Cf. Romans 9:11.
55. See note on §163.

178. We call this decree of election *eternal*, so that we avoid the errors of those who allege that election takes place solely in time.

179. We call it *free*, so that we exclude faith or foreseen works which impel God toward election. This is the opinion of the flesh, and it is insipid, directly contrary to the Scriptures.

180. We call it *immutable*, so that we might exclude all conditions upon which those outside of us think that this decree depends.

181. Likewise, so that we may defend the certitude of the hope of the faithful in this life. For if election is not immutable, then the *hope*[56] of the faithful is able *to be ashamed,*[57] which is most false.

182. We call it *of certain persons*, so that we ourselves may oppose those who think that election of conditions is firm, but not the condition of persons.

183. The end of election is this—that God may be glorified in His saints and wondrous works among all those who believe in Him.

184. Indeed, all these attributes which we predicate of election are contained in the consideration of the terms *decree,*[58] and *testament,*[59] and also the phrase *written in the book,*[60] by which election in the Scriptures is accustomed to be set forth for us. Concerning the testament, see the following sections.[61]

185. *Reprobation* is the eternal, free, and immutable decree of God for the revealing of the glory of His power and justice in the eternal destruction of certain men.

---

56. ἐλπίς.
57. καταισχύνει. Cf. Romans 5:5.
58. προθέσεως.
59. διαθήκης, *testamenti.*
60. Cf. Revelation 20:15.
61. E.g., §378–404; 426.

186. Most efficacious *teachings*[62] concerning this are discovered in Scripture for setting forth *the power of God*[63] before our eyes.

187. And so the liberty, immutability, and eternality of this decree is able to be conceived from these things which have been posited concerning election.

188. There is no certitude of this reprobation while man is living, which renders carnal man who hence seeks protection by his own sins *without excuse*.[64]

189. For no one is damned because he is reprobate, but because he freely sins and neglects to seek the grace of God, against the dictates of his soul and his conscience. *Let God be of the truth, and every man a liar.*[65]

190. And so, it is incorrect that this decree of predestination, in whatever way it is taught from the Word of God in our churches, denies any divine virtues, or is directly contrary to reason. On the contrary, all divine virtues are illuminated in the highest degree *fit for God*.[66] Indeed, these very attributes teach and would have taught this doctrine most powerfully *a posteriori*,[67] even if Scripture were silent.[68]

191. When a doctrine illustrates the power of God, it necessarily promotes the zeal for true piety, and so this one fulcrum and foundation is all for hope and faith, and it most powerfully arouses men called by God toward perpetual celebration of the divine name.[69]

---

62. ῥήσεις.

63. ὁ δυνατὸς τοῦ θεοῦ.

64. ἀναπολόγητον. Romans 1:20.

65. γινέσθω δὲ ὁ θεὸς ἀληθής, πᾶς δὲ ἄνθρωπος ψεύστης. Romans 3:4. *Doctrina*, 5.79.

66. θεοπρεπῶς.

67. See note on §136.

68. *Doctrina*, 5.80.

69. *Doctrina*, 5.81.

192. Indeed, one should struggle with this doctrine with care, partly because every sinner seeks a pretext for his own sin, and partly because men in this counsel of predestination are accustomed to consider the ends without the means.[70]

---

70. *Doctrina*, 5.82.

CHAPTER 6

Creation of the World, Angels, and Men

193. God began to execute this most wise counsel of His *decree*[1] through the creation of the world and of angels and men in the world.[2]

194. By *creation*[3] we understand the production of a thing through sheer power and command[4] of will, whether that thing may be a completely new thing and not existing before, or the totally unusual change of a presently existing thing for which an infinite power of will is required.[5]

195. And so for God *to create* is *to call something which does not exist into existence.*[6] And *to be created* is *to exist by the will of God*[7] or by *the Word of God.*[8]

196. Creation includes the idea of all-sufficiency or *eternal power.*[9] And since we do not have this, the concept of creation is exceedingly difficult for us to understand.

---

1. προθέσιν.
2. *Doctrina*, 6.1.
3. ברא ,בריאה.
4. νεῦμα.
5. *Doctrina*, 6.2.
6. καλεῖν τὰ μὴ ὄντα ὡς ὄντα.
7. εἶναι διά τὸ θέλημα τοῦ θεοῦ.
8. ῥῆμα τοῦ θεοῦ. *Doctrina*, 6.3.
9. ἀΐδιος δυνάμεως. *Doctrina*, 6.3.

197. So, it most surely follows that creation is such a work that can be understood by no one except an all-sufficient being such as God.

198. Now this is always true, since it is impossible that God give the power of creating to man unless you want to assume that God can give man an all-sufficient conscience, which is most absurd.

199. Nevertheless, it does occur that God displays a sign through man by which He wishes to work. This is evident in the execution of miracles. This work does not differ from creation.[10]

200. By *world* (Scripture uses the phrase[11] *heaven* and *earth*) we understand the complex of all bodies in a great chorus and wisdom of motions following certain laws. The Greeks call it the *cosmos*.[12]

201. That this world has not always existed, or that it was created by the will of God can be wholly understood by sound reasoning.

202. For we cannot conceive that anything is created or not to have a beginning since to be created is to begin to exist. But whatever begins to exist has its moments counted, and so it is not eternal.

203. So it clearly cannot follow that created things ought to be eternal since the will of God was eternal, because the concept of creation involves a finite existence, and for this reason it is contrary to eternity. Indeed, the concept of the decree or the will of God is not only inoffensive to the concept of eternity, but it most certainly requires it.

204. Whoever does not recognize that the world exists by a more powerful cause ought to understand that he, being in a brute and inert body which has no activity from itself, is given the sufficiency to exist, to be moved, and to be moved prudently. And

---

10. Cf. *Doctrina*, 6.7.
11. φράσει.
12. κόσμον. *Doctrina*, 6.8.

for this reason, it is absurd to say that there is nothing greater than him.

205. But in addition, experience thus abundantly shows that the world has not existed for a very long time, but rather it is recent in history. So you discover arguments for this everywhere if you diligently apply your soul.[13]

206. In accordance with this, no ancient histories are found among the peoples and nations who were eminent peoples, ruled over the world, and cultivated disciplines. And this can be demonstrated since all nations were born from the East, and so they have proceeded to settle the world more and more, first among the shores of the seas and rivers, then they proceeded into vast regions after multiplying further. And so, at this time we can explain the migrations of this expanding habitation. And it can be demonstrated that all languages have their origin from an Eastern nation, which is ancient Phoenicia.[14] And the literature and teachings of which I have spoken have thus far been easily preserved by inscribed pieces. But the arts, or rather the artifices, are uncovered and brought forth for man very much every day. We think, for example, *of sailing*.[15] But the inscriptions of their fables, which have been regarded by the nations as extremely old, are evidently able to be sought from the history of Moses, and so thence it is known that all their accounts hardly reach the age of the flood. And there are many others.

207. We cannot explain how much light they bring to the history of Moses, in which the creation of all things is clearly handed down to us by the giving of a conscience of such perfect testimonies

---

13. Cf. *Doctrina*, 6.17–18.

14. For Vitringa's fuller treatment of this point, see Vitringa, *Sacrarum Observationum*, vol. 1, chs. 1–2, 5–8.

15. The ancient Phoenicians are known for being master navigators at sea. Having sailed beyond the bounds of the Mediterranean, the ancient Phoenicians are credited with masterful ship designs and secured the praise of ancient writers such as Homer and Herodotus. See also Vitringa, *Hypotyposis Historiae*, 24.

that it best illuminates *the deity of God*[16] and so is most fitting to God.[17]

208. But to perceive these truths so simply from the Old Testament history and to confirm them with reasons does not thereby destroy that *understanding*,[18] attentive examination, and observation which Paul says is *of faith*.[19] This clearly requires the examination of the *end* to which all things have been ordained in the creation of the world, and of all brilliant divine power in the creation of the world toward such an end.

209. In that history of creation, in the order of works set forth by Moses (which have been summed up by *six days*), it ought to be observed that *light* was created on the first day while the *luminaries* were eventually founded on the fourth day.[20]

210. Likewise, *the foundation of the earth above the sea* was made on the second day and is considered in Scripture as a basis for the whole work of grace.[21]

211. From this it follows remarkably that this work on the second day was not able nor ought it to have lacked a blessing, and thus *and He said*,[22] which occurs in Genesis 1:9, ought to be translated as *and He had said*.[23]

212. In addition, it ought to be observed that this whole description of creation has been so fashioned so that it may be accommodated to our capacity.

---

16. τὴν θεότητα τοῦ θεοῦ.

17. For a fuller treatment of this point, see Vitringa, *Sacrarum Observationum*, vol. 1, chs. 8–9.

18. νόησιν.

19. πίστεως. Vitringa cites Hebrews 11:3 in *Doctrina*, 6.18.

20. Cf. *Doctrina*, 6.20–22. In *Doctrina*, Vitringa argues that Moses's account in Genesis 1 should not be understood allegorically (*allegorice*) on the grounds of the simplicity of the narrative and the reason of mystery.

21. See Psalm 24:1. *Doctrina*, 6.22.

22. ויאמר.

23. I.e., the *pluperfect* tense.

213. This ought also to be noticed in this continual procession from the more imperfect to the perfect, which is the rule of all natural working.[24]

214. The world has been founded as one and can be called *indefinite* since it does not overstep its own boundaries. Nevertheless, it does not seem to me that it ought to be called *infinite*, both because it consists of finite parts and because many other difficulties are born from this conception. I add that notions of a *finite* world seem to us to fit more with the Scriptures.[25]

215. Besides the bodies of which the world consists, it pleased God the Spirit to create finite beings who labor in the world, some of whom have been determined by His will to be certain corporeal beings who are called rational *souls* and produce men with a body, and indeed others who do not, who are called *angels*.[26]

216. By these beings [angels] we mean *finite thinking things, subsistences in themselves*.[27]

217. They are designated by various names in Scripture, but there are chiefly two: *spirits*[28] and *messengers*.[29] The Greeks call them *angels*.[30] One term expresses nature, the other office.[31]

218. By the term *spirit*[32] we understand their nature to be *to think*, that is, *to understand* and *to will*.[33]

219. Their *intellect* consists in the principles of truths impressed upon them by God, from which they can deduce conclusions

---

24. Cf. *Doctrina*, 6.23.
25. Cf. *Doctrina*, 6.24–25.
26. *Doctrina*, 5.26.
27. Cf. *Doctrina*, 5.27–28.
28. רוחות, πνεύματα.
29. מלאכים.
30. ἀγγέλους.
31. *Doctrina*, 5.29.
32. רוח.
33. *Doctrina*, 5.30.

according to the reason of a rational spirit. This understanding is increased from the perception of other truths which they learn through divine revelation, or which are in those who are executors of divine works, or in the churches. Perhaps also through communication which one makes with another.[34]

220. To their *will* we ascribe all things which we ascribe to the human will, except that *passions*[35] ought to be denied in them, which hold a place in the soul of man by the strength of a union with the body.[36] To *affections*, however, they are subject.

221. Their will is *effective*, and more effective than the human will, since we are able to effect understanding in our mind alone, but they in many, perhaps even in all bodies (even if not all at once). That is, they exist so that by their will they are effects in this or in that body. Nevertheless, it ought to be understood that their will is always subordinate to God.[37]

222. But we ought to diligently observe that such works from them which subvert the order of nature cannot occur. Thus, the accomplishing of miracles ought never to be ascribed to them, except those things which happen fittingly by the order of nature of which they are certainly far more knowledgeable than us since we ourselves may not know their causes.

223. Now when they operate by their will, then they are said to be present.[38]

224. Their works are certainly far more frequented to the human soul than we may persuade ourselves. Indeed, their mode of

---

34. *Doctrina*, 5.31–33.
35. "Passions" here do not refer to emotions, but rather to reactions that bypass the will. Passions are distinguished from "affections," which are reactions controlled by the will.
36. *Doctrina*, 5.34.
37. Cf. *Doctrina*, 5.35.
38. *Doctrina*, 6.42.

operating in our midst seems chiefly to consist in the representation of objects, or of *goods* or *evils*.

225. It is most likely that these beings were created on the first day.[39]

226. And certainly in enormous number.[40]

227. Likewise, we learn from Scripture that in the beginning all of them were made good. That is, we understand that they were fitting in order to God and to the creatures, but that they fell. Perhaps from envy of both the Son of God and created men.

228. They who persevered through divine grace by the eternal decree are called *elect angels, angels of light, of heaven*, or likewise *of God, holy*, etc.[41]

229. Those angels of divine grace now have a certain conscience in which sense we say that they are *confirmed* in that state of holiness. Nevertheless, if you look back to the divine decree, which has always been one and the same concerning their state, then you can remove this specification.

230. Their leader is the most high Son of God. They are considered His *associates* under the economy of the Old Testament (for He was sustaining the character of their will), and *ministers* under the new covenant. So Scripture says in numerous clear places.[42]

231. In addition, there is no doubt that these are more excellent than others, and so among them an order is maintained for excellence and nobility of offices and gifts. Nevertheless, the teachings of the Jews and the Papists are well beyond certitude.[43]

---

39. *Doctrina*, 6.43.

40. *Doctrina*, 6.44.

41. *Doctrina*, 6.47.

42. E.g., Deuteronomy 33:2; Daniel 10:13; 12:1; Galatians 3:19; Colossians 2:10; Hebrews 11:2; Jude 9; Revelation 12:7. *Doctrina*, 6.49.

43. *Doctrina*, 6.50. Vitringa here refers to the varying beliefs concerning the hierarchy of angels among the Jews and the Papists of his day. The Jews distinguished between many

232. The offices are prescribed to them principally by Christ and are surpassed by the faithful in different ways under the old and the new covenants. There is no certitude about the guardianship of specific angels for specific persons. And often they were summoned for punishing the reprobate.[44]

233. The state of *evil* angels or spirits which are specifically named in Scripture is distinctly described to us as *darkness*.[45]

234. It seems everywhere that there were some beliefs among the ancients that many things were brought forth through the air and in the air as if it were a place which was meant by these statements.[46]

235. In addition, we understand from the Scriptures that they were at one time exceedingly powerful in the rule of the world. This rule was then relinquished from them by divine judgment since God allowed the nations to walk in their own ways.[47]

236. There is one among them who is the leader of rebellion and is usually called in the sacred pages *Satan*,[48] *devil*,[49] *adversary*,[50] *evil one*,[51] *accuser of the brothers*,[52] *prince of this world, the prince of demons, the ancient serpent, Beelzebul*, and *Sammael* by the Jews.[53]

---

grades of angels: creatures of holiness, ophanim, chasmalim, seraphim, angels, gods, sons of God, cherubim, and ishim. The Roman Catholics, on the basis of the written corpus of Pseudo-Dionysus, held to three grades: in the first, *thronos*, cherubim, and seraphim; in the second, powers, dominions, and virtues; in the third, angels, archangels, and principalities. See Peter Lombard, *Sentences*, 2.9.1–2.

    44. Cf. *Doctrina*, 6.51.
    45. *Doctrina*, 6.53–54.
    46. See Ephesians 2:2. *Doctrina*, 6.55.
    47. *Doctrina*, 6.60.
    48. שׂטן.
    49. διάβολος.
    50. ἀντίδικος.
    51. πονηρός.
    52. ὁ κατήγορος τῶν ἀδελφῶν.
    53. *Doctrina*, 6.56.

237. They have an awareness of their present and chiefly of their future misery. Meanwhile, God permits according to His own justice and wisdom that they torment evil men and that they seduce them toward idolatry, superstition, and lust of the flesh. But they aim at and torment the faithful and the elect by trying to convince them that they are insignificant and that they have been rejected. We do not exclude deceit by apparitions.[54]

238. Spirits which are determined to certain bodies for their work and being united with these bodies are called *men*.

239. Their creation was wholly fitting to God since God was not able to make the world in vain.[55]

240. Scripture teaches us that men are called the *gladness* and *delight*[56] of the highest wisdom of the Son of God because, in the creation of man, the most high God gave a mark of His wisdom and power, and He even formerly determined that He would chiefly reveal His virtues to man before all His creatures through His most prudent governing in his various states.[57]

241. As for the *spirit*, or *his soul*,[58] which is a thinking thing, by a most distinct extension its beginning has been communicated, and so now also it is communicated through the sufficiency of God. For we do not admit the propagation of the soul.[59]

242. Besides a body, which has been made with the highest skill and which he has along with all the brutes, he has been raised on high to the end that he may understand that his office is above the brutes, *to see the things that are not seen and eternal.*[60]

---

54. *Doctrina*, 6.59.

55. *Doctrina*, 6.64.

56. שעשעים.

57. *Doctrina*, 6.65.

58. רוח, נשמת חיים.

59. *Doctrina*, 6.67. Today this idea is known as *traducianism*.

60. σκοπεῖν τὰ μὴ βλεπόμενα, καὶ τὰ αἰώνια. Cf. 2 Corinthians 4:18. *Doctrina*, 6.69.

243. The union of the mind and body not only signifies that our spirit rules our body by its will—even if it may be most different in essence from the body—but also that it cares for and loves our body as its own, that it is affected and suffers because of the body, and that it decides the movements of the body, and all other things which pertain to this.[61]

244. It because of this mind or spirit that man is said to be made *in the image of God.*[62]

245. This image is expressed in Hebrew by the terms *tselem* and *damuth*[63] which denote likeness. From this it is evident that these terms are of equal force. The words of God, *Let us make man in our image according to our likeness,*[64] really say: he who has a *similar image* as us.[65]

246. This image does not mean merely that man understands and wills, that is, that he thinks, because those who think are also those whom Scripture compares with animals and brutes which do not manifest the image of God. But this image consists in this: that man *rightly* thinks, understands, and wills.

247. Scripture describes this state of man possessing the image of God as *uprightness, holiness, goodness, holiness of truth,*[66] *knowledge,*[67] *love*, and the *understanding of God*. Likewise, *wholeness of spirit and soul and body*.[68] Theologians call this *original righteousness*.[69]

---

61. *Doctrina,* 6.70–71.

62. *Doctrina,* 6.72.

63. ‏דמות, צלם‎.

64. ‏בצלמנו כדמותנו‎. Genesis 1:26.

65. *Doctrina,* 6.73.

66. ὁσιότητα τῆς ἀληθείας. Ephesians 4:24.

67. ἐπίγνωσις.

68. ὁλοκληρίαν τοῦ πνεύματος καὶ τῆς ψυχῆς καὶ τοῦ σώματος. 1 Thessalonians 5:23.

69. *Doctrina,* 6.77.

248. They who conceive that man was made by God *innocent*, or *pure*, as they say, and ascribe to him *natural things*, or further attribute to him feebleness or concupiscence,[70] not only contradict the Scriptures, but they also disgracefully destroy the most excellent work of God, and they make it most intolerable by their "authority."[71]

249. Likewise, they who say that the image of God chiefly consists in dominion, speak *in error*,[72] since dominion belongs to no creature except those who are holy, and so it is a consequence of the divine image.[73]

250. And likewise, regarding the immortality of the whole man, it cannot be conceived that God has allowed the work of His hands to be destroyed in sin without intervening.

---

70. Concupiscence, in general, refers to sinful desire. See Muller, *Dictionary*, s.v. "concupiscentia."

71. *Doctrina*, 6.78. A subtle reference to the Roman Catholic Church.

72. ἀσύςατα.

73. *Doctrina*, 6.78.

CHAPTER 7

The General Preservation and Governing of Created Things, Especially of Man

251. Just as things cannot have their origin of existing without the efficacious will of God, so they cannot persevere in existing and be directed to their own ends without the power of this same divine will.[1]

252. This powerful work of God toward the creatures is usually expressed by the term *providence*[2] and refers to the *decree*. It means something different *than foreknowledge*[3] which refers to *foresight*.[4] The reason for this name is not wholly foreign to Scripture, although Scripture usually uses other words with negation. The Hebrews called it *oversight*.[5]

253. This providence, that is, this powerful work of God of *preserving* and *ruling* among the creatures, we attribute to God both because it is taught throughout all Scripture and also because the power of God—the foundation of created things, the most wise order which is discerned in all things, predictions, miracles, judgments of God, etc.—most clearly reveals it.[6]

---

1. *Doctrina*, 7.1.
2. προνόιας.
3. ἀπό τῆς πρόγνωσεως.
4. *praevidentiam.*
5. השגחה. Cf. Psalm 33:13–15. *Doctrina*, 7.2.
6. Cf. *Doctrina*, 7.3.

254. Indeed, besides the Epicureans (that sect of philosophers everywhere condemned)[7] most are not so absurd as to insist on denying providence to God, or at least the greater part of it.[8] The Stoics[9] conceived of *fate*[10] when they deny the liberty of the Supreme Being. Let the one who is favorably disposed to these ideas take heed.

255. The doctrine of providence is usually discussed in the schools by the terms *preservation*,[11] *concurrence*,[12] and *governance*.[13] Preservation refers to *the being*[14] of the creatures, concurrence to their *actions*, and governance to their *ends*.[15]

256. Preservation therefore wishes to express that God, who gives existence to the creatures, may give the same persevering in existing to them by the efficaciousness of His own will.[16]

257. This requires that the creatures are said to exist, to live, and to subsist in God.[17] But He is said to bear, to make alive, to renew, to satisfy, and to preserve the creatures, and indeed to give to them the Spirit. For He is called a *rock*[18] and *Lord*,[19] just as He seems to be a *place*[20] among the Jews.[21]

---

7. The Epicureans were a group of philosophers founded upon the teachings of Epicurus (341–270 BC). The Epicureans believed that one should seek the highest degree of pleasure (*hedonism*) while avoiding the most amount of pain. They denied the existence of prayer, miracles, and providence.

8. *Doctrina*, 7.5.

9. Stoicism was a philosophical school founded by Zeno of Citium (ca. 334–262 BC). The Stoics held to a very strong doctrine of fate, believing in a kind of naturalistic determinism in the world.

10. εἱμαρμένην.

11. *conservationis*.

12. *concursus*.

13. *gubernationis*.

14. τὸ εὖε.

15. *Doctrina*, 7.10.

16. *Doctrina*, 7.11.

17. Acts 17:28.

18. צור.

19. אדון.

20. מקום.

21. *Doctrina*, 7.13.

258. From these ideas we can say that preservation is not disagreeably called *continuing creation*, since those things which have been founded by the will of God proceed *to be* by the same.[22]

259. So in the same way it is clear that there is no small thing in this world, which is not preserved by God, since no small thing can begin to exist without the will of God.

260. Opposite to this preservation is *annihilation* of the creature, about which nothing has been revealed to us in the Word of God, and belief of which we think is problematic. Nevertheless, it seems good to understand by this idea that God may command by His own will that a thing exist for a certain time.[23]

261. We have said that concurrence refers to the actions of the creatures. Indeed, even though this term may not be found in Scripture[24] and we can conceive of this matter in a wrong way, nevertheless by this it is signified that God, who is the independent first cause, cooperates with the actions of secondary causes. Indeed, all such secondary causes are of the creature for the bringing about of existing and moving. The apostle signifies this when he says that we *move in God*.[25]

262. Hence it stands that this concurrence, which is considered by this term, ought not to be conceived as *simultaneous* in the sense that God concurs so that causes are joined unto actions, but as *prior* in the sense that He concurs in those creatures; or rather, by which He operates in those creatures.

263. Likewise, this concurrence is not vague and indifferent or indeterminate, but determinable by that creature itself; or even mediated, so that whatever things are now accomplished by

---

22. *Doctrina*, 7.14.
23. Cf. *Doctrina*, 7.15.
24. ἄγραφον.
25. Acts 17:28. *Doctrina*, 7.18.

strength of effort have been accomplished by God without the immediate working of God in them.[26]

264. This concurrence does not differ from the preservation of things since it is nothing other than the preservation of a thing with this or that *mode* of existing.

265. From this concurrence, free actions are not at all removed, nor contingencies of rational creatures, whether good or evil.

266. For contingency is nothing with respect to God, but it is only named among us because we do not know the binding of secondary causes.

267. God works good actions in us, so that not only that action, but even the quality of it ought to be ascribed to Him. *He works in us to will and to work.*[27]

268. But a foundational and natural act[28] holds evil actions together (which is their foundation), which is from God from whom is all being.

269. But they who state therefore that God is the author of sin *blaspheme*,[29] since what is a privation in man and indeed is sin in him only speaks of refusal or not giving of help with respect to God. Indeed, God, who is independent, does not give more or less to the creature than He understands to pertain to His glory, and so it is not possible that He sin, nor that He is conceived as such without manifest absurdity. To God, the law is His own glory to which He directs all things.[30]

---

26. Cf. *Doctrina*, 7.20–21.
27. Philippians 2:13.
28. See *Doctrina*, 7.45.
29. βλασφημοῦσι.
30. Cf. *Doctrina*, 7.27.

270. And so, it ought to be firmly insisted that sin has some reference to man and the law, and because the privation of man is a result of the denial of God. It suffices that the sinner is indeed damned, and that God is just. This is what the conscious creature is to himself: he sins freely against the dictates of his own conscience.

271. Indeed, it is true that the powerful work of God in regard to evil actions consists in denial, that is, in not giving or in a righteous removing of help for a time of allowance after sin had been committed, so that the most efficacious terms *to make blind* and *to harden*, and other *expressions*[31] similar to these (*to not give good precepts, to send efficacy of errors, to hand someone unto a debased mind in the heart of the reprobate, a mind lacking all judgment,* etc.) ought not to be abandoned in any way.

272. For it is evident in every one of these cases that God denies help in man because of preceding sins, and so He works in them less than He worked in them before. From this it follows that the creature must thereby fail more. Moreover, God, who is called the *instructor of the nations*,[32] after they sin, He also often removes from them the use of reason according to the principles of truth impressed upon their minds such that they attend to these principles no further. So the holy writers say.

273. We should not deny, however, that it is difficult for us to understand how we are conscious of the liberty of our actions such that we are regarded ourselves as the authors of those actions, and yet we are determined to these actions through the powerful will of God.

274. Indeed, since God works powerfully and wisely in all things, it cannot be the case that God does not direct the actions of the creatures to those certain glorious ends for Himself. This is called *governance*.[33]

---

31. φράσεις.

32. יסר גוים. Psalm 94:10.

33. *gubernatio.*

275. This governance extends itself equally in every direction just as the preservation of things, and so ought to be referred to all things, great and small, and both good and bad actions. Likewise, all free actions. For nothing can be in vain. All things owe response to God.[34]

276. Indeed, God governs the creatures according to certain laws and regulations from which He rarely withdraws. Scripture confirms this, when it teaches us that God has entered into, as it were, a *covenant*[35] with His creatures.[36]

277. The laws of divine providence are these: that certain means constantly produce this or that end. Yet it pleases God repeatedly to disregard ordinary means or to employ common means for effecting great things so that He is known as the highest author and arbiter of all things.

278. God rules rational creatures by prescribing to them precepts and by adjoining promises and threats to them. Likewise, by exhorting them toward good and deterring them from evil by whatever means that He has made. Think here of testimonies and vows. Finally, also by rewarding or punishing them.

279. Indeed, He governs the *good actions* of rational creatures by arranging them for the praise of His grace; and the *bad* ones by repeatedly impeding them (as we conceive of them in the mind); sometimes by permitting, and by determining them to certain objects, to certain positions, to certain ends, which at last result in the proclamation of His strength.[37]

---

34. Cf. *Doctrina*, 7.38.

35. Unless otherwise indicated, *foedus* will be translated as *covenant*, *pactum* as *pact*, and *testamentum* as *testament*.

36. See §280ff on the covenant of works.

37. Cf. *Doctrina*, 7.46–48.

CHAPTER 8

The Governance of Righteous Man, or the Covenant of Works

280. The governance of the rational creature in this state of uprightness is described by Moses. For *laws* were prescribed to him, and threats and rewards were added to those laws.

281. The first law is concerning the propagation of a holy seed through properly observed marital union. Along with this [law], justice and dominion were given to him over all created things which could be used by him. This dominion was confirmed to Adam by this sign—that he assigned names to the animals.

282. The law followed with *not eating from the Tree of Knowledge of Good and Evil,* to which was added the threat of death.[1]

283. Whether this tree was only one or a whole species of trees is not mentioned by Moses. Nevertheless, the latter is perhaps more likely. Of whatever species it might have been is uncertain. The reason for the name which it now has ought to cause no doubt about the event.

284. If we carefully examine the matter, it is clear that this precept served for the *testing* and *proving* of man. But what ought to be tested in man? Doubtless it was whether man loved God from his whole soul and heart, put nothing before Him, and willed to abandon all things for His sake.

---

1. Cf. *Doctrina,* 8.4, 24.

285. That one law (as we call it) contains many precepts in its force: first, that he recognize God alone is Lord of all things; second, that he recognize his own dominion depends on God; third, that he should not seek his own true and necessary good and His communion outside of God; fourth, that he should desire nothing outside of God or not in God and to God; fifth, that he should regard the rule of all desirable things as the word and law of God; sixth, That he render to God the obedience of both his soul and members in a full posture of love; finally, that he seek a holy seed through perseverance in uprightness.[2]

286. Hence it follows that man was under the law written on his heart which is found in all men. The sum is this: *that he love God from his whole heart and his neighbor as his own self.*[3] That he seek the glory of his God, and that he tend to Him with all strength of his will in all his actions. He should *desire* (ἐπιθυμεῖν)[4] nothing besides God nor before God.

287. Moses explains that man was placed in this state when he says that man was made in the image of God. But who would deny that it was his duty to *preserve* the image of God? Certainly, it cannot be conceived that the creature is rational, and that God does not display Himself as a model for man's imitation and copying.

288. Adjoined to this precept is the threat of death, through which comes some explicit understanding of death in Scripture. *Abandonment*[5] of the soul by God resulted in that it is no longer able to be a work to the glory of God. Corruption of the body through miseries, calamities, deaths, misfortunes, accidents, affections, labors—thus, every part gradually becomes unfitting for serving the soul until it may finally be separated from it. Finally, there is that state in which God afflicts the soul and body in a horrible way.

---

2. *Doctrina*, 8.9.
3. Leviticus 19:18; Matthew 22:36–40; Mark 12:30–31; Luke 10:27.
4. Cf. Galatians 5:17.
5. *abalienatio.*

That is, that the whole man has no hope of a greater life, and he is separated from the presence of the glory of God.

289. All this death begins to dominate to a degree with sin, and so that statement of God is most true: *On that day...*[6]

290. The threat sufficiently proves that man, if he had not sinned, would not have died, and so he would live, or more correctly, *live into eternity*, since the one who does not sin does not die.[7]

291. But how is it living into eternity? Was it by animal life only in the same way he was now living? It certainly does not seem that his *earthy*[8] body was ordered for it.[9]

292. Further, since eternal death, which is the merit of sin as is clear from the event because God in His judgment was terrible against the whole man, who doubts whether this reward for obedience would come so that God would also be marveled and glorified in the whole man?

293. And so it seems that man's body, at whatever moment would be pleasing to God, was to be changed into something *incorruptible*,[10] and the soul filled with the glory of God which is the highest salvation and blessedness of man.[11]

294. So it is therefore confirmed that God is described to us as a *rewarder*.[12]

295. And a promise of eternal life is tied to the observation of this same precept of love toward God for the human sinner, by faith.[13]

---

6. Genesis 2:17.
7. *Doctrina*, 8.13.
8. χοϊκὸν. 1 Corinthians 15:47.
9. *Doctrina*, 8.14.
10. ἄφθαρτον. 1 Corinthians 15:52.
11. *Doctrina*, 8.15.
12. μισθαποδότης. Hebrews 11:6. *Doctrina*, 8.17.
13. *Doctrina*, 8.18.

296. In this also God extended Himself as the true pleasure of the first man, because it was ever fitting for him to be satisfied by God.

297. Likewise, it was signified to man by the *Tree of Life* and *Paradise*, which cannot be considered as anything other than sacraments which confirm and represent the promise. In our judgment, the *Tree of Knowledge of Good and Evil* is wrongly identified as a sacrament.[14]

298. The Tree of Life is elsewhere summed up as a whole species of tree. By a certain strength, it seemed to have offered the body a gift of reviving from God, so that in it we might see the antitype more clearly—the Son of God, the author of eternal life.[15]

299. We think that Paradise (perhaps from *to bear fruit*[16] and *grass*[17]) was a most ample space of the earth, rich in metals by the special providence of God, which He destined as the domain[18] of man. It is called *Eden*[19] for *pleasure*. Its location can be ascertained particularly from the names of the rivers.[20]

300. It is legitimate to conclude from the holy writers that *Paradise* with its rivers and with its flowing and irrigating streams was a symbol of heaven.

301. It is pleasing to theologians to understand and describe this state of the first man as *covenantal*,[21] in which were also included friendship and certain conditions between God and man. But

---

14. Cf. *Doctrina*, 8.21–25. Interestingly, Vitringa avoids using the term *sacramentum* with reference to the Tree of Life and Paradise in *Doctrina*. Yet he does describe Paradise as "figuring" the heavenly state of the church, and the Tree of Life as "exhibiting" Christ and eternal life.

15. Cf. *Doctrina*, 8.23.

16. פרה.

17. דשא.

18. *sedem.*

19. עדן.

20. Genesis 2:10–14. Cf. *Doctrina*, 8.25.

21. *faederalem.*

it is usual to call this a *covenant of works* and *of nature*, and so distinguished from the *covenant of grace*.[22]

302. *Covenant* (the Hebrews call it a *berith* from the verb *barah*[23] which means *to choose*, and the Greeks use *diatheke* and *homologia*[24]) is understood as a kind of agreement[25] between God and man, by which God under certain conditions (by prescription of law) gives an expectation to man of certain good, but man joins himself to God and awaits the reward by the strength of the covenant.[26]

303. And so, the parts of the whole covenant on the part of God are *precept*[27] or *commandment*[28] and *promise*.[29] On the part of man, *confirmation*[30] and *obligation*.[31]

304. God is said *to make* or *to cut a covenant*[32] when He invites man to friendship with Him. This invitation always obligates man toward a constant habit by the calling of God since God is his Lord. For the covenant of God with man ought to be considered as *unequal*.[33]

305. But Adam lived in this state of friendship with God and expected a certain good under certain conditions before he was defeated. It should not be doubted that that state can be called a *covenant* and a *covenant of works*. Yet it ought to be acknowledged that

---

22. *Doctrina*, 8.27–28.
23. ברה, ברית.
24. διαθήκη, ὁμολογία.
25. *conventione*.
26. *Doctrina*, 8.29.
27. παραγγελία.
28. ἐντολή.
29. παγγελία.
30. ὁμολογία, *adstipulatio*.
31. ἐπερώτησις, *restipulatio*.
32. כרת ברית.
33. *Doctrina*, 8.32.

this label does not explicitly appear in Scripture. But what else does the *law of works*[34] appear to mean in Paul?[35]

306. The law concerning the Sabbath was not given to Adam except insofar as the *Sabbath rest of God*[36] was set forth for his imitation so that he would in turn rest in God, bless Him, and sanctify Him.[37]

---

34. νόμος ἔργων.
35. E.g., Romans 2:15; 3:20; Galatians 2:16; 3:5. *Doctrina*, 9.33.
36. σαββατισμός τοῦ θεοῦ. Hebrews 4:9.
37. *Doctrina*, 9.34.

CHAPTER 9

The Result of the Governance of Righteous Man, or the Fall of Man

307. By reporting the result, the sacred history teaches that the first man did not persevere very long in that state of friendship with God, but he destroyed it by transgressing the precept about the Tree of Knowledge of Good and Evil.[1]

308. The first man could perish in that state by reason of the habitual condition of his own nature, since he was made *mutable* by God. This mutability proceeds from the *nothingness*[2] of the created mind.[3]

309. This possible mutability of man ought wholly to be distinguished from his *liberty*. For the liberty of the rational creature is not always joined with mutability, but rather liberty in the highest degree excludes mutability. For mutability always has an accompanying fear, but the highest liberty has security. Therefore, a creature is more free when he is more holy and more confirmed in good.[4]

310. Likewise, with respect to God, created man was able to fall, since we perceive that God did not restrain him, and that He always works in man for the highest perfection.

---

1. *Doctrina*, 9.1.
2. οὐδένεια.
3. *Doctrina*, 9.2.
4. *Doctrina*, 9.3.

311. The transgression of the law did not happen without the preceding temptation of the devil who invaded man as a living serpent.[5]

312. In this temptation, the *craftiness*[6] and deceit of that temptation ought carefully to be considered so that we may learn to recognize the *schemes of the devil.*[7] For there is no doubt that by this method he began to seduce men, and he proceeds to seduce many more.[8]

313. This cunning includes first that he used an instrument of this kind [i.e., a serpent] which is a symbol of *prudence.*[9] I call it an *instrument* since it is certain that the devil was present in the serpent.

314. From this it seems that Eve convinced herself that a good angel had entered into conversation with her, an angel that could be trusted by living beings without absurdity, even before she had experience with good angels.

315. Likewise, he assailed the woman, a holy but weaker vessel.[10]

316. And indeed, she was separated from her husband.[11]

317. It was not very long after she was made that the circumstances induced her. Nevertheless, it is difficult to believe that man was tempted and fell on the sixth day of the week of creation.[12]

318. We also need to understand that [Satan] attempted to lure man not in one great moment but through various antecedent and

---

5. Cf. *Doctrina,* 9.5.

6. πανουργία.

7. τὰς μεθοδείας τοῦ διαβόλου. Ephesians 6:11.

8. *Doctrina,* 9.5.

9. φρόνησεως.

10. 1 Peter 3:7. *Doctrina,* 9.7.

11. *Doctrina,* 9.8.

12. *Doctrina,* 9.9.

differing works when he is alone. This is the continual method of the devil in all seduction.[13]

319. The particles *indeed that*[14] mark the beginning of the sermon of the devil. These ought to be received as part of a longer discourse which appeared to her to be true.[15]

320. These particles were used so that the sermon of the devil might be *suspicious*,[16] but it most certainly pertains to his *cunning*.[17]

321. First, the devil calls the Word of God into doubt such that he excites in man *reasonings and murmurings*[18] against the Word of God which greatly injure *faith*.[19]

322. But when the woman sufficiently repeated her firm memory of the word of God (for it is not evident to us how much she omitted) he began to displace the threat adjoined to the divine precept, and he suggested another explanation by reporting a plausible argument and by confirming it with an oath.[20]

323. His explanation was a lie, even if he spoke ambiguously.

324. Those who believe that the devil attributed hatred and envy of fellowship to God by these words do not speak fittingly with respect to the cunning of the devil, nor to the state of the first man.

325. This reasoning of the devil gave birth in the woman to *many notions*,[21] enough so she finally fell. For her will, having not been strengthened enough with the fear of and care for the Word,

---

13. *Doctrina*, 9.10.
14. כִּי אַף. Genesis 3:1.
15. *Doctrina*, 9.11.
16. Λοξὸς.
17. *Doctrina*, 9.12.
18. τοὺς διαλογισμοὺς καὶ γογγυσμοὺς.
19. *Doctrina*, 9.13.
20. Cf. *Doctrina*, 9.14.
21. חשבונות רבים. Ecclesiastes 7:29.

and having been tickled by the lust of apparent good, fell first. And her will received concupiscence instead of love, and it ruled over the intellect so that it might devise reasons for accomplishing transgression. Having been tested by God, and by the devil, finally the woman tested her own self, so that she tested God and so that she destroyed patience, power, and of all her virtues in this forbidden thing. She is responsible for destroying her goodness of obedience and fear.[22]

326. Adam, it seems, by these same reasons was led to the same sin by the woman.[23]

327. The reason for violating this precept (which is set forth above) and the many circumstances made it so that this sin of the first men ought to be judged most seriously.[24]

328. The cause of this ought in no way to be found in God who *tempts no one*,[25] but in man only who knowingly and willingly committed this deliberately by neglecting the Word and help of God to which one ought to hasten in troublesome times.[26]

329. God did not remove His grace or help in the temptation of man before He purified them, but He did not add a greater grace which was required at this time to overcome temptation, since man did not desire it.[27]

330. Yet the eternal foreknowledge and providence of God concerning this act of man was deeply involved effectively but also with holiness, although the *how*[28] is hidden from us. We do not penetrate *the depths of God*.[29]

---

22. *Doctrina*, 9.18.
23. *Doctrina*, 9.19.
24. *Doctrina*, 9.20.
25. James 1:13.
26. *Doctrina*, 9.25.
27. *Doctrina*, 9.26.
28. πῶς.
29. βάθος τοῦ θεοῦ. Romans 11:33. Cf. *Doctrina*, 9.27.

331. Whoever dares to accuse God here, let him investigate his own conscience as to whether he knows the cause of this first sin, and how even now he often neglects the help of God and gazes at his own soul with such idol curiosities which the conscience should not search, and thus seriously sins. And let him who dares to excuse our first parents see whether he can excuse himself before his own conscience.

CHAPTER 10

Sin and Its Consequences

332. So *through one man sin entered the world, and death through sin.*[1]

333. *Sin*[2] is any disposition, action, inquiry, or motion of the rational creature which, contrary to the law of God, does not have the testimony and praise of a good conscience.[3]

334. Sin is described by John as *lawlessness*,[4] that is, a questioning of the dominion of God. For lawlessness is just as strong a term as *apostasy*.[5]

335. Even if Scripture expresses the nature of this term with various words and phrases, nevertheless it is accustomed to use three distinct terms since it wishes to lay every kind of sin to us before our eyes: *sin*,[6] *iniquity*,[7] *transgression*,[8] all of which are strong terms. The Greeks answer with the terms *unrighteousness*,[9] *lawlessness*,[10]

---

1. ἡ ἁμαρτία εἰς τὸν κόσμον εἰσῆλθεν καὶ διὰ τῆς ἁμαρτίας ὁ θάνατος. Romans 5:12. *Doctrina*, 10.1.

2. ἁμαρτία.

3. Cf. *Doctrina*, 10.2.

4. ἀνομίαν. 1 John 3:4.

5. ἀποστασία.

6. חטאה.

7. עון.

8. פשע.

9. ἀδικία.

10. ἀνομία.

and *sin*.[11] That final term *sin*[12] expresses the most serious kind of sin.[13]

336. Sin is not something real or positive, or merely even relative, but some *privation*, which makes it so that the conscience perceives that such a disposition or action is repulsive and unfitting for it.

337. For sin is not only called an indifferent transgression of the law which has been given by a higher power, but a transgression of the law which the conscience praises, so that the good, right, and holy are declared to be their contrary: corrupt, iniquitous, and unjust.[14]

338. So it is clear that sin is committed against God alone, since the conscience, the judge of the fair and the good, can be bound by nothing except God.

339. And so, sin is not only evil actions done by deliberate decisions, but also every most trivial motion of our own longings such that this concupiscence in occupying our soul and body is a disgrace to man.[15]

340. Nevertheless, this sin is not therefore defined as *voluntary*, although the will does decide first by receiving and then by considering.

341. It has been said now that every sin committed has a *sense of repulsiveness* which makes it so that God hates the sinner, men hold Him in contempt, and He makes them ashamed. This is called *dishonor*.[16]

---

11. ἁμαρτία.
12. חטאה, ἁμαρτία.
13. *Doctrina*, 10.10.
14. *Doctrina*, 10.14.
15. Cf. *Doctrina*, 10.12.
16. Cf. *Doctrina*, 10.13.

342. His companion is another *accuser*,[17] that is, the conscience, *that those who do such things are worthy of death.*[18] Here the cause against the sinner is fear and escape from God.[19]

343. The distinction of this twofold effect of sin (dishonor and accusation) is most useful both for understanding the various phrases of Scripture and the distinctions forming the concepts of *justification* and *sanctification.*[20]

344. The distinction of the Papists between the *reatus culpae* and *reatus poenae* is unsatisfactory. But our common distinction between *potential* and *actual guilt* is useless since the actual can hardly be distinguished from the penalty.[21]

345. The *penalty* (the threefold consequence of sin) is the harsh punishment of evil on the sinner by God, the judge, on account of the demerit of sin for the satisfaction of His righteousness.[22]

346. From this it is clear that [the penalty] is not *correction*[23] unless exceedingly loose and unsuitable, and not *testing*,[24] nor the highest grade of testing,[25] since we are called by God to the truth of the testimonies given in our death, and to deserve the debt of the penalty.[26]

---

17. *reatus.*

18. ὅτι οἱ τὰ τοιαῦτα πράσσοντες ἄξιοι θανάτου εἰσίν. Romans 1:32.

19. *Doctrina*, 10.17.

20. *Doctrina*, 10.18.

21. *Doctrina*, 10.19. Some theologians such as the medievals made a distinction between the "liability to punishment" (*reatus poenae*) and the "liability to guilt" (*reatus culpae*). They argued that the obedience of Christ only removes the liability to guilt of the sinner, but the liability to punishment must be removed by works of satisfaction. The Protestants rejected this distinction. See Muller, *Dictionary*, s.v. "reatus."

22. *Doctrina*, 10.20.

23. παιδείαν.

24. δοκιμασίαν.

25. μαρτύριον.

26. *Doctrina*, 10.22.

347. This penalty for every sin is death, as mentioned before.[27] Yet chiefly *eternal death*, in the flames and *inextinguishable fire*, and *the worm which does not die*, etc. as set forth in Scripture.[28]

348. This *just penalty*[29] not only consists in that man will be made an alien from the face of God into eternity and from the glory of His strength (which is called the *penalty of damnation*), but also that the magnitude of the anger of God, which is only expressible to us in soul and body (for in what other way is there a union of these parts?) is brought forth with utmost horror before which one ought to tremble. This is called the *penalty of sense*. Present in this condition is blasphemy, torture, and suffering of the conscience—the most troublesome thoughts of incitements with the highest grade of despair.[30]

---

27. §292.
28. Mark 9:48.
29. δίκη.
30. *Doctrina*, 10.27.

CHAPTER 11

The Effects of Sin, Both in the First Man and in His Posterity

349. These effects or consequences of sin were already visible in the fall of man to the extent that it is evident from the sense of nakedness and his zeal being laid bare. These were marks of the laying bare of his conscience, horror, fear, and fleeing from God, the expulsion from Paradise, the denial of the fruit of the Tree of Life, the malediction of the earth, the beginning of labor and pain to which the man and woman were bound by the sentence of the judgment of God, the binding unto destruction of the soul by the body, etc.[1] The symbol of the anger of God was the flaming sword separating man from Paradise. Nevertheless, God added various restrictions to the inflicted penalty, since in the fall of man His counsel was to make the hope of a new salvation and to the extent that it appeared true, to redeem the first men to be partakers of Him.

350. Likewise, this sin, with all its effects from the just law of God, the upright judge, transmitted the sentence to all of Adam's posterity which are included in the force of this statement: *Be fruitful and multiply*,[2] namely, those who were born of him. This is called *original sin*.[3]

351. Certainly, God, the governor of the world, established this law

---

1. *Doctrina*, 11.1.
2. Genesis 1:28.
3. *Doctrina*, 11.7–8.

that man might procreate children in his specific state according to man's image, that is, his own likeness.[4]

352. But even if it were not necessary that God the governor would retract for us the rule of His laws, yet we can understand that this statute of His was just and holy, since it is constantly observed in the nature of things that likeness procreates likeness, and since it would be intolerable to God for the sinner to seek a holy seed, to give a holy seed, or for God to accept the seed of the sinner when He had condemned that sinner, and also since there is such a relationship between the parents and the children that the children are able to be considered as least good and a possession of the parents, and so the parents punish them.

353. Therefore, in connection with this law, our first parents procreated according to their own likeness. So flesh and concupiscence began to reign in them in some way and thereby rendered the beauty of the image of God void and unworthy though they once lived in communion and friendship with God. This corruption, or sin which predominates in all human nature, is called *inherent original sin*.[5]

354. Now we should consider that inherent sin (or *habitual vice*) is just according to the most holy ordinance of God because of the first sin of Adam. It is called *imputed original sin*. For Adam was justly deprived of the image of God.[6]

355. This state of sin and of accusation in which we are born is thus forced upon us efficaciously and emphatically throughout all the Scriptures. It is evidently confirmed by continual experience. It is also heaped up through consideration of help and of divine grace which is required for the sanctification of man. Finally, it is illustrated through various economies by God, by which it

---

4. *Doctrina*, 11.5–6.

5. *Doctrina*, 11.6.

6. *Doctrina*, 11.7–8. This statement about Adam being deprived of the image of God is not repeated in *Doctrina*.

was pleasing to Him to rule His church, so that we might be astounded at the strength of the divine judgment, and the arts of the devil with which the devil persuaded the Pelagians long ago[7] and the Socinians[8] in our day.[9]

356. But we must now attend to the more notable terms and phrases by which this state of sin is expressed in Scripture, such as *alienation from the way of God*,[10] *darkness*,[11] *powerlessness*,[12] the *old man*,[13] the *outer man*,[14] *sin*,[15] *impurity*,[16] *dirt*,[17] *inventor of evil*,[18] *death*,[19] *abhorrence*,[20] *core bearing poison and wormwood*.[21]

357. But most frequently the term is *flesh*[22] and *concupiscence*,[23] since our corruption is most powerfully seen in that man perpetually *longs* after other things before God, which Scripture calls *not-God*[24] for the satisfaction of his flesh, to such a degree that all

---

7. Pelagius (ca. 354–418) was an ascetic from Britain who, after objecting to a prayer written by Augustine, argued that if God commanded man to do something, man must have the ability to do it. Pelagius and his followers (most notably Coelestius) therefore rejected any notion of original sin and the imputation of Adam's guilt to his posterity. Some even went as far as to reject the idea that God's grace is necessary for salvation. According to the Pelagians, man may earn his salvation through obedience.

8. Faustus Socinus (1539–1604) is known for his anti-Trinitarian theology and his Adoptionist Christology. The Socinians were rationalists, and they rejected the divinity of Christ, positing that Jesus provides believers with a kind of example to show them how to be saved. Much of the teaching of the Pelagians was embraced by the Socinians.

9. Cf. *Doctrina*, 11.6.

10. Ephesians 4:18.

11. Ephesians 5:8.

12. Matthew 26:41; Romans 5:6; 6:19.

13. Romans 6:6; Ephesians 4:22.

14. 2 Corinthians 4:16.

15. Romans 6:12.

16. Job 14:3; Isaiah 64:6.

17. Psalm 103:14.

18. יצר רע. Genesis 8:21.

19. Job 5:24. Vitringa thinks that "you shall not miss" (לא תחטא) refers to death.

20. Psalm 58:4.

21. Deuteronomy 29:18, *Doctrina*, 11.10.

22. σάρξ.

23. ἐπιθυμία.

24. לא אלהים, *non-Deum*.

his wishes and all his desires terminate *in himself* and earthly and perishable things *outside himself* which he strives for *because of himself.* But since this longing is chiefly described through the body and flesh, even our body is called a *body of sin.*[25]

358. This longing so strongly rules in every sinner and has for a long time ruled among the gentiles that there is no work of the sinner or of the gentiles (even of the best kind) which may be called *good*, because it is not born from this font. It is always the case that no sinner seeks the glory of God, nor is he able to, and so all his works terminate in himself and not in God. That is, those works proceed from an inordinate love of himself and strive for his own glory, but not from love for God and for the glory of God.[26]

359. The *state of guilt*, in which the sinner is born, is described as a state of *anger, hate, hostility, condemnation*,[27] but by reason of man being a *sinner*,[28] it is called *accusation because of sin*, and he *is under sin*,[29] and *subject to the judgment of God.*[30] Likewise, he is called *dead in Adam.*[31]

360. Likewise, this state of sin and accusation in which the sinner finds himself is called *slavery to sin*, since man is justly subject to sin, and has been conquered by it. Thus, it is elegantly expressed that man by the just sentence of God is in that pronouncement because he can do nothing nor will to do anything except to sin.[32]

361. This state of servitude to sin does not destroy the *liberty of our will*, which properly and specifically consists in that man operates by willingness, and that he has, by his own will, the faculty of choosing what he pleases from objects which he observes, such that he is not forced by something outside of himself.[33]

---

25. σῶμα τῆς ἁμαρτίας. Romans 6:6. Cf. *Doctrina*, 11.13.
26. *Doctrina*, 11.13.
27. κατακρίματος.
28. ἁμαρτωλός.
29. ὑφ᾽ ἁμαρτίαν εἶναι. Romans 3:9.
30. ὑπόδικος τῷ θεῷ. Romans 3:19.
31. 1 Corinthians 15:22.
32. Cf. *Doctrina*, 11.15–17.
33. *Doctrina*, 11.16.

362. *Liberty*, strictly speaking, helps the creature equally in whatever state he is. For God, who can work by His powerful grace so that holy man may consistently choose good freely, is also able to work by His powerful justice so that the sinner freely chooses evil, and that consistently.[34]

363. But if you understand by *liberty* that man with a full approval of his conscience and peace of his own mind operates without fear concerning a most noble object (which is the highest kind of liberty), then we can say that man is more holy in that by which he is more free, and he sins more severely in that by which he is more severely a *slave*.

364. They who conceive of liberty as *indifference toward two things*[35] or confuse it with mutability and so call the state of immutability of the first man the state of *liberty* as opposed to other states, truly and seriously err.[36]

365. But the *propagation* of humankind in this state which was under the long-suffering and tolerance of God for the illustration of His glory cannot be unworthy and unfitting to God since God in this holy and just propagation observes the *laws of generation* which He had fixed in the creation of things for His own glory.

366. Now the mode of propagation is this, that God denies created souls the grace and habit of good which would be fitting to give to an upright creaturely mind. But in the body through generation, He allows there to be such a disposition through which the soul is subjected to certain concupiscence of the flesh.

367. But inborn concupiscence produces continuous sins, that is, evil acts which are called *actual sins*.[37]

368. The apostle John renders all these things with three terms:

---

34. *Doctrina*, 11.18.
35. ὁπότερον.
36. *Doctrina*, 11.17.
37. *Doctrina*, 11.20.

concupiscence of the flesh,[38] *concupiscence of the eyes*,[39] and *pride of life*.[40] But most other distinctions fitting with Scripture have been used among theologians,[41] by reason of the part, subject,[42] mode,[43] effect,[44] etc. But the distinction between *mortal* and *venial* sins is not correct. In this the Papists engage in the flattering of the flesh.[45]

369. For mortal sin, or *sin unto death*[46] is called the *blasphemy of the Holy Spirit* (which does have a place) only when someone firmly denies or blasphemes *truth of extreme importance* from which he is convicted by the most evident and firm demonstrations of the Holy Spirit or by clearly adjoined reasons or miracles, out of a hatred of the truth such that (if he were able) he would not need God.[47] This sin is described as a *raised hand*,[48] or the *bearing of the name of God in vain*,[49] or as *voluntary*[50] without which there is no sacrifice. Thus, God has taught that the creature should fear the magnitude of His anger and come humbly before His face.[51]

370. So you should not reduce any action in Scripture by which the Holy Spirit is said to *afflict painfully*.

---

38. ἐπιθυμία τῆς σαρκὸς.

39. τῶν ὀφθαλμῶν.

40. ἀλαζονεία τοῦ βίου. 1 John 2:16.

41. *Doctrina*, 11.21.

42. *Doctrina*, 11.25.

43. *Doctrina*, 11.23.

44. Cf. *Doctrina*, 11.27.

45. According to Rome, *mortal sins* are sins which destroy the grace of justification, while *venial sins* do not. *Doctrina*, 13.30.

46. πρὸς θάνατον. 1 John 5:16.

47. Vitringa's definition of the blasphemy of the Holy Spirit is very similar to that given by Zacharias Ursinus (1534–1583) in *The Commentary of Dr. Zacharias Ursinus on the Heidelberg Catechism*, trans. Rev. G. W. Williard, 2nd ed. (Columbus: Scott and Bascom, 1852), 40.

48. ביד רמה.

49. בשוא.

50. ἑκούσιον.

51. *Doctrina*, 11.29–30.

CHAPTER 12

That Which Is Called the Annulling of the Covenant of Works

371. From what was said above, it is sufficiently proven that by the transgression of the precept into the constituted *state of accusation*, the way of arriving to the state of perfection which God prescribed to Adam[1] was blocked.[2]

372. This was sufficiently shown to him by the denial of the use of the Tree of Life, the expulsion from Paradise, and the employing of a blockade by the flaming sword.[3]

373. They who call the state of friendship in which Adam lived with God a *covenant*[4] and certainly a *covenant of works* can also call this disqualification to the hope of salvation (which was accomplished by Adam after committing this sin in that way which God prescribed to him) the *annulling of the covenant of works*. Yet it ought to be noted that Scripture does not use this *expression*[5] concerning the removal of the Adamic covenant of works.[6]

374. The covenant which was erected between God and man is said to be annulled because through the substitution of the new covenant, it is declared useless for producing the effects which are

---

1. *ipsi.*
2. *Doctrina,* 12.1.
3. Genesis 3:24. *Doctrina,* 12.2.
4. *foedus.*
5. φράση.
6. *Doctrina,* 12.3.

expected by the covenant between God and man in a legal pact, that is, *justification*, *sanctification*, and *glorification*.[7]

375. But it ought to be carefully avoided, although we apply the term *annulling* or *abrogation* to the Adamic covenant, we do not extend that annulling to all parts of this covenant in whatever way may be elsewhere, since the covenant at Sinai is called *annulled*.[8]

376. For justice was not deprived of requiring obedience from man by his sin, nor was man released from the debt of obedience, nor was the binding between the observation of the law and the way of love destroyed. On the contrary, the effects of disobedience (which are called the *breaking of the covenant*) are extremely grave, and only through grace are they conquered at various moments and stages.[9]

377. But the annulling ought specially to be tied to the production of the anticipated effect: *eternal life*. Even if we can lack this clear conclusion in this discussion, Scripture does not lack the statement.

---

7. *Doctrina*, 12.9.
8. Cf. *Doctrina*, 12.9.
9. Cf. *Doctrina*, 12.11.

CHAPTER 13

The Testament of the Father and the Son in Grace for the Sinner[1]

378. Man has now been reduced to such a state in which there is no hope for him except in the all-sufficiency of God, if his hope has not been extinguished in fear and in terror of the Judge, which we rightly anticipate.[2]

379. But now at last, in God the occasion has given birth to the riches of His wisdom, power, sufficiency, and goodness for unfolding *salvation* in the fall of man. But His righteousness and holiness are plainly for the working for the *damnation* of sin and of all flesh which perseveres in sin.[3]

380. So it stands that the fall was *permitted* by God for most serious reasons.[4]

381. And so it pleased God according to the riches of His own *kindness*[5] toward fallen man who was now stirring in great fear to make with Himself a *counsel* concerning a certain seed from men propagated after the fall under the power of sin by *sanctifying* and *glorifying* His Son under the power of death, who would finally come in the flesh and triumph over the devil and sin.[6]

---

1. In *Doctrina*, this chapter is titled "On the Testament of Grace."
2. *Doctrina*, 13.1.
3. *Doctrina*, 13.2.
4. Cf. *Doctrina*, 13.3.
5. φιλανθρωπίας. Titus 3:4.
6. *Doctrina*, 13.3.

382. This whole counsel of grace, if we accept it in most simple and particular terms, is nothing other than the *will of the Father* for giving a seed of sinners to the Son who would acquire them from Him through the suffering of death, and would sanctify them through the *Spirit of the Son*, and *the will of the Son* who assumed a human nature, in which He sanctifies His Father through suffering in the place of and for the good of the elect seed, and through His Spirit would reign over this elect seed into all eternity. Can I speak now with more clarity and simplicity? It is the will of the Father through the Son for the sanctifying of His name and demonstrating Himself miraculously by this means unto such miserable sinners who are sanctified through His Spirit and eternally blessed in an ineffable way.[7]

383. But even if this may be one and the same eternal and most simple will of the Father and Son, which is often set forth through common terms like *good pleasure*[8] and *purpose*,[9] yet it was pleasing to the Holy Spirit, so that we may distinctly perceive the attributes of this one eternal and most simple will of the Father and the Son, to express it to us through various parts and modes of speaking for the sake of *the eyes*,[10] but chiefly by the testament of the Father and the Son.[11]

384. The *testament of the Father* (or the first part of this one will of God) is that by which the Father *appoints by a testament*[12] to the Son (in vain do you turn elsewhere, if you wish to be satisfied by the Scriptures) *a kingdom*.[13] From this the Son in Scripture is called the *heir*, and the good having been awarded to Him (that is, the kingdom) is called the *inheritance*.[14]

---

7. Cf. *Doctrina*, 13.4.

8. εὐδοκίας. Luke 12:32.

9. προθέσεως. Romans 8:28.

10. I.e., what is generally and easily understood.

11. *Doctrina*, 13.5.

12. διέθετο.

13. βασιλείαν. Luke 22:29.

14. *Doctrina*, 13.9.

385. In this testament, the Father is considered and is also able to be considered as the *testator*, the Son as *the heir*, and the elect, being called by Christ with the highest of glory for being sanctified, ruled, and saved, as the *inheritance.*[15]

386. And so, this testament is the will of the Father for giving to the Son a seed of sinners, whose King is in glory unto all eternity.

387. This will is called a *testament*, both for expressing the *immutability of this counsel*,[16] and for representing that the Father *according to the dispensation*[17] is the beginning of every work and of all efforts of grace concerning the sinner, and also since it has been confirmed in death.[18]

388. For even if the Father Himself, the testator, did not die for the confirmation of the testament, nevertheless by the death of the Son the whole gracious will of God was confirmed concerning the sinner, and more the Father Himself by the death of His Son (for the Father does all things through His Son) permitted that this His will be confirmed concerning the giving of the *inheritance* to the Son. For the sinner would not be able to be the heir of the good things of God and coheir with the Son of God without the death of the Son of God.

389. This testament is rendered in the form of a *covenant*, since the testator stipulates a *condition* in a testament which he wishes to be kept by the heir before he can have and possess the full lawful inheritance.[19]

390. The condition expressed in this testament was this—that it was necessary for the Son to sanctify His Father *through the suffering*

---

15. *Doctrina*, 13.10.
16. τὸ ἀμετάθετον τῆς βουλῆς. Hebrews 6:17.
17. κατ᾿ οἰκονομίαν.
18. *Doctrina*, 13.12.
19. Cf. *Doctrina*, 13.14.

of death[20] in a human nature, on a raised altar, and be united with Him.[21]

391. Since Scripture wishes to explain to us that the Son of God consented to this condition, and undertook this precept unto Himself (that is, from eternity He willed the same glorification of God with this means which the Father willed) so Scripture is accustomed to express this testament by the term *counsel of peace*,[22] or *contract*[23] or covenant, which was, as it were, made between the Father and the Son.[24]

392. Likewise, since Scripture wishes to signify to us that the Son of God consented to this will of the Father freely, voluntarily, and gladly, and that He concurred *equally with the Father*[25] for this work of grace, so it describes the Son to us under the terms *redeemer*,[26] *sponsor, priest, intercessor,* and *mediator*.[27]

393. Again, lest we understand that the Son, since He is related to us under the title of mediator, willed the salvation of the elect before the Father willed it, He is called the *mediator of the testament*.[28]

394. The Holy Spirit also willed through many modes of speaking to teach us that it is of such a great work to intercede with God for the sinner, and yet confidently to promise his liberation, then it is glorious to save the sinner and to lead him from extreme misery to the highest glory.

395. Likewise, we know that no one can be the mediator and redeemer

---

20. διὰ τὸ πάθημα τοῦ θανάτου. Hebrews 2:9.

21. Cf. *Doctrina*, 13.15.

22. סולש תצע.

23. *contractum.*

24. *Doctrina*, 13.16. As proof texts in *Doctrina*, Vitringa lists Psalms 40:7–9 and 89:29; Isaiah 49:3–5; and Zechariah 6:13.

25. ἴσον τῷ πατρί. Cf. John 5:18.

26. לאוג.

27. *Doctrina*, 13.17–19.

28. διαθήκης μεσίτης. Hebrews 9:15.

of the sinner except God Himself, who is able to appear, suffer, and be glorified in the flesh, that is, in a human nature.

396. But since the Holy Spirit depicts before our eyes such emphatic ways of speaking, one is sufficiently able to be astounded at the highest judgment of God against the Jews and the Christians who desire to say such that they insist that the mediator is not God. *Our redeemer*[29] is the *Holy One of Israel*.[30] This is the hope of the sinner.

397. They who conveniently believe that by His own *purpose*[31] the Son of God at one point was able to renounce the *pledge*[32] subvert the whole counsel of God and every mode and reason of divine wisdom.[33]

398. Glory and a kingdom ought to be given solely to Christ by the power of the pact after the completed condition of the pact. For the reward, which Adam expected after the completion of obedience, was plainly of another nature, which the Sponsor, indeed even the human nature of the Sponsor, receives by the strength of the singular contract with the Father.[34]

399. *The testament of the Son* is that same eternal and irrevocable will which is of the Father for the sure giving of grace and glory to a seed elected from sinners. The Father willed to give to the Son a certain seed for salvation. This is the *testament of the Father*. The Son willed to save by Himself a certain seed. This is called the *testament of the Son*. "I," says the Son, "appoint[35] a kingdom to you."[36]

400. But even if the will of decreeing a kingdom to the certain seed

---

29. ונלאוג.
30. לארשי שודק.
31. προθέσει.
32. *sponsioni.*
33. *Doctrina,* 13.32.
34. Cf. *Doctrina,* 13.24.
35. *dispono.*
36. Ἐγὼ διατίθεμαι ὑμῖν βασιλείαν. Luke 22:29. *Doctrina,* 13.34.

were equally of the Father and the Son, yet *according to the economy*[37] it is first of the Father, and then of the Son, but the Son in this *testament of grace* chiefly is considered as the testator, since He by His own death makes this will established.[38]

401. The good things ascribed in this testament are *grace* and *glory*, *sanctification* and *glorification* of the sinner.[39]

402. In addition, they are expressed by various terms and phrases in Scripture: *God; Christ having accomplished righteousness, sanctification, and redemption; all things; inheritance of the world; the nations; a kingdom; what God is to the one who is in God; that God knows and loves; circumcision of the heart;* etc.[40] All these things ought to be explained prudently.[41]

403. The heirs of these good things are certain sinners who have been expressed previously by us under the name *the elect*.[42] These people in Scripture are called *the people*,[43] *sheep*,[44] *church, Israel, remnant*,[45] *preserved of Israel*,[46] *little flock*.[47]

404. This testament of grace is rendered in the *form of a covenant*[48] since it is written that there is a prescribed *condition* to the testament (or rather, a *quasi-condition*, lest we think that God weighs this condition by the power of sinners) without which God does not will that the inheritance be given.[49]

---

37. κατ᾿ οἰκονομίαν.

38. *Doctrina*, 13.35.

39. Cf. *Doctrina*, 13.36. Vitringa includes justification in 13.41a.

40. Genesis 17:7; Deuteronomy 30:6; Luke 12:32; Romans 8:17; 1 Corinthians 3:22.

41. *Doctrina*, 13.36.

42. ἐκλεκτῶν.

43. Matthew 1:21.

44. Acts 20:28.

45. λεῖμμα. Romans 11:5.

46. לאֹרשי תרוצנ. Isaiah 49:6.

47. Luke 12:32.

48. *formam foederis*. Vitringa references the word νενομοθέτηται, which appears in Hebrews 7:11 and 8:6, and describes the old covenant and the new covenant, respectively.

49. *Doctrina*, 13.39–41. Vitringa clarifies that this quasi-condition is *faith*. See the next chapter.

CHAPTER 14

❦

Faith

405. This condition or quasi-condition is *faith*. By the Hebrews it is called *belief*,[1] and by the Greeks *faith*.[2] Others call it *assent*.[3]

406. The full prescription of this condition is this: *If you profess with your mouth that Jesus is Lord and believe in your heart that God raised Him from the dead, you will be saved*.[4]

407. Faith is the soul submitting in assent to the truth of some matter or testimony which is offered for judgment.[5]

408. And so the nature of faith is to give or to hand itself over to something, just as someone rests on someone else, such that we rightly wish to use the word *trust*.[6]

409. The testimony to which I assent, since I call it *to believe*, is a wholly divine testimony in any manner which may be proposed and concerning any matters it may address (including those

---

1. אמונה. This Hebrew word in Scripture can mean faithfulness, truth, belief, loyalty, etc.

2. πίστις.

3. ὁμολογία. Vitringa translates this word as *adsensus*. In *Doctrina*, he uses *assensus* and cites Hebrews 3:1 in 14.1.

4. Romans 10:9.

5. Cf. *Doctrina*, 14.1.

6. אמונה. *Doctrina*, 14.2.

things which can be deduced from principles of reason) and also in any manner which has been told to me.[7]

410. All conclusions and consequences which are clearly deduced from it also belong to this testimony.[8]

411. But since the full head of every word and of all truth revealed by God is the *testimony*[9] that the Son of God ought to be and was sent for the reconciliation of the sinner to God through His sufferings for his salvation, so he who *receives this testimony*[10] is said in Scripture *to believe.*[11]

412. But no one can receive this testimony of the Son and accept it in the judgment of his own mind unless he has understood through certain external means like the preaching or reading of the Word, etc.

413. From this it is clear, that knowledge is required for the end of faith, and therefore it has thus been well said that an *implicit faith* and the *faith of colliers*[12] does not merit the name of faith.[13]

414. Indeed, it is difficult to explain how much ignorance in a Christian may be damnable, since we are not able to understand the power of divine grace nor the secret operations of the Spirit. But it is certain that someone is not able to be ignorant of salvation without being damned.[14]

---

7. *Doctrina*, 14.3.

8. *Doctrina*, 14.4.

9. μαρτύριον.

10. τοῦτο τὸ μαρτύριον λαμβάνει. Cf. John 3:33.

11. *Doctrina*, 14.5.

12. Vitringa is referring to the Roman Catholic teaching that if one has faith in what the church teaches without actual knowledge of the content of that teaching, it is still genuine faith. Reformation Protestants rejected this notion, arguing that implicit faith, "the faith of colliers" (namely, the faith of a coal miner who knows nothing about the content of Scripture), is not genuine faith.

13. *Doctrina*, 14.8.

14. *Doctrina*, 14.10–11.

415. This aspect of faith in Scripture is called *knowledge*,[15] often used for the full act of faith.[16]

416. After the testimony is understood, it is necessary that it be *explored* by the conscience, not only whether it may be *of God*[17] in its whole essence and content (about which the conscience is able to judge), but especially how the witnesses agree among themselves, and how the truth of this may be confirmed by the signs, works, arguments, and effects, etc. So Christ says. For God does not lead us as human beasts. *Demonstration*[18] ought to belong to faith.[19]

417. This exploration of divine testimony does not so much regard the object *which* God has spoken, but *whether* God has spoken that which is offered to us under this heading. Therefore, if it is evident according to the true sense of this testimony that God has spoken, then Christians ought to reject all *thoughts*[20] and contrary murmurs of the flesh.[21]

418. Therefore it pleased the Holy Spirit, the only author of faith, *to reveal* the beauty, the becomingness, and the attractiveness of this testimony openly to our mind (which He does sometimes in one way, sometimes in another, sometimes by many arguments, sometimes by few) to such a degree that man, being convicted of his own misery and regretting with a full consent of his will, being deeply moved by the divine strength, embraces it. He gives his whole self to it, naturally considering this one instrument of his salvation, then he is said *to believe*, to accept that God is truly speaking.[22]

---

15. דעת, γνῶσις.
16. *Doctrina*, 14.12.
17. θεωπρεπὲς.
18. ἔλεγχος. Hebrews 11:1.
19. *Doctrina*, 14.12.
20. διαλογισμοὺς.
21. *Doctrina*, 14.14.
22. *Doctrina*, 14.15.

419. But since the sum of this testimony which is related to us for belief is *Jesus Christ, and Him crucified for our sins*,[23] it is therefore not possible that someone would be able to be said to accept this testimony who does not *receive*[24] Christ Himself nor commit himself to Him with whole acceptance and affection as the only Savior.[25]

420. The proper *actus fidei*[26] is expressed chiefly and with the principle and most elegant phrases of Scripture, and it ought to be properly explained for understanding the justification of the sinner.[27]

421. In addition, this *actus fidei* receives various names in the sacred Scriptures, because it is considered in various ways. For from this we conceive that the full consent of the will belongs to it, and *full assurance*,[28] binding by firm arguments and *demonstration*[29] and *foundation*,[30] and with highest desire, hunger, and thirst,[31] and with the highest love of the object which is set forth for belief, and love,[32] with the rest of the mind delighting in that which is believed, and it is called *eating and drinking*.[33]

422. Faith having taken good root leads to *trust*.[34]

423. But true faith is always discerned from its most certain fruit, which is the *zeal for the good and true*,[35] that is, for the glory of

---

23. 1 Corinthians 2:2.

24. λαμβάνει.

25. *Doctrina*, 14.16.

26. The "act of faith" is a technical term in scholastic theology. It refers to the actualization of faith in the heart of a believer. The term comes from Aristotle's distinction between *actuality* and *potentiality* (*potestas*). See Muller, *Dictionary*, s.v. "actus," "actus fidei."

27. *Doctrina*, 14.18.

28. πληροφορία. Hebrews 6:11; 10:22.

29. ἔλεγχος.

30. ὑπόστασις. Hebrews 11:1.

31. Isaiah 55:1; Matthew 5:6.

32. Deuteronomy 6:5; 2 Thessalonians 2:10.

33. Proverbs 9:4–5; Isaiah 55:1–2; John 6:53. *Doctrina*, 14.20.

34. *fiduciam*. Cf. *Doctrina*, 14.22–24.

35. חסד.

God and whatever most leads to the glory of God. The apostle calls this *charity*.[36]

424. Other similar terms are *wisdom*[37] and *prudence*[38] which are called something other than *knowledge*.[39]

425. These fruits, from which true faith can and ought to be distinguished from other acts of the mind in a Christian, and which also come under the name of faith and are often so called, are *historical, temporal faith*, and *the faith of miracles*, either active or passive.[40]

---

36. Galatians 5:6. *Doctrina*, 14.25.
37. חכמה.
38. בינה.
39. γνῶσις. *Doctrina*, 14.26.
40. *Doctrina*, 19.28–30.

CHAPTER 15

The Covenant of Grace Which Was Made in an Eternal Testament, and Its Various Dispensations

426. Since the good things of the testament of grace are either promised or exhibited to sinful man under this condition of faith and are said to be exhibited, the testament is said to be rendered in the form of a covenant.[1]

427. And from this the sinner is called to this condition, that is, by true faith he is stipulated to a communion of his own good by God's calling of him, so God is said to make a covenant with the sinner. This is the *covenant of grace*.

428. For the covenant of grace is an agreement between God and the sinner, in which God offers to the sinner the goods of the eternal testament under the condition or through the command of faith and repentance. But the sinner is stipulated by God's inviting him through the Spirit of God who works faith in him, and so thus in a good conscience he expects the fulfillment of the divine promises.[2]

429. The form of the covenant of grace is eloquently expressed by Moses: *You have spoken of Jehovah today concerning Him, that He shall be your God, and that you shall walk in His ways, and you shall keep His statues and His precepts, and His rules and you will*

---

1. *Doctrina*, 19.1.
2. *Doctrina*, 19.3.

obey His voice. And Jehovah has declared to you today that you are a peculiar people for Himself.[3]

430. Therefore, those parts in this covenant ought to be distinctly observed which we have said before have a place in every covenant.

431. This covenant of grace is one substance in every age of the church, since the *same goods* (namely, Christ, with bringing righteousness through Him, and salvation thence coming forth) have been offered to the sinner under the same condition or by the same command of faith and repentance.[4]

432. But we ought to observe that the goods of the testament have been offered to the sinner either as *being brought about* at a certain [future] time or as *having been brought.*[5]

433. For God willed that there would be *proper times*[6] of the dispensation of His grace. This dispensation of divine grace at various times and states of the church defined by Him is called the *dispensation of times.*[7]

434. The time (in which the goods of the testament had been received as being brought in a [future] time but yet the sinner was able to have the firstfruits at that time through the gracious dispensation of them by God) in general is called the time *of promise.*[8] But in [another time] the goods are announced as having been brought, the time *of fulfillment.*[9]

435. It also ought to be noted that the condition of the covenant in these two dispensations of the times was fittingly called by

---

3. Deuteronomy 26:17–18. Vitringa's translation. *Doctrina*, 19.4.
4. *Doctrina*, 19.7.
5. *Doctrina*, 19.8.
6. ἴδιοι καιροί.
7. מועדים, οἰκονομία καιρῶν. *Doctrina*, 19.9.
8. ἐπαγγελίας.
9. εὐαγγελίου. *Doctrina*, 19.10.

various other names. For in the time of *promise* it was chiefly called *hope*, but in the time of *fulfillment* it is emphatically[10] called *faith*.[11]

436. Now the general reason why God was pleased that the time of promise preceded the time of fulfillment is that God first willed to set before the eyes of sinful man his utmost weakness and defect to excite in him a most ardent desire for true righteousness.[12]

---

10. ἐμφατικῶς.
11. *Doctrina*, 19.11.
12. *Doctrina*, 19.12–13.

CHAPTER 16

The Time of Promise, and Its Three Intervals Stated

437. The time of promise lasted from *Adam to Christ*. In this time, it ought to be observed generally that the goods of the testament of grace were displayed more and more clearly with time.[1]

438. Now this time has three distinct intervals. The first is that in which the promises of the testament of grace were only *heard*. This flowed from *Adam to Abraham*. The second is that in which, besides the promises of the testament of grace, the promises of another testament were heard, which later is called *old*, concerning the giving of the land of Canaan, etc. This flowed from *Abraham* to *Moses*. The third is that in which the promise of the land subsequently began to be fulfilled to the inheritors under the condition of the fulfillment of the law concerning which the covenant was made on Mount Sinai and the plains of Moab.[2]

The First Interval of the Time of Promise: Adam to Abraham

439. The manifestation and promise of the goods of the eternal testament was made first to *Adam and Eve* by these words: *The seed of the woman*, etc.[3]

---

1. *Doctrina*, 20.1.
2. *Doctrina*, 20.2.
3. Genesis 3:15. *Doctrina*, 20.3.

440. Adam and Eve not only understood this writing of Moses, but they believed it, as is evidenced by various proofs in the writings of Moses.[4]

441. The propagation of this promise from Adam and Eve to their children is clear from the offering of sacrifices by *Cain* and *Abel*, which seem to have been of divine institution for the confirming of faith in the promise.[5]

442. For the sacrifices represented the same thing which is commonly meant by *the word of promise*.

443. And Moses shows that Abel did a gracious thing by sacrificing, since in a kind of testimony he sacrificed by faith.[6]

444. In place of Abel, the son of promise, because of the exclusion of Cain, *Seth* was given to our first parents through whom the word of promise was propagated.[7]

445. At the time of *Enosh*, his son, *some began to call on the name of Jehovah.*[8] That is, the church began to exist in the world by being distinguished from the assemblies of the reprobate because it proclaimed the word of promise, and it was widely known for this faith in God.[9]

446. From this church *Enoch, Methuselah, Lamech,* and *Noah* were born. They learned these testimonies of their faith and were famous heralds of righteousness and condemners of wickedness, iniquity, and faithlessness.[10]

---

4. *Doctrina*, 20.4.
5. *Doctrina*, 20.5.
6. *Doctrina*, 20.6.
7. *Doctrina*, 20.7.
8. הוחל לקרא בשם יהוה. Genesis 4:26.
9. *Doctrina*, 20.9.
10. *Doctrina*, 20.10.

447. We ought to mention here that the apostle Jude refers to the prophecy of Enoch.[11] But it ought not to be believed that any prophecy of Enoch existed outside of Moses.[12]

448. The signs, by which it was pleasing to God to illustrate and signify the promise, were not only *Noah* himself, an eminent type of the Messiah, but also the ark and the flood.[13]

449. But particularly here there was a greater covenant enacted which God made with Noah and annexed the sacrament of the rainbow to it.

450. Moreover, in the new world, noble *Shem* had to preserve the promise from the prophecy of Noah. But it was accomplished chiefly when God called Abraham.[14]

The Second Interval of the Time of Promise: Abraham to Moses

451. It was pleasing to God to call *Abraham* from the family of Shem. At this time faith in the promise was greatly diminishing. For God was always accustomed to direct things by His providence so that the manifest corruption of the world might precede the eminent working of His grace.[15]

452. Abraham was twice called by God, first he came out from Ur with his parents, and second at the death of his parents in the land of Canaan when he was seventy-five years old. From this time 430 years ought to be calculated until the Israelites departed from Egypt.[16]

---

11. Jude 14–15.
12. *Doctrina*, 20.11.
13. *Doctrina*, 20.12.
14. *Doctrina*, 20.14.
15. *Doctrina*, 20.15.
16. *Doctrina*, 20.116–17.

453. Now the *promises*[17] of the goods of the eternal testament of grace were repeated to Abraham with such copiousness and clarity as had not existed in what was said before. These shining promises ought diligently to be noted through all of history. But it was singularly proclaimed to him that they would be for the blessed seed, or rather, for the blessed and sanctified.[18]

454. Also his faith, added to the promise, was truly brilliant, so that he would be set forth as the parent and example of all the faithful.

455. In addition, it was pleasing to God to tell Abraham that it was His will to give some earthly good to his carnal seed before He fully revealed the testament of grace and confirmed it by the death of the testator.

456. This good was the peaceful, prosperous, delightful possession of the land of Canaan as the pledge of a better inheritance of the testament of grace.

457. This will of God, since it is certain and immutable, was called a *testament*. Chiefly so because by the typological death of animals, a greater one was confirmed.

458. That testament receives the name *Old Testament* or *covenant*, since the good assigned in it to the heirs began to disappear and to be destroyed, and still more is given to the heirs by the strength of this testament by substituting it for the *better goods* of the better testament.[19]

459. The heirs of this [Old Testament], as we call it, have been written as only the sons of Abraham according to the flesh. But on the contrary, it was revealed to Abraham, that the heirs of the testament of grace, with the advent of the testator uncovered,

---

17. αἱ ἐπαγγελίαι.
18. *Doctrina,* 20.18.
19. *Doctrina,* 20.24.

would be all who believe in the one whom Abraham himself believed, either Jews or gentiles, but chiefly gentiles.[20]

460. These promises of every kind (both of the testament of grace and of the so-called Old Testament later) were confirmed to Abraham through various and most wonderful signs.[21]

461. Among these was *circumcision, a seal of righteousness by faith*[22] by which both sanctification and multiplication of his seed were signified to Abraham in a most wise way.[23]

462. Likewise, the twofold dispensation[24] of the church was proclaimed along with the twofold testament through the twofold marriage of Abraham, and from that a twofold seed was indicated.[25]

463. The *word* of all these promises and along with it the word *faith* Abraham transferred to *Isaac*, the son of promise, an eminent type of Christ, with whom the promises of both kinds were repeated, and the heirs of them were spread out again in a new and domestic way.[26]

464. The heir of the blessing of the parents was *Jacob*, to whom the promises of the leading were increased anew by shining evidences.[27]

465. He was the parent of twelve sons, from whom *Judah* (because *Reuben*, *Simeon*, and *Levi* despised the law) was constituted as the leader by the declaration of Jacob that *the seed to whom the*

---

20. *Doctrina*, 20.25.

21. *Doctrina*, 20.27. In *Doctrina*, Vitringa calls these marks "symbols" (*symbolis*) and "sacraments" (*sacramentis*).

22. σφραγῖδα τῆς δικαιοσύνης τῆς πίστεως. Romans 4:11.

23. *Doctrina*, 20.28.

24. οἰκονομία.

25. *Doctrina*, 20.29.

26. *Doctrina*, 20.34.

27. *Doctrina*, 20.35.

promises were made[28]—namely, Christ would descend from this parent.[29]

466. These with Jacob the parent went down into Egypt and fixed their camp in that very place which was the occasion that oppressed their seed with the great harm of the divine oracles of Egypt.[30]

467. Now it ought to be observed in this last dispensation of the promise that the gentiles who did not belong to the family of Abraham were not yet excluded from the hope of the goods of the testament, since Melchizedek and Job stand as illustrative examples.[31]

The Third Interval of the Time of the Church Under Promise: Moses to Christ, or the Old Testament

468. At this time, which was defined by divine speech, God stirred up *Moses*, the son of Amram, the great grandson of *Levi* (fourth generation from Jacob), to the good of the testament, which afterward was called *old* because [the future good] was being brought.[32]

469. In his birth and education divine providence so primed him that he was prepared already from the beginning for coming great things.[33]

470. He, having been called by God in a special way and having been confirmed in his faith in the promise by the knowledge of the name of God, freed the heirs of this testament from Egypt through various demonstrations of divine power and righteousness.[34]

---

28. τὸ σπέρμα, τῷ ἐπήγγελται. Cf. Galatians 3:19.
29. *Doctrina*, 20.36.
30. *Doctrina*, 20.37.
31. *Doctrina*, 20.38.
32. *Doctrina*, 20.39.
33. *Doctrina*, 20.40.
34. *Doctrina*, 20.41.

471. This *liberation*,[35] insofar as it was a complete type, points to the liberation from slavery to the devil and sin promised in the *testament of grace*. And it was pleasing to God on this occasion that by the sacrament of the Paschal lamb, this *redemption*[36] would remarkably represent and signify what the faithful have through the blood of Christ.[37]

472. The people having been liberated from Egypt were not immediately led into the land of Canaan, but by the command of God they were led to Mount Sinai so that they would understand by what condition they would take the inheritance of the land of Canaan.[38]

473. There, therefore, after the repeated promise of the goods of the eternal testament of grace, God began to prescribe to the people various laws, but mixed, both for religion, and for governing the state, among which some were of natural law and many of His will. He required the keeping of these laws with faith and love.[39]

474. The most noble and excellent of these laws which God included are the *Ten Commandments*,[40] which along with the angels in the midst of various signs, the God of Israel, the Son of God, announced these collected laws to excite reverence for Him in a stiff and carnal people.[41]

475. For these Ten Commandments contain the roots and foundations of all the laws of Moses.[42]

---

35. Λύτρωσις.
36. ἀπολύτρωσιν.
37. *Doctrina*, 20.42.
38. *Doctrina*, 20.43.
39. *Doctrina*, 20.44.
40. δεκαλόγῳ.
41. *Doctrina*, 20.45.
42. *Doctrina*, 20.46.

476. For this reason, these ten precepts were handed over on stone tablets unlike all the others.[43]

477. The laws which pertain to religion (which are called *ceremonial,* though somewhat inconsistently, since even the political laws are largely ceremonial) can be placed under four heads—that is, *persons, affairs and what must be done,*[44] sacred *space,* and *time.*[45]

478. Among the sacred persons, the priests and Levites ought chiefly to be considered, and their leader the high priest, and their order, prerogatives, consecration, clothing, and duties.[46]

479. Regarding what ought to be done, they observed the sacrifices, the kinds of which are numbered by Moses according to a provided description: *whole burnt offering,*[47] *gift offering,*[48] *sin offering,*[49] *guilt offering,*[50] *satisfactions,*[51] and *sacrifice of thanksgiving.*[52] Compare with this latter kind, a *vow offering.*[53]

480. Note that the most worthy among these kinds were *the guilt offering*[54] and *sin offering*[55] which were not known before this institution. Indeed, after this institution their use was necessary. But distinguishing them is most difficult.[56]

481. The power of offering these on the altar belonged to no one except the priests who were descended from Aaron.

---

43. *Doctrina,* 20.47.
44. I.e., rites and ceremonies.
45. *Doctrina,* 20.48.
46. *Doctrina,* 20.49.
47. עולה.
48. מנחה.
49. חטאת.
50. אשם.
51. מלואים.
52. זבח שלמים.
53. נדר. *Doctrina,* 20.50.
54. אשם.
55. חטאת.
56. *Doctrina,* 20.51.

482. This also includes firstfruits and the tithe which ought not to be excluded from the priests.[57]

483. With regard to *space*, one should think of the tabernacle and the temple along with all of its apparatus of instruments, especially the ark, a complete compendium of religion, and also the *synagogue*.[58]

484. *Sacred time* consists in days consecrated to God according to a rule, either one or many, to be observed with joy, abstaining from work, and penitence. These recurred either as a single out of seven, like the seventh day Sabbath; or monthly, like the new moon; or annually, like the three festival celebrations[59] and the days of public penitence; or many years long, as the seventh year and Jubilee.[60]

485. Besides these laws many others were commanded to the Israelites in their private lives: clothing, food distinctions, cultivating of fields, cleanness, and uncleanness, and even many others concerning the civil constitution.[61]

486. The highest of all these laws was the *law of faith and love* from which God never willed that these laws should be observed if their observation did not include the law of love and faith.[62]

487. It is this same reason why the *precept of the love of God and neighbor* is so frequently mixed with the recitation of these precepts, and why the Decalogue, which contains the sum of all these laws, chiefly comprehends such precepts which pertain to the law of love and faith.[63]

---

57. *Doctrina*, 20.52.
58. *Doctrina*, 20.53.
59. Cf. Leviticus 23.
60. *Doctrina*, 20.54.
61. *Doctrina*, 20.55.
62. *Doctrina*, 20.56.
63. *Doctrina*, 20.57.

488. These precepts of the law of love and faith are usually called the *moral law* (even if the term is somewhat unsuitable). Not only do they comprehend the Decalogue, but they are diffused throughout the whole corpus of the Mosaic laws as the foundation for the rest.[64]

489. For even if the distinction of these precepts may be understood by theologians as the love of God and neighbor, and others as the exercise of external religion and civil constitution, nevertheless it ought not to be held that God prescribed laws to the people in this way, nor that Moses distributed and separated them in this way. Rather, it ought to be held that every law of this kind (to which we give various names according to the various consideration of its origin and use, especially as enumerated by Moses) was in one rendered body, so that the city of the people of God should be constituted and ruled under them.[65]

490. All these laws were received in common. But particularly those which began to be given on Mount Sinai were not accustomed to be understood before the time of prescription (for the precept of love and of faith, contrary to what had already been heard before, was hardly comprehended by the term *law*, since its observation was not tiresome and burdensome, but pleasing). For the apostles (especially Paul in the epistles to the Romans and Galatians) speak *concerning the law of works*,[66] and *works of the law*.[67] *The law was given through Moses*, etc.[68] That precept of circumcision, which had not been regarded as a species of law before that time, now began to be a heavy and burdensome law, since circumcision bound a certain observance to the rest of the laws.[69]

---

64. *Doctrina*, 20.58.
65. *Doctrina*, 20.59.
66. περὶ τοῦ νόμου ἔργων.
67. ἔργων νόμου. Romans 4:2; Galatians 2:16.
68. John 1:17.
69. *Doctrina*, 20.60.

491. But it ought to be noted that the word *law*[70] in the Old Testament writings and especially in the Psalms is often used widely for every word of God whether proclaimed through the patriarchs, continued through the prophets, or repeated through Moses, which shows the sinner the way of coming to the enjoyment of the highest good. In a word, it sums up the whole theology of this time and of the future time.[71]

492. The particular ends, on account of which all of these laws were introduced, were: first, to restrain and to make plain the strength and efficacy of sin and of corruption; second, to reexcite the memory of sin, and even its presence; third, to display the necessity of being led *to Christ and righteousness* through Him; and finally, that they represent and depict Christ, and His righteousness with the goods distributed to the church by the power of the coming righteousness of Christ, so that they excited the most brilliant desire for them in the souls of the faithful. *The end of the law is Christ unto righteousness for all who believe.*[72]

493. Now, God works most prudently, because He desired to restrain the reckless and childish lasciviousness of the Israelite people with a yoke of this kind and to contain them within His limits, while they were plainly in sin with the commission of the golden calf.[73] But nonetheless, it ought not to be supposed that God at length willed to impose this yoke on Israel on this occasion, since before this sin the laid foundations of all the ceremonial laws were already established.[74]

494. All of these laws (some of which were already given, others had yet to be given) and their diligent observation God prescribed to the Israelites in faith as a *condition* by which they would at

---

70. תורה.

71. *Doctrina*, 20.61.

72. τέλος γὰρ νόμου Χριστὸς εἰς δικαιοσύνην παντὶ τῷ πιστεύοντι. Romans 10:4. *Doctrina*, 20.62.

73. See Exodus 32.

74. *Doctrina*, 20.63.

length have the fulfilled right of approaching the inheritance of the Old Testament and of expecting in their time the acquisition of the full goods of the testament of grace.[75]

495. Since the Israelites were joined to this condition first on Mount Sinai by the administrator or mediator, Moses, and again on the plains of Moab (since all the precepts were certainly given already; for this is the same covenant elsewhere) so what is called the *Old Testament* was cast in the form of a covenant, which is called the *old covenant* and was subordinate to the Old Testament.[76]

496. This covenant in no way ought to be thought of as a repetition of the covenant of nature, and neither can it be called a *mixed covenant of grace*, but a covenant of grace mixed with strictness, accommodated to the condition of the church at this time.[77]

497. The formulae of this covenant of Sinai are: *He who does these things* (i.e., all the precepts given through Moses in faith and a good conscience) *shall live by them.*[78] And: *Cursed is he who does not remain in all those things which have been written in the book of the law, so that he does them.*[79]

498. This covenant was not ratified without the blood of slaughtered animals and of its *sprinkling*, which the apostle calls the *initiation of the first testament.*[80]

499. From this *initiation*[81] of the Old Testament which was accomplished on Mount Sinai in a unique way, the time of the Old Testament was set up to flow forth. For it is said that every testament includes a beginning, since there is nothing more contrary

---

75. *Doctrina*, 20.64.
76. *Doctrina*, 20.65.
77. *Doctrina*, 20.66.
78. Leviticus 18:5. Vitringa's translation.
79. Deuteronomy 27:26. Vitringa's translation. *Doctrina*, 20.67.
80. ἐγκεκαινισμὸν τῆς πρώτης διαθήκης. Cf. Hebrews 9:18. *Doctrina*, 20.68.
81. ἐγκεκαινισμῷ.

than that the heirs would not approach the inheritance of this written testament. For elsewhere it is certain that every divine testament (properly understood) is eternal since the will of God is eternal.[82]

500. Now the time of this testament or covenant flowed up until the manifestation of Christ in the flesh, whose good promises were made in this interval of time much clearer than before. For *the law was not contrary to the promise*.[83]

501. For beside promises of the testament of grace which had been repeated on Mount Sinai, the same were also signified by various new sacraments instituted by God for that time. They were: the passing through the Red Sea, manna, the rock, the bronze serpent, the Sabbath, the sacrifices for sin and guilt, and all the rest of the ceremonial laws.[84]

The Defects of the Old Testament, and of Its Annulling

502. It is impossible to deny that there was the greatest *privilege for the Jews*[85] under this covenant, such as, the promises of the eternal testament of grace were made known only to the fleshly seed of Abraham unto the spurning of the gentiles, that the goods of this testament were represented to them through types and shadows, and that the land of Canaan was given to them as their down payment.[86]

503. But the apostles rightly declare that this testament was not *free from all blame and charge*[87] which one could deservedly infer against it. Now we can think of this claim strictly concerning that testament, or somewhat more broadly as the testament as it

---

82. Cf. *Doctrina*, 20.69.
83. Cf. Galatians 3:17. *Doctrina*, 20.70.
84. *Doctrina*, 20.71.
85. περισσόν τοῦ Ἰουδαίου.
86. *Doctrina*, 20.72.
87. ἄμεμπτος. Hebrews 8:7.

had then been cast in the form of a covenant and according to the state of those living Israelites under that covenant.[88]

504. With regard to this Old Testament in a strict sense, the faithful achieved no other goods by the power of the Old Testament than corporal ones. For the pure goods of grace—namely justification, sanctification, and glorification which the Fathers secured—were given to them by the power of the testament of grace.[89]

505. With regard to the [Old] Testament more widely understood, a condition was most harshly prescribed to the heirs. For the law was imposed upon the faithful which was a very great burden and tire, committing them to times, places, ritual matters, often greatly shameful and costly and under a heavy threat. They were squeezed and constrained, appointed and set forth according to the rigor of the messenger and of the specific office. Yet from their observation of the law (I am now considering the law strictly given through Moses) which expected no consolation or sanctification but rather a *reminder of sin*,[90] it was greatly unpleasant, and it stole liberty from the faithful, along with the peace and happiness of approaching God. This is that *slavery* concerning which the apostle everywhere speaks. To this pertains the *spirit of slavery, fear of death, elements of the world*, and so forth.[91]

506. As for the state of the faithful who were living under that covenant, there was a common wall from the overthrowing of this covenant in place of the gentiles; a smaller measure of knowledge and grace in place of the full acquisition of the goods of the testament of grace; famines, thirst, and a desire of good things in place of the full distribution of them; hope in place of faith, etc.[92]

---

88. *Doctrina*, 20.73.
89. *Doctrina*, 20.74.
90. Hebrews 10:3.
91. *Doctrina*, 20.75. See Romans 8:15; Hebrews 2:15; Galatians 4:9.
92. *Doctrina*, 20.76.

507. Indeed, these defects (i.e., these *faults*[93] concerning which one who was an heir of this testament could justly lament) were of its nature so that it plainly could not provide full access to the testament of grace and acquisition of those goods and promises.[94]

508. The reason was that all the prophets preached that this testament would be *annulled*. That is, that the laws annexed to that covenant as a condition would no longer be observed, and the inheritance of *this testament* would be replaced with the inheritance of *a better testament*.[95]

509. Therefore, this testament grew old and faded away (as the apostle puts it),[96] and so it is called *old*.[97]

510. Likewise, it is called *first*[98] since the goods of this testament were first available to the heirs when the testament of grace was plainly revealed.[99]

---

93. μεμφόμενα.

94. *Doctrina*, 20.77.

95. *Doctrina*, 20.78. In *Doctrina*, Vitringa lists the following texts on this point: Psalm 110:4; Jeremiah 3:16–17; 31:31–33; Ezekiel 16:60–62; Daniel 9:27; Habakkuk 2:3–4; and Haggai 2:6–7.

96. Hebrews 8:13.

97. *Doctrina*, 20.79.

98. ἡ πρώτη.

99. *Doctrina*, 20.80.

CHAPTER 17

The Gospel, or the Testament of Grace Revealed, and the Acquired Goods of This Testament Which Were Promised[1]

511. The [time of] the *gospel*,[2] as opposed to the [time of] *promise*,[3] describes the happy announcement concerning the acquired goods of the testament of grace which were promised and foreshadowed. This is another great dispensation or administration of the covenant of grace.[4]

512. We said before that the goods of the testament of grace were grace and glory,[5] or Christ manifested in the flesh acquiring *everlasting righteousness*,[6] by whose power the faithful are *called, justified, sanctified,* and *glorified*,[7] and by His strength are liberated from slavery, restored to the state of sons of God, possessing God Himself and all things which are of God and Christ (the whole world), along with a complete conscience, peace, faith, happiness, expecting the fullness of all these things in a future life.[8]

513. Now the goods of this testament were so set forth *in many times and in many ways*[9] in the writings of Moses and of the prophets

---

1. This chapter received considerable reorganization in *Doctrina*, 23.
2. εὐαγγέλιον.
3. ἐπαγγελίαν.
4. *Doctrina*, 23.32.
5. See §388–401.
6. δικαίωμα.
7. Romans 8:30.
8. Cf. *Doctrina*, 23.28.
9. πολυμερῶς, πολυτρόπως. Hebrews 1:1.

such that they could not very easily be counted. But besides the phrases noted above, the testimony of Jeremiah ought to be noted above the rest, from which Paul proposes this doctrine.[10]

514. Likewise, it ought to be observed that after the times of Moses, the prophets plentifully described the goods of this testament with the methods and ways of speaking which were entirely opposite to the troublesome defects of the Old Testament. So, for this reason there is frequent mention of peace, liberty, and delight in the writings of the saints of this time.[11]

515. In general, therefore, the good of this testament is *salvation*[12] and *eternal life*[13] in which sense the Holy Spirit uses this phrase. *Life*, I say, in which we exercise communion with God without fear in a good conscience from the dominion of sin and every other kind of spiritual slavery, with trust and in peace, little by little stretching toward our *consummation*.[14]

516. To say it in another way, if you wish, the good of this testament is the abolition of sin with all its effects on account of the present *righteousness of Christ*.[15]

517. But in particular, note distinctly that the goods of this testament are, first, the acquiring of righteousness of Christ, and second, the payment of the iniquity of the whole earth. From this, third, the full justification of the sinner, which is called *justification*,[16] *redemption*,[17] *remission of sins*.[18] By this God now declares there

---

10. Hebrews 8:7–9. *Doctrina*, 23.8.
11. *Doctrina*, 23.6.
12. σωτηρία.
13. ζωή αἰώνιος.
14. τέλειοσιν. Cf. *Doctrina*, 23.10.
15. δικαίωμα τοῦ Χριστοῦ. *Doctrina*, 23.9.
16. Δικαίωσις.
17. ἀπολύτρωσις.
18. ἄφεσις τῶν ἁμαρτιῶν.

can be no *condemnation*[19] for the faithful, and there remains no argument, sign, or sin.[20]

518. First, from this justification from sin follows liberty from the dominion of sin. This is the *sanctification* of the sinner. To this sanctification pertains the full outpouring of the gifts of the Holy Spirit, and His working toward a clear knowledge of the ways of God (for it is every *protection*[21] from sin), and toward happiness, liberty, and a perfect conscience, which is called the *Spirit of adoption.*[22]

519. Second, from this justification from sin follows the payment of all slavery, which had been imposed on the church by the occasion of sin which had not yet been committed. From this comes the *abrogation* of the ceremonial laws along with all threats attached to them (this is liberty from the elements of the world), *liberation* from fear which is born from the threats, *abolition* of authorities of the world[23] and magistrates who press and force laws, and *cessation* of the distinction between the land of Canaan and the rest of the parts of the world, including the temple and synagogue.[24]

520. Third, from this justification from sin follows peace with God, the one who bears testimony in our consciences, and ourselves. This is the *perfect conscience.* There is no accusation of the conscience against him who exercises faith. Next, is peace between us and those who are in heaven, that is, both angels and blessed spirits. All have been made one through Christ. And finally, there is peace between us and the rest of men dispersed throughout the whole globe, Jew and gentile. So any faithful person has

---

19. κατάκριμα.
20. Cf. *Doctrina*, 23.40.
21. κάλυμμα.
22. Romans 8:15. *Doctrina*, 23.11–12.
23. κατάργησις τὰς ἀρχὰς τοῦ κόσμου.
24. Cf. *Doctrina*, 23.10, 12.

this peace through faith in Christ, wherever and whoever he may be in the end.[25]

521. Fourth, from this justification from sin follows happiness, born from the conscience of possession of present things and from the sure hope of future goods.[26]

522. Finally, from this justification from sin follows eternal glory, to which we are gradually led through the possession of these primary things, consummated with the resurrection of our bodies, since every effect of sin shall cease.[27]

523. For eternal glory, salvation, and eternal life are not specifically distinguished from the goods of the New Testament by the Holy Spirit. But they are considered as the highest grade of the possession of these goods.[28]

524. For all of these goods considered together without distinction are called *eternal inheritance,*[29] *that which cannot be shaken,*[30] *unmovable kingdom,*[31] *kingdom,*[32] *all things,*[33] etc.[34]

525. Therefore, the goods of the New Testament are the goods of this testament of grace which we have described before.[35]

526. For we do not believe that it is consistent with Scripture that the so-called *common testament of grace* in which salvation fell on the faithful of all times and ages, is distinct from the New

---

25. *Doctrina,* 23.13.
26. *Doctrina,* 23.14.
27. *Doctrina,* 23.15.
28. *Doctrina,* 23.16.
29. κληρονομία αἰώνιος.
30. μὴ σαλευόμενα. Hebrews 12:27.
31. βασιλεία ἀσάλευτος. Hebrews 12:28.
32. βασιλεία. Luke 22:29.
33. τὰ πάντα. 1 Corinthians 3:21.
34. *Doctrina,* 23.17.
35. See §399–402. *Doctrina,* 23.18.

[Testament], which is the gracious disposition of God (which the faithful had under the Mosaic dispensation) for those who lived in this world after the birth of Christ by the gracious giving of the goods.[36]

527. For Scripture calls that testament which was confirmed by the death of Christ the *New Testament*. But who doubts that it was this same testament by which salvation was decreed to the faithful of all ages? For it is called a *testament* by the apostle, confirmed through the death of Christ, by which the eternal inheritance is given.[37]

528. Therefore, nowhere in the Scripture are more than two testaments mentioned which pertain to the church: one by which *earthly* goods are given, the other by which *heavenly goods* are given.

529. From this also the state of those who live under the New Testament is called the *heavenly state, kingdom*, and *kingdom of heaven*.[38]

530. *This singular testament* (as Cocceius says) *is the disposition of the Father and the Son concerning the inheritance of heaven and of the nations through the blood of the Son as the blood of the testament. This is introduced through the promise made known to the Fathers by the abrogating of the Old Testament, that is, as if by a changed will of the Israelite people they would have a better inheritance through the blood and death of the Testator, instead of the land of Canaan.*[39] But it ought not to be understood for this reason only, namely, that the will of God is *one* and simple, appointing all things (with which everyone agrees), but by this also, that Scripture does not portray that one will of God to us by many

---

36. *Doctrina*, 23.19.

37. Cf. *Doctrina*, 23.20.

38. *Doctrina*, 23.23.

39. Vitringa hear appears to paraphrase from one of his mentors, Johannes Cocceius (1603–1669). See Cocceius, *Summa Theologiae*, 52.13 (p. 535).

parts. Therefore, we say, in speech and in writing, that the Holy Spirit resembles a teacher.[40]

531. Now this testament of grace is called *New*, after it was confirmed by the death of Christ since its goods began to be distributed with utmost abundance and fullness after the annulling of the *Old Testament.*

532. Its heirs are *emphatically*[41] all those who take possession of the goods of this testament by faith after the death of the Testator. But in general, from the *teaching*[42] of Scripture all the faithful who lived before Christ and who had the firstfruits of these good things received justification, adoption, and sanctification in this life, and salvation after this life. For those good things were not given except by this testament.[43]

533. Now the reason why they also are called the heirs of this testament is: first, since by their vows, desires, faith, and hope they were marked out at that time; second since they were not provided with the goods which they received except by the power of the *righteousness*[44] of Christ, which at this time was yet to be acquired, and only acquired now; finally, since because they had the same faith as we do, and they had the same body that we do, in accordance with us they were conceived as having been made heirs of the good promises.[45]

534. This is the reason why Paul asserts that the faithful ancients *would not be made perfect without us*,[46] and why Abraham, Isaac, and Jacob are said by Christ to preside in the kingdom of heaven.[47]

---

40. *Doctrina*, 23.25.
41. ἐν ἐμφάσει.
42. φρασει.
43. *Doctrina*, 23.26.
44. δικαιώματος.
45. *Doctrina*, 23.27.
46. Hebrews 11:40.
47. *Doctrina*, 23.28.

535. Therefore, the way that Scripture proposes the matter is that these goods were promised to be acquired in all their fullness after the death of the Testator, to be possessed by those in the church and with the church which would be assembled after the death of Christ in utmost fullness, and that meanwhile it was pleasing to the Father, on account of the present surety[48] of the Son and of His death definitely coming, that they be the written heirs of the testament.[49]

536. Therefore, Abraham and the faithful before Christ from that testament were heirs of the firstfruits of the goods of justification, sanctification, and glorification, from which we are heirs of all the goods which we possess at this time. As he was the father, we are his sons.[50]

537. The covenant which is built upon the acquired goods of this testament is specifically called the *new covenant*, in which God invites the sinner to communion of the goods of the testament, which have now been acquired in all their abundance, under the condition of faith. This, strictly called, is opposite to the hope of the ancients.[51]

538. Now, the proclamation of these goods through the voices and writings of certain men who have been destined to this end is called the *gospel*, as we said before.[52]

539. The sum of this is that He concerning whom Moses and the prophets spoke has appeared in the flesh and has brought the *eternal cause of righteousness*.[53]

540. The first of these was John the Baptist, priest, chief of the prophets,

---

48. *sponsionem.*
49. *Doctrina*, 23.29.
50. *Doctrina*, 23.30.
51. *Doctrina*, 23.31.
52. See §511. *Doctrina*, 23.32.
53. δικαιώμα.

who proclaimed the way to the Lord Christ to restore the hearts of the sons to the fathers and the fathers to the sons, and he preached that the Christ was at hand, and that they should repent and believe by being baptized. He was Elijah who was to come.[54]

541. But the proper authority of this proclamation was Jehovah Himself, the Son of God, appearing in the flesh, at which time He was preached by John, baptized, and inaugurated to His office. At this chief beginning, salvation was announced through the Lord Himself.[55]

542. The sum of the gospel announced through the Son is, *The time has been fulfilled and the kingdom of God has come: repent and believe in the gospel.*[56]

543. Likewise, that word was repeated and explained by the apostles and Evangelists who were sent by Him.

544. Now from the sum of the gospel announced through the Son of God it is evident that the term *gospel* as commonly used not only includes the promises, but also the precepts. For it comprehends every word spoken by Christ and the apostles as opposed to the word which was announced to the people by God through Moses.[57]

545. This matter also stands on its own since the goods of the testament, the giving of which the gospel announces, are never offered with a condition which is included in the precepts of the gospel.[58]

546. The precepts of the gospel (though it speaks abundantly concerning the promises) are explained with various expressions in the writings of the New Testament. But they can be summed up

---

54. Malachi 4:5–6. *Doctrina*, 23.41.
55. *Doctrina*, 23.42.
56. Mark 1:15. *Doctrina*, 23.33.
57. *Doctrina*, 23.34.
58. *Doctrina*, 23.35.

with *faith*, *repentance*, and *charity*, or the exercise of love toward God and neighbor. To faith pertains that one deny himself, follow Christ, etc.[59]

547. Indeed, these precepts of the gospel had been intermixed with the precepts given by Moses, but they cannot be called equal with those which Moses gave for this reason. Yet we ought rightly to hold that these same precepts in the old covenant plainly occur elsewhere in the new covenant. But with other and more powerful arguments we can argue that formerly, then just as now, that they belong to the covenant of the New Testament, which is the reason that the same ancient precept of love is called *new*.[60]

548. For formerly, it was observed by most excellent men that every law given by Moses was abrogated, not as if all the Mosaic precepts completely ceased, but all the precepts of the Mosaic law which had a special relationship to the civil government constituted by Moses ceased.[61]

549. But wherever the gospel is most widely accepted, not only the precepts, but even the threats pertain to the gospel as from the decree of Christ. By disobedience to the gospel, anger, condemnation, and severe judgment are announced more severely than is pronounced in the Mosaic law. For in place of the size of a good offering, a penalty is required.[62]

550. Therefore, let us repeat that every word that is understood as the gospel was spoken by Christ and the apostles.[63]

551. The elegant statements of Holy Scripture of both the Old and New Testament pertained to this.

---

59. *Doctrina*, 23.36.
60. *Doctrina*, 23.37.
61. *Doctrina*, 23.38.
62. *Doctrina*, 23.40.
63. Cf. *Doctrina*, 23.43

CHAPTER 18

The Messiah, Jesus the Nazarene[1]

552. We believe that the Christ, who was the author, cause, and foundation of this *proclaimed happiness*, is Jesus, who was called the *Nazarene*, Son of Mary—a betrothed virgin, of the lineage of David and of humble birth, who was joined to Joseph in marriage, her holy husband of eminent lineage.[2]

553. That He is the true Messiah ought to be demonstrated from His *teachings* joined with His *deeds*. Now we can certainly demonstrate this with any most certain truths. Secondly, from His teachings and deeds together with those prophecies which foretell of the teachings and deeds of the Messiah.[3]

554. Likewise, from the most brilliant effects which followed His teachings and deeds, such as the resurrection from the dead, ascension into heaven, and demonstration of His session at the right hand of the Father through the pouring out of the Holy Spirit, the rejection of the Jews, the conversion of the gentiles, etc. Again, these things ought to be compared with the prophecies.[4]

---

1. The contents of this chapter are found in *Doctrina*, 21, which is entitled, "On the time of fulfillment of the promises made to the fathers, or on the *Testament of Grace* revealed."

2. *Doctrina*, 21.4.

3. Cf. *Doctrina*, 21.5.

4. Cf. *Doctrina*, 21.6.

555. Further, it ought to be demonstrated that the state of His origin, birth, education, family, etc. lacked nothing of those things that the prophets sought in the Messiah.[5]

556. After this it ought to be argued that He came in a common state, at a precipitous time in which it was necessary for the Messiah to come. To this pertains an explanation of the *signs of the times*.[6] This argument, if it is prudently instituted against the Jews, is invincible.[7]

557. Finally, the Jews who foster false imaginings about the Messiah in their own skulls ought to be confounded at this.

Names of the Messiah

558. This Savior is described by the prophets with various names which all signify the same *thing*s to be fulfilled by Him, or the same *truths* accomplished in Him. These are *Immanuel*,[8] *Goel, Angel of the Covenant, Branch, David*,[9] *Solomon, Counselor, Prince of Peace*,[10] *Jehovah our Righteousness*.[11] Others can be joined to these.[12]

559. But there is a singular reason that the Jews in the ancient way of speaking chose the term *Son of God*, or what is much more familiar, *Messiah*.[13]

560. So we certainly understand how for a long time the Second Psalm and the prophecy of Daniel were clearly interpreted.[14]

---

5. *Doctrina*, 21.7.

6. In *Doctrina*, 21.8, Vitringa cites the following biblical texts: Deuteronomy 30:1–2; Jeremiah 3:15–16; 30:18–19; Haggai 2:9–10.

7. *Doctrina*, 21.8.

8. Isaiah 7:14.

9. Jeremiah 23:5.

10. משיח. Isaiah 9:6.

11. Jeremiah 23:6.

12. *Doctrina*, 21.13.

13. *Doctrina*, 21.15.

14. Vitringa's theological disputation at Leiden on the interpretation of Psalm 2

561. The name *Messiah*[15] as is evident for all who know Hebrew means the same as *Christ*[16] or *anointed one.*[17]

562. By this name it is indicated that the Savior has long been ordained by the Father unto the offices of *king* and *priest*, which includes *prophet*, and ought to be *inaugurated* to them in His time.[18]

563. This inauguration was accomplished in various parts. We will treat these shortly.

564. But the proper name by which God willed that His Son appear in the flesh and be designated by a sign in circumcision is *Jesus.*[19]

565. This corresponds with the Hebrew *Joshua*[20] (for who today thinks it comes from the Greek language?). This is either a simple form, as *to save*,[21] or a composite form of *Yahweh*[22] and *he saves*,[23] so that it is satisfying to some men learned in this language to note *Savior* from the interpretation of an angel.[24]

566. Now this name has been given to Him not only so that we might know by this term that our Savior would be a twofold *antitype*[25] of *Joshua* (for *Joshua*[26] is expressed by the Greeks with *Jesus*[27]),

---

was published in 1679 under the title *Disputatio Theologica Inauguralis de Genuino Sensu Versu VII. Psalmi Secundi.* The disputation demonstrates a remarkable skill with the Hebrew and Greek as well as various Jewish sources.

15. משיח.

16. Χριστός.

17. *Doctrina*, 21.16.

18. *Doctrina*, 21.17.

19. Ἰησοῦς. *Doctrina*, 21.18.

20. יהושע.

21. ישע.

22. יהוה.

23. ישע.

24. *Doctrina*, 21.19. See also Martin Vitringa's footnote "e" (21.18).

25. ἀντίτυπον.

26. יהושע.

27. Ἰησοῦς.

but chiefly on account of the occasion since [the meaning of the name] is most fitting with the prophecies of the prophets.[28]

567. And besides this, since this name most accurately expresses the work that would be performed by Christ, which is to save His people from their sins. For all the benefits which Christ presents to His church are comprehended in these words.

568. Now His surname, the *Nazarene*, was often given since the prophets described this kind of Savior.[29]

Person of the Messiah, and His Two Natures

569. The person of the Messiah is God manifested in the flesh.[30]

570. By *God* we understand the *divine essence*, subsisting in the second person of the Holy Trinity, that is, the Son of God.[31]

571. That God is our Savior can be demonstrated in the first place, as they say, as it has been taught in previous places.[32] But indeed that this office pertains to the Son of God is understood further from the *counsel of peace*, since in that we are able to perceive the infinite wisdom of God.[33]

572. The reason is that the Savior is called the *Son of God* in the writings of the New Testament.[34]

573. By *flesh*, we mean a human nature consisting of a soul and body, born from a woman.[35]

---

28. Cf. *Doctrina*, 21.20–21.
29. *Doctrina*, 21.22.
30. *Doctrina*, 21.23.
31. Cf. *Doctrina*, 21.25.
32. E.g., §53–54, §164, §393.
33. Cf. *Doctrina*, 21.28.
34. *Doctrina*, 21.26.
35. *Doctrina*, 21.27.

574. For that the Savior had to be man has been observed earlier.[36]

575. The Messiah had a true and holy soul distinct from the divine nature. Many heretics have argued against this.[37]

576. Likewise, His body was truly a body, just as it says everywhere in Scripture, subjected to the infirmities of our bodies in every manner, yet free from every reproachful effect of concupiscence and from every sin.[38]

577. The reason why the Messiah is called the *Son of man* is from the use of this expression[39] in the Psalms.[40]

578. Now, by the *manifestation of the Son of God in the flesh* we understand this: that the Son of God willed to fashion a special human nature for Himself, in a very certain way, and to work by a special grace to complete the whole task of our salvation, and finally He wished to be adored and glorified into eternity as in His temple and tabernacle. This is called by theologians the *personal union of two natures in Christ.*[41]

579. This mystery so expressed is proclaimed with such variety and efficacy of phrases in the Scriptures of both the Old and New Testaments that it not only astounds the blindness of those who do not admit this great *mystery,*[42] but it also greatly critiques the theologians who dispute the clear and easy ways of speaking that Scripture uses which often neglect the use of philosophical terms.[43]

---

36. E.g., §390, §395, §398. *Doctrina*, 21.28.

37. *Doctrina*, 21.29. Vitringa has in mind the Arians (who denied the deity of Christ) and the Apollinarians (who argued that God, or the Logos, replaced the human soul and spirit of the human Jesus).

38. *Doctrina*, 21.30.

39. φράσει.

40. Psalm 8:4. *Doctrina*, 21.31.

41. *Doctrina*, 21.33.

42. μυστήριον.

43. *Doctrina*, 21.34.

580. Scripture teaches that the Mediator is *one*, that is, that the Son of God dwells with a human nature, or, as David says, *it inhabits the Son of man*, that is, He exists by the operation of a singular human nature with both grace and glory, such that it follows that the works performed by His human nature are rightly ascribed to the Son of God.[44]

581. Since we clearly perceive these things insofar as they can be perceived, so the disputes concerning *personhood* and those discussions about the *assumption of the human nature into personhood* (and *of the Logos*[45]) do not seem to be useful. These discussions are also not able to be conducted except by the definitions which are given to them by the philosophers, often at their own pleasure.[46]

582. First and foremost, the errors of Nestorius[47] and Eutyches[48] ought to be carefully avoided.[49]

583. From the human nature of Christ, by the power of the union with the divine nature, follows a question concerning the *charismata*, or the *habitual grace* through which not only the holiness and impeccability of the human nature of Christ are understood, but additionally the various gifts of the Holy Spirit such as His knowledge, wisdom, *self-control*[50] communicated in this life above the rest of His brothers by the divine nature which inhabited it. And after this life, the highest glory above His brothers, to which pertains the adoration of the Son of God in this human nature. Also, it ought to be repeated here that

---

44. *Doctrina*, 21.35.

45. τοῦ λόγου.

46. *Doctrina*, 21.36.

47. Nestorianism, often credited to the archbishop of Constantinople, Nestorius (ca. 386–450), was a Christological heresy which argued that Christ had two natures and two persons.

48. Eutychianism was another early Christological heresy which taught that Christ's divinity was absorbed into his humanity, thus confusing the two natures of Christ.

49. *Doctrina*, 21.37.

50. σωφροσύνης.

these were the very graces of the inhabiting of the divine nature because they were the highest privilege of the human nature of Christ.[51]

584. Another effect or consequence of the inhabiting of the divine nature in the human is called the *communicatio idiomatum*,[52] by which we mean that the *properties*[53] of each nature can be predicated of the whole person. Likewise, when the person of the Mediator is named according to one nature, not only is the completion or work itself described, but even what is proper to the other nature. For example, *God obtained His church by His own blood.*[54]

585. Most recently, this is proposed by modern advocates of the *Augsburg Confession*,[55] since they in fact contend that certain properties of the divine nature are communicated to the human, such as omnipresence,[56] omniscience, omnipotence, the power of remitting sins and of making alive.

586. Also, the *communication of works*[57] is applied to this consequence of the inhabiting of the divine nature in the human. Through this they understand that those manifest works which pertain to the office of mediatorship—like, for example, redemption and sanctification of the sinner, which theologians call *works*[58]—are attributed to the whole Mediator according to each nature, with one nature being united to the other for that work accomplishing what pertains to mediatorship.[59]

---

51. *Doctrina*, 21.38.

52. *communication of properties.*

53. ἰδιώματα.

54. Acts 20:28. *Doctrina*, 21.39.

55. Vitringa here refers to the Lutherans. See Augsburg Confession, Art. 3; Formula of Concord, Art. 8. Vitringa probably has such theologians as Johann Gerhard (1582–1637) in mind. *Doctrina*, 21.39.

56. Emending *omnipotentia* here to *omnipraesentia* per *Doctrina*, 21.40.

57. *communio apotelesmatum.*

58. ἀποτελέσματα.

59. Cf. *Doctrina*, 21.40.

Offices of the Messiah

587. The offices to which the Messiah was ordained from eternity and to which He was to be inaugurated in His time, which we said before were indicated by the title *anointed one*[60] are *prophet, priest,* and *king.*[61]

588. For even if under the Old Testament[62] hardly anyone was anointed except priests, kings, and prophets, yet the office is not only attributed to Christ by the power of words, but also it pertains especially to the priestly office.[63]

589. For that Christ would be a prophet and teacher is preached most clearly in the Scriptures of the Old Testament. And the prophet Isaiah proclaimed to a greater extent that the Messiah would speak under the name and *form*[64] of a *gentle prophet* and *teacher.*[65] Recall that Moses marked Him out with this special title.[66]

590. But let it be rightly observed and added against the Jews that this surely was done to convince them of the truth of the gospel.[67]

591. Now it was pleasing to the first prophets that Christ be depicted with the highest title, since Christ in His public life all the way to His own death had to undertake this most important persona.[68]

592. Now every book of the New Testament teaches that Christ was a prophet.[69]

---

60. משיח. §559–61.
61. *Doctrina,* 21.41.
62. Clarifying *Instrumento* as *Testamento* per *Doctrina,* 21.41.
63. *Doctrina,* 21.42.
64. σχέσει.
65. Isaiah 55:4; 61:1.
66. Deuteronomy 18:18. *Doctrina,* 21.43.
67. *Doctrina,* 21.45.
68. *Doctrina,* 21.46.
69. *Doctrina,* 21.47.

593. To the prophetic office of Christ pertains teaching, doctrine of miracles, power over death, and foretelling the future.[70]

594. Christ taught the Old Testament church through His Spirit. He teaches the New Testament church through His same Spirit, though more abundantly. But He especially exercised the office of prophet when He spoke face-to-face with the people of Israel at the time of His ministry and explained the whole will of His Father more clearly.[71]

595. This institution of Christ surpasses that of the preceding prophets not only in clarity, but also in authority and efficacy, or convincing power. It was also more excellent than the giving of the law on Mount Sinai.[72]

596. Also, it ought not to be excluded from this prophetic office of Christ that He gave laws and formed a new *citizenship*[73] with them distinct from that of Moses, although this can also be attributed to the office of kingship.[74]

597. But it should be avoided, lest we understand this like the Socinians, who believe that the precept of most perfect love in the Mosaic law does not continue, and in the same manner, they allege that the laws of Christ are more perfect than the laws of Moses. If it is understood in this sense, it is false.[75]

598. The Papists err too when they speak of the *counsels of the perfect gospel*.[76]

---

70. *Doctrina*, 21.48.
71. *Doctrina*, 21.49.
72. *Doctrina*, 21.50.
73. πολιτείαν.
74. *Doctrina*, 21.51.
75. *Doctrina*, 21.52–53.
76. *Doctrina*, 21.54. Vitringa refers to the Roman Catholic notion of *consilia evangelica*, or "evangelical counsels." This is "ecclesiastical advice" which is not commanded in the moral law, such as special vows or acts common to monasticism and asceticism. The completion of such acts earns the believer additional merit for or above salvation.

599. The miracles by which Christ, as Teacher, confirmed His institution surpass those of Moses and the prophets because He accomplished them Himself by His own power, that is, *by the Spirit of God*,[77] through His divine nature, by which others accomplished those same things in His name.[78]

600. They also surpassed the miracles of the prophets in number, variety, and magnitude of effects.[79]

601. Likewise, they were most fitting to the office of Christ which was to save men, since Moses and the rest of the prophets brought ruin on many under that more severe government with their miracles.[80]

602. But besides these marks, the teaching of Christ was confirmed by His death and resurrection; and further by brilliant signs which followed His advent. These are called *His session to the right hand of the Father* and *coming on the clouds of heaven*. For these are certain proofs because Christ sits at the right hand of His Father.[81]

603. The prophets made known signs concerning the things of a future time of the church after the coming of Christ, but principally concerning the fates of gentile and Jew. Further, it was pleasing to the apostle John himself, in distinct order, to pronounce the more notable events of the church all the way up to the age of consummation.[82]

604. That the Messiah would be a priest was splendidly foretold by the first prophets,[83] and it was confirmed by the writers of

---

77. ἐν τῷ πνεύματι θεοῦ. Matthew 12:28.

78. *Doctrina*, 21.57.

79. *Doctrina*, 21.58.

80. Matthew 11:5. *Doctrina*, 21.59.

81. Cf. *Doctrina*, 21.60.

82. *Doctrina*, 21.61.

83. In *Doctrina*, 21.62, Vitringa cites the following biblical texts: Psalms 40:7, 9; 110:4; Isaiah 53:10; Zechariah 6:13.

the New Testament, and chiefly by Paul in the epistle to the Hebrews.[84]

605. He was prefigured as a priest not only by Aaron, but even by all the rest of the priests if we consider them individually.[85]

606. But if they are considered together, then Aaron and the rest of the faithful priests were types of Christ.[86]

607. But for a certain reason, the priesthood was represented by Melchizedek. It was done for this reason, so that we might conceive Christ to be a priest who is simultaneously a king, and at the same time being born from that family which were kings. A priest, he says, *by the power of an incorruptible life.*[87]

608. The parts of this office of priest are *offering, intercession,* and *blessing,* although these last two do not differ very much with respect to Christ.[88]

609. *Offering* consists in this, that the Son of God, the Mediator, erected a human nature in which He inhabited both morally and rationally for the offering of a sacrifice on the cross, as a *demonstration of the righteousness of God,*[89] and of *atoning*[90] for the sins of the elect.[91]

610. It is evident from this thesis that the Mediator, insofar as He is God, executed the priesthood, and insofar as He is man, the sacrifice.[92]

---

84. *Doctrina,* 21.62.
85. *Doctrina,* 21.63.
86. *Doctrina,* 21.64.
87. κατὰ δύναμιν ζωῆς ἀκαταλύτου. Hebrews 7:16. *Doctrina,* 21.65.
88. *Doctrina,* 21.66.
89. ἔνδειξιν τῆς δικαιοσύνης τοῦ θεοῦ. Romans 3:25.
90. *expiandum.*
91. *Doctrina,* 21.67.
92. *Doctrina,* 21.68.

611. Likewise, a priest is represented by an *altar*. For the reason is that priests offered their sacrifices to God on altars since the sacrifices were not able to be burned in their hands.[93]

612. But it is not inconsistent that the cross and the lifting up of the human nature of Christ on the cross is represented by the altar, insofar as the altar bears the sacrifice.

613. By the *fire* we should understand something that consumes the human nature of Christ, but especially the will of God, the Judge, who vindicates sins, and the burning desire of Christ to be subject to the righteousness of the Father. But the desire in Him was excited by the inhabiting divine nature and by the Holy Spirit.[94]

614. His *intercession* is the *intervening appearance*[95] of Christ in heaven with the Father with the will of applying the effects of eternal righteousness to His elect seed. This is called *arbitration* because of its effect.[96]

615. The eternal *surety*[97] of the Son of God ought not to be excluded from this, which is His will of being sanctified in His human nature by His Father, not just His frequent repetition made in the days of the Old Testament before the assumption of His human nature (Scripture so pronounces this matter to us, though the will of the Son of God is always one and the same), but also the prayers and the weeping of His human nature which flowed for the church in all time which it survived on earth. These remain even now by that same will which was glorified in His human nature.[98]

---

93. Cf. *Doctrina*, 21.69.
94. *Doctrina*, 21.70.
95. ἐμφανισμὸς.
96. *Doctrina*, 21.71.
97. *sponsio*.
98. *Doctrina*, 21.72.

616. And so, it is clear that to this intercession of Christ, the Mediator, pertains also the *priestly blessing*.[99]

617. All these acts of the priesthood of Christ were excellently foreshadowed a long time before through the offering of Isaac and of the sacrifices of this kind, but chiefly through the public Day of Atonement.[100]

618. The effect of this offering and intercession of Christ is the *consummation*[101] of all the faithful of all time. We will treat this later under *satisfaction*.[102]

619. The errors of the Socinians ought to be carefully avoided, who hardly distinguish the offices of Christ from anything other than king. And they destroy all the true effects of the sacrifice of Christ. That is, they destroy our hope, and they weaken these things throughout all of Scripture.[103]

620. All the prophets teach that the Messiah would be a king, the Evangelists teach the most brilliant marks and effects of His kingdom.[104]

621. None of the prophets describe an *earthly* kingdom to the Messiah, neither will it ever be earthly, although the church will become more blessed in the world, even as it is now.[105]

622. The beginning of the kingdom is stated in the prophets as the *glorification of the Mediator*, or His *session at the right hand of the Father*. For this reason, the church for all this time is called the *kingdom of heaven*, or the *kingdom of God*.[106]

---

99. *Doctrina*, 21.73.
100. Cf. *Doctrina*, 21.74.
101. τελείωσις.
102. Ch. 19.
103. Cf. *Doctrina*, 21.75.
104. *Doctrina*, 21.77.
105. *Doctrina*, 21.78.
106. *Doctrina*, 21.79.

623. But Christ did not rule His church as Lord before that time, since: first, at this time He acquired the full right for Himself by His blood to rule over the church; second, at this time His kingdom was published throughout the whole world and hence, third, at this time He began to have a great multitude of subordinates throughout all the lands of the globe; fourth, at this time He alone ruled the church, because all the other institutions of Mount Sinai were abolished by all of His power over His church; finally, at this time He rules His church not as an *ambassador of His Father*[107] as He was under the Old Testament, but as an *equal to the Father*,[108] which He is called because of His session at the right hand of the Father. So it is also understood that every task of the kingdom has been handed over to the Son. These things are understood to have been before the manifestation of the Son by reason of the *dispensation*[109] with the Father.[110]

624. The parts of this kingdom are that He *gathers*, *rules*, and *defends* His church and people.[111]

625. To the kingdom of the church pertains the giving and execution of the law.

626. Likewise, to the kingdom of the church pertains the whole reign of the world with regard to the church, since the church is not able to be ruled nor defended unless at the same time the whole world is governed in which the church is, out of which it is collected and in which it ought to be defended.[112]

627. From this it is evident that a distinction between the *natural* kingdom of the Son of God and the *mediatorial* kingdom is

---

107. ἄγγελος τοῦ πατρός.
108. ἴσος τῷ πατρὶ.
109. οἰκονομίας.
110. *Doctrina*, 21.80.
111. *Doctrina*, 21.81.
112. Cf. *Doctrina*, 21.82.

not of very great importance, since Scripture does not pay more attention to the natural kingdom of the Son of God than to the mediatorial one.

628. This mode of ruling which is through the gathering of the church out of the world and of its defense in the world which has been joined with the defeating of her enemies must endure until every enemy has been defeated, which also includes the death of the body. This will happen in the resurrection of the dead.[113]

629. At this time, the Son of God will cease to reign, that is, He will no longer gather the church, and having collected the church, He will not protect and defend it, that is, His grace will have no regard for subjugating enemies any longer. For where there are no enemies, there is no need for defense. And where the gathering has been fully completed, there is no longer any need for gathering.[114]

630. But He never ceases to be the head, the Lord, and the king of His church which will survive in every time through His Spirit, and the church shall worship Him as the cause of her salvation, and as her firstborn brother.[115]

631. The *ordination* of the Son of God to these offices has been accomplished from all eternity. But Scripture sets the *inauguration* in various degrees of which the first is at the manifestation of the Son of God in the world. The second is when he was thirty years old when He was baptized, when the solemn declaration of the Father appeared. The third was at His ascension into heaven, when He was given possession of full glory and happiness. One passage says: *He was anointed with the oil of gladness before His kindred.*[116]

---

113. Cf. *Doctrina*, 21.83
114. *Doctrina*, 21.84.
115. *Doctrina*, 21.85.
116. Psalm 45:7. *Doctrina*, 21.86.

632. This can be confirmed from the types also. Consider the history of David.[117]

633. Indeed, these offices, being never to be separated from each other, were executed in turn, separately from each other, by the Mediator. Now the Mediator exercised the prophetic office in the course of His public life, the priestly office chiefly at the time of His life, and the kingly office after His glorification.[118]

634. But the natural order of the offices is this, that the priest precedes prophet and king.

Twofold State of the Messiah

635. Now the difference between these offices which are executed by the Messiah introduces the difference between the *states of the Messiah*, which are two: *self-emptying* and *exaltation*. These are often joined in the Old and New Testaments and clearly represented to the Jews through a *twofold Messiah*.[119]

636. Two parts of the self-emptying are aptly set forth as *emptying*[120] more specifically, and *humiliation*.[121]

637. To *self-emptying*[122] it pertains that the Son of God assumed the form of a servant, and He appeared *in the likeness of sinful flesh*.[123] For the assumption of the human nature and union with it is not able to constitute the self-emptying of the Son of God.[124]

---

117. 1 Samuel 16:13; 2 Samuel 11:4. *Doctrina*, 21.87.

118. *Doctrina*, 21.88.

119. By *twofold Messiah*, Vitringa means the *son of Joseph* and the *son of David*. *Doctrina*, 21.89.

120. κένωσις.

121. ταπείνωσις. *Doctrina*, 21.90.

122. κένωσιν.

123. ἐν ὁμοιώματι σαρκὸς ἁμαρτίας. Romans 8:3.

124. *Doctrina*, 21.91.

638. The assumption of the human nature, commonly called *incarnation*[125] and *appearing*,[126] is the preparation of a human nature for this: that it might be an instrument and organ of the Son of God (and likewise through this it also might be a singular work of the Son of God in that prepared nature so that He is rightly said to be united with this nature), that it deserves to be called the temple and tabernacle of the divine nature, and finally that the works of this human nature be conceived as the works of the Son of God, as we said before.

639. The Holy Spirit uses in His Word various and most efficacious ways of speaking to us about this mystery placed before our eyes. The possibility of this is most clear by sound reason. Who opposes that God would not be able to use man as an instrument?

640. To this *incarnation*[127] pertains *conception* and *birth* which is described to us by the Evangelists.[128]

641. His *conception* was accomplished in the Virgin Mary through the most powerful working of the Son of God and the Holy Spirit. Indeed, Scripture even attributes this working to the Father.[129]

642. His physical substance in conception was not separated from the flesh and blood of the Virgin Mary. This is very necessary to believe.[130]

643. His *birth* was wrought in the Virgin Mary in accordance with the prophecies and promises according to the stated course of nature, and not without pain, yet still from virginity.[131]

---

125. ἐνσάρκωσις.
126. ἐπιφάνεια.
127. ἐνσάρκωσιν.
128. *Doctrina*, 21.92.
129. See Jeremiah 31:22; Hebrews 10:5. *Doctrina*, 21.93.
130. *Doctrina*, 21.94.
131. *Doctrina*, 21.95.

644. This birth happened under Augustus, before Quirinius was *governor*[132] of Syria,[133] having been encircled with the circumstances of this kind which would plainly be the future situation of the Messiah.[134]

645. At His birth, He was made under the law, *a servant of dominions*,[135] for a brief time lower than the angels, and hence obligated to all the precepts to which the Israelites were subject.[136]

646. Besides this, a special mandate was assigned to Him by the Father: to be the Mediator of humankind, for which He came into the world to carry out.[137]

647. Because of this subjection to the law, He was made to be circumcised on the eighth day and presented to God in the temple according to the custom, and He studiously observed the rest of the Mosaic laws.[138]

648. Circumcision (as with the other sacraments) greatly applied to Christ just as every other Israelite since it was the mortification of sin in His flesh with pain for the sanctification of the church.[139]

649. Next, he was educated in Nazareth according to the prophecies. And, although little concerning his childhood and adolescence is told to us (and not without good reason), yet, from those things which are written it is evident that He lived in chastity, purity, and holiness, and diligently cared for those things *which were of His Father*.[140]

---

132. ἐπίτροπον.

133. Luke 2:2.

134. *Doctrina*, 21.96.

135. עבד מושלים.

136. *Doctrina*, 21.97.

137. John 10:18. *Doctrina*, 21.98.

138. *Doctrina*, 21.99.

139. *Doctrina*, 21.100.

140. τὰ τοῦ Πατρός αυτοῦ. *Doctrina*, 21.101.

650. His private life ran up until His thirtieth year when He was inaugurated to His offices by being baptized by John through the voice of His Father and the shining *symbol*[141] of both the appearing of the Holy Spirit and the opening of heaven.[142]

651. Again, *baptism* denotes a particular meaning for Him, and hence it was rightly permitted for Him.[143]

652. After His most grave temptation which He underwent, He went forth in public, traveling everywhere in Judea and Galilee not even neglecting Samaria and spreading His gospel everywhere with utmost tenderness to the elect, besides the apostles and Evangelists who were doing the same.[144]

653. He lived this time of public life in poverty, infirmities, temptations, afflictions, and tears, sustaining the hatred and jealousy of the leaders and teachers, yet without any pause in His duty.[145]

654. He endured that time of public ministry for a few years (three it seems) since the Messiah is said to endure most great sufferings in which He had to demonstrate obedience to His Father. The apostle calls this *humiliation*[146] or *humbling* which includes two kinds: *death* and *death on a cross*.[147]

655. That the Messiah had to suffer is clearly written in the prophecies. Yet the Jews through their *sorrows of the Messiah*[148] seem to have meant something else.[149]

---

141. σύμβολον.
142. *Doctrina*, 21.102.
143. Cf. *Doctrina*, 21.103.
144. *Doctrina*, 21.104.
145. *Doctrina*, 21.105.
146. ταπείνωσιν.
147. Philippians 2:8. *Doctrina*, 21.106.
148. חבלי המשיח.
149. *Doctrina*, 21.107.

656. This hour of darkness (that is, the time of the most vehement sufferings of Christ) and the binding and *oppression*[150] to which Christ was handed down consists in this: first, He had the most grave sense of divine wrath inexpressible to us such that most troublesome thoughts, anxiety, highest sadness, and horror arose in His soul, from which the labor of soul is ascribed to Him, and the terrors of God are said to wave over Him; second, the devil powerfully tempted Him in this state, placing before His eyes with skill and vigor the difficulty of undertaking this work, and urging Him to desert the cause of God in this way; third, the future afflictions, temptations, and struggles of the church which He loved so tenderly (as we can say) were presented to Him so that it would make Him dread it, not less than Abraham long before;[151] fourth, He saw His own brothers according to the flesh whom He was not able to pursue with utmost love as a man and a Jew perish in disobedience, and even on this occasion in which salvation was announced to them chiefly through Him; fifth, these Jewish brothers of His, along with the gentiles, incited by the devil, afflicted Him with disgrace, bitterness, and most grave sorrows to His body before His death; finally, He watched His most dear disciples abandon Him to His shame, and on His own had to undergo injustices, and all manner of insults, words, and sufferings which were most grave.[152]

657. This was the reason and cause of the *just fear*[153] which assaulted Christ and the *agony*[154] of supplication and tears and sweat of blood in the garden, and His exclamation on the cross. This time was one of grief and battle with the devil which was foretold of old.[155]

---

150. עצר. Isaiah 53:8.

151. Namely, when Abraham dreaded bringing Isaac to the altar (Genesis 22:1–10).

152. *Doctrina*, 21.108.

153. τῆς εὐλάβειας.

154. ἀγωνία.

155. *Doctrina*, 21.109.

658. But in this temptation, He did not sin, but rather in the midst of sorrow, horror, and fear He exerted a most constant and pure love toward God and His brothers. Through God He at last escaped the devil as the superior. *He learned obedience from those things which He suffered.*[156]

659. From these words it is evident that Christ not only suffered in His soul, but He suffered there more greatly than in His body.[157]

660. These sufferings in the soul can be called the *descent into hell,* even if it is evident that the Fathers used this phrase in another way.[158]

661. The terminus of these sufferings was death on the cross on which Christ's death was foretold and prefigured by various types. For it is necessary that Christ would die by that death in which it can be demonstrated that there would be a *curse*[159] in His death — that is, a *proof*[160] — of the righteousness of God who punishes sins.[161]

662. Not only did the Messiah have *to die* according to the prophecies and types, but also He had *to be buried* since His death not only had to be a demonstration of the righteousness of God, but also a testimony reversing the curse on account of this demonstration of the righteousness of God in Him.[162]

663. This lowest state of self-emptying had to be followed by the state of *exaltation*[163] or *glories*[164] which were owed to Christ as the reward for His obedience after His *sufferings.*[165] About this

---

156. ἔμαθεν ἀφ ὧν ἔπαθεν τὴν ὑπακοήν. Hebrews 5:8. *Doctrina,* 21.110.
157. *Doctrina,* 21.110.
158. *Doctrina,* 21.111.
159. κατάρα.
160. ἔνδειξις.
161. *Doctrina,* 21.113.
162. *Doctrina,* 21.114.
163. ὑψώσεως.
164. αἱ δόξαι.
165. τὰ παθήματα.

reward we have already spoken when we treated the covenant of the Father and the Son.[166]

664. The first part of this state of *exaltation*[167] is the resurrection of Christ from the dead, accomplished in the early morning on the first day. For the Evangelists do not differ here.[168]

665. The prophets foretold that the Messiah would rise again, and illustrious types foreshadowed it.[169]

666. They add most weighty reasons which press it, since without the resurrection of Christ, no perfection, no *justification*[170] of Christ and the church could be devised. For on the resurrection, it plainly hangs that either the devil through eternal death would triumph over Christ and the church, or indeed that Christ and the church would triumph over the devil and death.[171]

667. It can and ought to be made solidly clear from the Evangelists that Christ *rose again*, since this is for the proving, demonstrating, and vindicating of the truth of the whole gospel.[172]

668. Christ rose again by the infinite strength of His own power. And this is the reason why that same resuscitation of the human nature of Christ is ascribed to the Father and to the Holy Spirit.[173]

669. Now He rose again on the third day, after the example of Jonah, who seems to have been in the fish for the same amount of time that Christ was in the grave.[174]

---

166. §391–98. *Doctrina*, 21.115.
167. ὑψώσεως.
168. *Doctrina*, 21.116.
169. *Doctrina*, 21.117. See also 21.119.
170. δικαίωσις.
171. *Doctrina*, 21.118.
172. *Doctrina*, 21.120.
173. Ephesians 1:20; Romans 8:11. *Doctrina*, 21.122.
174. *Doctrina*, 21.123.

670. Christ, when resuscitated for forty days, revealed Himself to His disciples and conversed with them, although in such a way which was presently fitting for a body prepared for glory.[175]

671. In accordance with the prophecies and images of the former times,[176] He ascended into heaven, [entrusting] the faith of His work to those who make confident testimonies.[177]

672. Now, first and foremost, it ought to be repeated here that this most worthy *mystery*[178] is the approaching of the high priest into the holy of holies on the public Day of Atonement. He who *ascended* was one who first *descended*.[179]

673. This kind of glory of the Mediator is called in one way *assumption*[180] and *presentation*[181] and in another way *ascension*[182] for good reasons.[183]

674. The place on which the ascension took place is the Mount of Olives. [He ascended] to the highest heaven, that is, the destined place of the blessedness of the faithful.[184]

675. The Lutherans weaken this ascension of Christ into the heavens, which is so clearly explained to us in Scripture, when they interpret it through the disappearance of the body of Christ so that it serves their hypothesis.[185]

---

175. *Doctrina*, 21.124.
176. Psalm 47:5; 68:18.
177. *Doctrina*, 21.125.
178. μυστήριον.
179. John 3:13. *Doctrina*, 21.126.
180. ἀνάλημψις.
181. εἰσαγωγὴ.
182. ἀνάβασις.
183. *Doctrina*, 21.127.
184. Cf. *Doctrina*, 21.128.
185. τῇ ὑποθέσις. *Doctrina*, 21.129. See Martin Vitringa's anthology of Lutheran sources in footnote "1."

676. Besides many other reasons, this ascension of Christ into heaven was plainly necessary so that the Messiah would become a partaker of the glory which was decreed to Him by the Father. This is called the *session to the right hand of the Father*.[186]

677. For by the session to the right hand of the Father the reward of obedience is understood which the Son, the Mediator, has received from the Father by the power of the eternal pact which was between Him and the Father. This reward is the *highest exaltation*,[187] or the uncovered kingdom of Christ without any partners in His church which is dispersed throughout the whole world and brought forth by His blood. For to sit at the right hand is to reign. Let those who are said to be of the kingdom of Christ be brought together.[188]

678. Now it ought to be carefully noted that the conquering of the enemies of Christ pertains to His session at the right hand in a particular way. For the phrase used in Psalm 110:1 is thus only used of Christ.[189]

679. Now this phrase ought to be explained from the custom of kings who often gather their subjects with a scepter to their right hand to whom they desire to give their authority. Thus, the session to the right hand denotes the communication of authority.[190]

680. But it should be noted that Christ is described to us in Scripture not only as sitting at the right hand as a king, but also as a priest, interceding for us, although these, rightly explained, do not completely differ. See *intercession* in previous sections.[191]

---

186. *Doctrina*, 21.130.
187. ὑπερύψωσις.
188. *Doctrina*, 21.131.
189. *Doctrina*, 21.132.
190. *Doctrina*, 21.133.
191. §608–34. *Doctrina*, 21.134.

681. The first demonstration of the session of Christ at the right hand of the Father was in the pouring out of the Holy Spirit on the day of Pentecost. Further, all the blessings given to the church and the judgments against the enemies of the church ought to be considered as its fruits and effects.[192]

---

192. *Doctrina*, 21.134.

CHAPTER 19

Firstfruits of the Death and Obedience of Christ, or Satisfaction

682. We have said before that the reason for the manifestation of the Son of God in the flesh is the acquiring *of righteousness*[1] (that is, of the cause of righteousness and of eternal life for the faithful) which was promised by all the prophets and foreshadowed by many types.[2]

683. We say that this is the same condition which the Father had stipulated in the pact with the Son.[3]

684. Now we have stated that the cause of the justification of the faithful is this *righteousness*[4] in the obedience, suffering, and death of Christ through which also divine justice was satisfied.[5]

685. The word *satisfaction* is not found explicitly in Scripture, but we do find the word *payment* which is plainly like and equal to it. For this reason, it ought not to be regarded as *absent from Scripture*.[6] Therefore it is not necessary that we change our view. On

---

1. δικαιώματος.
2. §512. *Doctrina*, 22.1.
3. *Doctrina*, 22.2.
4. δικαίωμα.
5. *Doctrina*, 22.3.
6. ἀγράφῳ. I.e., unbiblical.

the contrary, we find the idea in the word *guilt offering*[7] which includes the meaning of *satisfaction*.[8]

686. By satisfaction we understand that the Son of God *as surety*,[9] by His sufferings and His death for the elect who would come to believe in time, presented and offered everything which the most holy righteousness of God demanded for the vindication of sin in the sinner. This payment had for the faithful the effect of *redemption*,[10] or as we say in court, *liberation*. That is, by His power the elect were declared to be immune from the penalty and are regarded just for eternal communion and happiness with God.[11]

687. It was pleasing to God, by His singular providence, that this truth which clearly and manifestly lies on every page of Holy Scripture might chiefly be revealed in this present age with open light by occasion of the errors and the contrary teachings of either the Papists who variously obscure it, or the Socinians who thoroughly pervert it by leading astray the fragile and feeble with their handsome sayings, or the Remonstrants[12] who are zealous to tear out its root.[13]

688. Now although Scripture is most abundant in this matter with the variety of testimonies and efficacy of expressions, it is not necessary for us to be worried about this dispute except that we formulate arguments of highest clarity, utility, and efficacy and that we explain them in a proper order.[14]

---

7. אשם.

8. *Doctrina*, 22.4.

9. *sponsor*.

10. ἀπολύτρωσεως.

11. *Doctrina*, 22.5.

12. The Remonstrants were a group that rejected the classical Reformed teaching on predestination, stirring up controversies in the early seventeenth century which sparked the monumental Synod of Dort (1618–1619). Jacob Arminius is often credited as the founder of the movement.

13. *Doctrina*, 22.6.

14. *Doctrina*, 22.7.

689. Indeed, it seems that that best order is that which flows from the very nature of things. Therefore, it ought to be examined in this way.[15]

690. First, according to the teaching of the Holy Spirit, the righteousness and sanctity of God demand that sin may not be dismissed unpunished, and the sinner may not be admitted to His communion.[16]

691. Further, the truth of God demands the same, and death is threatened to the sinner.[17]

692. Second, the Son of God as surety has interceded for a certain seed of sinners and has begun to bring them to Himself and free them because the sinner is in debt. To this also pertains an inquiry of whether the Son of God under the Old Testament sustained the persona of a *fideiussor* or an *expromissor*.[18] Likewise, see what has been said in the sections of the Mediator, Goel, Priest,[19] and the pact between the Father and the Son.[20]

693. After this, we ought to consider this payment to divine justice which was made in the obedience of Christ by the Son's fulfilled

---

15. *Doctrina*, 22.8.

16. *Doctrina*, 22.9.

17. *Doctrina*, 22.10.

18. These terms are left untranslated because they are technical terms in the history of Reformed theology. The debate rests on the question of the precise nature of the forgiveness that the Old Testaments saints received. The question arises because Christ offered satisfaction *after* they lived. On one side of the debate, the Cocceians understood Christ's *surety* (*sponsor*) as a *fideiussor*, or a *guarantee* of sins being paid before the coming of Christ. In this way, God "passed over" the sins of Old Testament saints until Christ came, and at the death of Christ their sins were paid. On the other side of the debate were the followers of Gisbertus Voetius. The Voetians argued for Christ's surety as an *expromissor*, or an absolute forgiveness of sins even before Christ's death in time. See Baugus, "Covenant Theology," 392–95. See also Willem J. van Asselt, "Expromissio or Fideiussio?: A Seventeenth-Century Theological Debate between Voetians and Cocceians about the Nature of Christ's Suretyship in Salvation History," *Mid-America Journal of Theology* 14 (2003): 37–57. For Vitringa's further thoughts, see Vitringa, *Sacrarum Observationum*, vol. 3, cps. 3–4.

19. §392.

20. §512. *Doctrina*, 22.11.

subjection to the Father under the law, and His *self-emptying*[21] and *humiliation*[22] *unto death, even death on a cross.*[23]

694. This demonstration being rightly understood, the testimonies of Holy Scripture ought to be laid out most brilliantly in which Scripture considers the death of Christ as a price by which a debt was paid, or as a *ransom,*[24] by the strength of which captives were liberated from prison.[25]

695. By this deed it ought to be declared what the Holy Spirit understands by the soul, blood, and death of the Son of God, since He portrays those things as the price of redemption of the faithful. For the shedding of blood, death, giving the soul, and laying down of life (if understood properly) cannot produce the price which may satisfy divine justice. Rather, no one except the Son can accomplish the shedding of blood with the demonstration of highest obedience to the Father with the most constant love for glorifying God and of being sanctified for the good of the church.[26]

696. For the further confirming of this thesis, it is necessary to prove that the suffering human nature of Christ is compared in Holy Scripture with the sacrifice, and certainly with the sacrifice for sin, since He is called the *sin offering.*[27] Christ, the Mediator, as a priest stands as this kind of sacrifice.[28]

---

21. κενωσί.
22. ταπεινώσι.
23. Philippians 2:8. *Doctrina*, 22.12.
24. כפר, λύτρον.
25. *Doctrina*, 22.13.
26. *Doctrina*, 22.14.
27. אשם, ἁμαρτία, περί ἁμαρτίας. Isaiah 53:10; John 1:29; Romans 8:3; 2 Corinthians 5:21; Hebrews 9:28; 1 Peter 2:24 (cited in *Doctrina*, 22.15).
28. *Doctrina*, 22.15.

697. Further, the prepositions *in place of*[29] and *for*[30] which correspond to the Hebrew word *tachath*[31] ought to be understood, since Christ is said to have died *for* us. And they also mean that Christ not only died for our good, but also in our stead, and in our place.[32]

698. Likewise, the prepositions *from,*[33] *on account of,*[34] *on behalf of,*[35] and *for*[36] are paired with the word *sin*. For example, it says that *Christ died on account of sin* or *for sin*. These prepositions denote the impulsive cause,[37] not the final cause.[38]

699. It also pertains to confirming this thesis with an even greater dictum that Scripture considers the crucifixion of Christ and His death as an *exemplary penalty,*[39] and states that it is a *demonstration of the righteousness of God*.[40]

700. Along with these arguments let us add a solid explanation of the phrases which are found in Isaiah 53.[41]

701. Finally, this thesis is most stable in that this truth ought to be treated from the effects of the death of Christ which are true effects and not an imaginary payment. These are such: expiation

---

29. ἀντί.
30. ὑπέρ.
31. תחת.
32. *Doctrina*, 22.16.
33. מן.
34. διά.
35. ὑπέρ.
36. περί.
37. The *impulsive cause* refers to a cause which provides the occasion for the efficient cause.
38. *Doctrina*, 22.17.
39. מוסר, παράδειγμα.
40. ἔνδειξιν τῆς δικαιοσύνης τοῦ θεοῦ. Romans 3:25. *Doctrina*, 22.18.
41. *Doctrina*, 22.19. See also Vitringa, *Commentarius in Jesaiam*, 2:767–97.

and oblation of sin as *debt*,[42] or *redemption of the captive from prison, reconciliation*,[43] *justification*,[44] or *nonimputation of sin*.[45]

702. These effects of the death of Christ so surely flow from His death and obedience that they are owed to and possessed by all those for whom Christ died.[46]

703. Therefore, it follows that we cannot say that Christ died equally for all, since these effects are not obtained by all.[47]

704. Also, the death of Christ ought to be considered as the death of the *surety*.[48] Therefore, He died for none other than those for whom He sponsored.[49]

705. It is for this reason that in Holy Scripture the death of Christ is applied to the remnant, elect seed, church, people of Christ, sheep, little flock, Jacob and Israel, etc.[50]

706. So it is most clear that Christ is not said to have died in any sense for *all* or for the *world*, except that He died for an indeterminate number of those who are *in the world*, and for a great multitude of gentiles without discrimination who have been dispersed throughout the whole world, which is different from the dispensation of the church under the Old Testament.[51]

707. For at this time of the church, the preaching of the gospel and the offering of salvation is for everyone without discrimination

---

42. ἱλασμός, גאולה.
43. ἀπολύτρωσις.
44. δικαίωσις.
45. *Doctrina*, 22.20.
46. *Doctrina*, 22.21.
47. *Doctrina*, 22.22.
48. *sponsoris*.
49. *Doctrina*, 22.23.
50. *Doctrina*, 22.24.
51. *Doctrina*, 22.25.

of people group. *Whoever believes will be saved,*[52] even if everyone will not be saved.[53]

708. Therefore, the opinion of the Remonstrants[54] concerning this article ought to be rejected. And we cannot approve of the ways of speaking of those who presently argue for a universal grace. We always need to accept that the obtaining of salvation and its application cannot be extended equally or extensively.[55]

709. The death of Christ, by which divine justice was satisfied for the elect, ought to be considered as the cause of the just attaining of the communion of God and life, which Scripture calls *righteousness,*[56] or *the right to become children of God.*[57]

710. This ought to be properly preserved and solidly defended against the Papists and Remonstrants who establish the right to eternal salvation in works by merits and observation of evangelical precepts.[58]

---

52. Cf. Mark 16:16.

53. *Doctrina*, 22.26.

54. For *Remonstrants*, see §687.

55. *Doctrina*, 22.27. Vitringa probably has theologians like Moïse Amyraut (1596–1664) in his crosshairs, who argued for a hypothetical and universal atonement. Vitringa may also be thinking of Roman Catholics and Lutherans. See Martin Vitringa's footnote "l" in *Doctrina*, 22.22.

56. δικαίωμα.

57. ἐξουσίαν τέκνα θεοῦ γενέσθαι. John 1:12. *Doctrina*, 22.28.

58. *Doctrina*, 22.29.

CHAPTER 20

Calling, Regeneration, and Repentance

711. It was said in the previous chapter (and more specifically in §401–2, 517–21) that from the *obedience and death of Christ*[1] flows forth the goods of justification, sanctification, and glorification, and to these pertain other things such as peace, happiness, and freedom. These eternal goods are of the testament of grace, the surety[2] of which is Christ.[3]

712. It has also been said that God invites the sinner to the possession of these goods under the condition of faith which we described in chapter 14.[4] This is the proposition of the covenant of grace.

713. But we have warned that God does not weigh this condition as being brought about by the sinner's own power.[5] Indeed, the sinner is a slave to sin, and inept to any spiritual good on his own.

Calling

714. Now since in sinful man faith is the beginning of justification, sanctification, and glorification and it is not fitting that God should make man a participant of His goods without faith (which the very nature of the matter demands), and since sinful

---

1. δικαίωμα τοῦ Χριστοῦ.
2. *sponsor.*
3. Cf. *Doctrina*, 15.1.
4. §405.
5. §404.

man is unable to believe by his own nature, it is evident that God must work faith in sinful man out of His own grace by the Holy Spirit through the power of the obedience of Christ.

715. By this *grace* we mean the most powerful working of God in us by the power of His eternal and gracious will toward us, through which we believe, repent, love Him, and are sanctified. Concerning this there has been a long dispute with the Pelagians and the semi-Pelagians,[6] and in our present age with the Papists and the Socinians[7] and Remonstrants.[8]

716. Now *economically*[9] this work ought to be attributed to the Holy Spirit. For the Father decreed this salvation for us, the Son procured it, and the Holy Spirit applies it to us through the means of faith.[10]

717. This work of faith in the sinner through the power of the Holy Spirit is described with various terms and is expressed to us with various *parts*[11] such as *calling, regeneration, sanctification, circumcision of the heart*, and *purification*.[12]

718. *Calling* is a most powerful act of God in which those who are elect of God and redeemed by Christ from the state of sin are invited and infallibly led to communion with God in Christ through the word of the gospel which has been disclosed and persuaded to their minds through the Holy Spirit.[13]

719. The transfer of the sinner from the state of misery and sin to communion with God through the power of God is called

---

6. The semi-Pelagians were a modified group of Pelagians who recognized the necessity of divine grace for salvation but yet rejected Augustine's doctrine of predestination.

7. For Socinian note, see §355.

8. Cf. *Doctrina*, 15.2. For Remonstrant note, see §687.

9. κατ᾽ οἰκονομία.

10. *Doctrina*, 15.3.

11. σχέσει.

12. *Doctrina*, 15.4.

13. *Doctrina*, 15.5.

calling in various places in Scripture, both since approaching God is effected by calling (for in Scripture the Holy Spirit usually gives a name to things because of their effects), and since it is through the mode of calling.[14]

720. For in the same way that the *terminus a quo*,[15] *terminus ad quem*,[16] and the voice are considered with respect to a calling (by which someone is led from one terminal place and state to another) so it is with respect to the divine calling.[17]

721. The *terminus a quo* in this place is the state of alienation from the life of God which is depicted as *darkness*, *kingdom*, or the *power of darkness*,[18] etc.[19]

722. The *terminus ad quem* is communion with God in Christ—that is, Christ with all the goods which have been acquired by Him. Indeed, the angels, blessed spirits, the faithful, and the rest of the called, are possessed in Christ, and even *all things*.[20] The Holy Spirit calls this state *the kingdom of the beloved Son of the Father*,[21] and the *marvelous light of God*.[22]

723. The voice by which the transition from one state into the other occurs is the word of the gospel (the fullest acceptance of the gospel according to every gracious word) received by the external senses.[23]

724. Indeed, since the human sinner is described in the Scriptures as *deaf, dead, a hater of God, incapable of any good, having a heart*

---

14. *Doctrina*, 15.6.
15. "the point from which" or the beginning point.
16. "the point to which" or the ending goal.
17. *Doctrina*, 15.7.
18. Cf. Ephesians 6:12.
19. *Doctrina*, 15.8.
20. τὰ πάντα.
21. βασιλείαν τοῦ υἱοῦ τῆς ἀγάπης τοῦ πατρός. Cf. Colossians 1:13.
22. τὸ θαυμαστὸν φῶς τοῦ θεοῦ. Cf. 1 Peter 2:9. *Doctrina*, 15.9.
23. Cf. *Doctrina*, 15.10.

of stone, it is plainly evident that the external sound of the gospel and the moral persuasion of the truth in the soul of man is not sufficient to fully lead sinful man to God and communion with Him.[24]

725. And besides this, it is most clearly evident from the course of the preaching of the gospel.[25]

726. On account of this, it is clear that the real and singular working of the Holy Spirit in the soul of the sinner is utterly necessary, by which He illumines the mind and persuades the will of the sinner to subjecting himself to the joining of the gospel of Christ, and to loving God in Christ, and to seeking Him gladly with every affection and inclination of the will.[26]

727. Since these are the *actus fidei*,[27] it is clear that the working of the Holy Spirit is the working of faith in the soul of the sinner.

728. This working of the Holy Spirit is of such power and efficacy in the soul of the sinner that it always has most certain efficacy. It is inconsistent to say that the creature cannot will when God wills. Likewise, it is inconsistent that the creature would be able to resist when God draws.[28]

729. This power of divine working in the mind is set forth to us in the Word of God by so many devices and phrases that all the Pelagianizers[29] ought to be pronounced as withdrawing from God His greatest glory because they deny it. The glory of

---

24. *Doctrina*, 15.11.
25. Cf. *Doctrina*, 15.12.
26. Cf. *Doctrina*, 15.13.
27. See note on §420.
28. *Doctrina*, 15.14.
29. For *Pelagians*, see §355.

Christ is that He has *subjected*[30] *all things*[31] *to Himself* by His Spirit.[32] Let us hold fast to this confession if we desire to be Christians.[33]

730. Now, the term *calling* is used for no other reason than that the Holy Spirit signifies this working of God in the sinner is analogous to that calling by which God *called those things which did not exist to exist*,[34] and so to rejoice in the same event. It is for this reason that *calling* is called *new creation*.[35]

731. Now in the same way that the will of God by which the world was created and all things which now exist were called is eternal, so also this calling, which is temporal, depends upon the eternal will of God concerning the determined heirs of this calling to communion of His goods. Therefore, the eternal decree of God concerning calling is often called in the Scriptures *calling*.[36]

732. For the word of the testament of grace by which the elect are called in time is nothing other than the declaration of God concerning the eternal purpose of giving certain goods to certain heirs.

733. Now this calling ought distinctly to be considered as being accomplished in various ways according to the particular *dispensation of the times*.[37] We have treated these before.[38]

---

30. ὑποτάσσειν.
31. τὰ πάντα.
32. Philippians 3:21.
33. Cf. *Doctrina*, 15.15.
34. ὡς ὄντα. Romans 4:17.
35. καινὴ κτίσις. 2 Corinthians 5:17. *Doctrina*, 15.17.
36. κλῆσις. Romans 8:28. *Doctrina*, 15.18.
37. οἰκονομίας καιρῶν.
38. §426. *Doctrina*, 15.19.

Regeneration

734. This calling is called *regeneration*,[39] *new birth*,[40] and *second birth*[41] since the Holy Spirit willed to teach us that those who are said to commune with God begin to live anew.[42]

735. That is, the sinner who is called *dead* and *fallen in sins* since he is not active for the glory of God receives a new faculty, a new principle (to which Scripture refers in various ways) from which the sinner produces living actions worthy to God.

736. For against the Pelagians and Socinians[43] we ought to firmly believe that the *new habits*[44] and new faculty are given to sinful man in regeneration, and so it does not simply consist in a change of actions.[45]

737. The origin of these habits is *faith*. Therefore, it is evident that regeneration is the giving of faith.

738. The seed of this regeneration is the word of grace joined with the highest power of the Holy Spirit. For the Spirit is the author and cause of this generation.[46]

739. In this first regeneration, which occurs in a moment, man is *passive*. For there are no preparations for it by man himself with his own strength. In a loose sense, they can be said to exist in him by God. But the transition from death to life is not able to happen except in a moment.[47]

740. The various degrees and states of regeneration which God ordains

---

39. παλιγγενεσία.
40. ἀναγένησις.
41. δεύτερα γένησις.
42. *Doctrina*, 15.20.
43. For notes on the Pelagians and Socinians §355.
44. ἕξεις.
45. *Doctrina*, 15.26.
46. *Doctrina*, 15.28.
47. Cf. *Doctrina*, 15.29.

to the praise of His glory ought to be understood by the minister of the gospel and explained for the confirmation and edification of those who have been made participants of this grace.[48]

741. However, the states of regeneration ought to be explained with utmost care, and none other than those which are certain and searched out.[49]

742. Regeneration, though common to all the faithful of all times, is to some extent given its special appearance in the New Testament, about which Christ discussed with Nicodemus.[50]

743. Since Christ reproached Nicodemus for ignorance of this as a vice, He was not thinking of those customary expressions concerning proselyte baptism,[51] but rather the various names for this regeneration which are expressed in Moses and the prophets.[52]

744. For this regeneration does not differ from circumcision of the heart, inscription of the law on the heart, giving of a heart of flesh, or being made holy.

745. Also, regeneration is the beginning of sanctification.

Repentance

746. Scripture expresses *repentance, to regret,*[53] and *to turn away*[54] as common terms for either true or false repentance, and of either its whole or its part.

747. Now the word *repentance* is peculiar, since it expresses the decision of the called and regenerated soul of man at which moment

---

48. *Doctrina*, 15.32.

49. *Doctrina*, 15.33.

50. John 3. *Doctrina*, 15.34.

51. Proselyte baptism was ritual washings practiced during the time of intertestamental Judaism.

52. *Doctrina*, 15.35.

53. נחם, μεταμέλεσθαι.

54. שוב, μετανοιεῖν, ἐπιστρέφειν.

God either first gives this grace to him or restores His grace in a fall after regeneration. For repentance has been joined with sorrow and detesting of the former vice and actions.

748. Now it consists in two parts: the *putting off*[55] of the old man and the *putting on*[56] of the new man, which we will explain.

749. The true signs of repentance which the Papists set forth are not satisfying according to their interpretation.

750. *Repentance from dead works,*[57] about which Paul speaks to some extent, is simply called *repentance.*[58]

---

55. ἐκδύσει.
56. ἐνδύσει.
57. Μετανοίας ἀπὸ νεκρῶν ἔργων. Hebrews 6:1.
58. *Doctrina,* 14.31–38

CHAPTER 21

Justification of Sinful Man by Faith, Peace, Adoption, Liberty, and the Effects

751. *Faith*, which is implanted in man in regeneration and calling by the powerful working of the Holy Spirit, is the means of justification, the foundation of sanctification, and the symbol and down payment of glorification. These goods of the testament of grace, which are described in §517–19, flow forth from the righteousness of Christ.[1]

752. There is a most certain foundational distinction concerning justification that we ought to hold, namely, that the word *to justify*[2] is forensic, and in Scripture it denotes the act of a judge in which he absolves someone from a crime or declares that someone be regarded as just with respect to one matter or another.[3]

753. This can even be thoroughly proved from Paul's Epistle to the Romans in which is the seat of this argument.[4]

754. Next, the force of the terms ought to be explained which the

---

1. *Doctrina*, 16.1.
2. הצדיק, δικαιοῦν.
3. *Doctrina*, 16.2.
4. *Doctrina*, 16.3. In *Doctrina*, Vitringa cites Romans 2:13; 5:16, 18; 8:33–34.

Holy Spirit used when He set forth the matter: *justification,*[5] *justice,*[6] *righteousness,*[7] *righteous.*[8]

755. With these words the apostles skillfully set forth that *God justifies the ungodly.*[9]

756. By *God*[10] we understand that this work belongs to the Father *according to the economy*[11] who is described as the Judge of all flesh, which is plainly evident from all places of Scripture and from the whole mystery of salvation.[12]

757. By *the ungodly*[13] we mean the sinner, not simply the one who has an impure heart, but who has merited condemnation and who has no right to approach eternal life. Such a person is called *wicked*[14] in Hebrew.[15]

758. But not every sinner [is condemned], (for no one asserts this), but only some sinners, as is clear from the following:[16]

759. By justification of this kind of sinner, we mean an act of God the Father as Judge by which the sinner, a son of wrath, who does not have any right of himself to approach the heavenly goods, is declared to be immune from all guilt and condemnation, and to have the right of claiming his own communion

---

5. Δικαίωσις.

6. δικαιωσύνη.

7. צדיק, צדיקה, δικαίωμα.

8. צדיק, δίκαιος. *Doctrina*, 16.3. For Vitringa's analysis of these terms, see *Doctrina*, 16.4–13.

9. Deus justificat impium, Θεός δικαιοῖ τὸν ἀσεβῆ. Romans 4:5. Vitringa's translation.

10. θεὸν.

11. κατ᾽ οἰκονομίαν.

12. *Doctrina*, 16.14.

13. τὸν ἀσεβῆ.

14. רשע.

15. *Doctrina*, 16.15.

16. *Doctrina*, 16.16.

with eternal salvation and with all the goods which pertain to it.[17]

760. In this way justification may be summed in two parts: a) the acquittal of guilt and *condemnation*.[18] By this term I mean all the effects of divine anger on account of sin; and b) judicial order of eternal life. By this term I mean all the goods of grace which flow from communion with God.[19]

761. In Holy Scripture, these two parts are expressed very frequently in one *expression*[20] as *remission of sins* because of the highest and inseparable connection which they have in grace.[21]

762. Likewise, this remission of sins is usually described with most significant terms.[22]

763. Since every judgment of God is according to truth and since it is our duty to justify the ways of God, here it must chiefly be sought by what pact God was able to absolve the sinner, a natural son of wrath, from guilt, and declare him to have the right of communion with Him.[23]

764. Now lest someone object, we carefully respond that this ground of justification cannot at all be located in man who is considered as *ungodly*,[24] having no right *from himself. By works of the law, no flesh is justified before God.*[25]

765. For even if the apostle Paul who was disputing against the Jews who sought to be justified from observation of the external law,

---

17. *Doctrina*, 16.17.
18. κατακρίματος.
19. *Doctrina*, 16.18.
20. φρασει.
21. *Doctrina*, 16.19.
22. *Doctrina*, 16.20. See also 16.43.
23. *Doctrina*, 16.24.
24. ἀσεβῆ.
25. Cf. Romans 3:20. *Doctrina*, 16.25.

it would seem very possible that he was speaking about the ceremonial law. However, it ought to be held firmly that he was powerfully refuting the Jews because this testimony was in the ceremonial law: *no flesh can be justified by itself.* It is evident that the proofs of wrath were in the ceremonial law and powerful demonstrations of the *infirmity of the flesh.*[26]

766. Therefore, let us hold that no flesh can discover *in* itself nor produce *from* itself the cause and foundation of justification. This is what Paul argues against the Jews.[27]

767. It is necessary for us to argue for this foundation since we defend the truth set forth there clearly and firmly by Paul against the Socinians, Papists, and Remonstrants[28] who seek the foundation of justification either wholly or partially in man.[29]

768. Therefore, *righteousness*[30] ought to be sought—namely, on what basis the sinner is justified. It is outside the sinner in the obedience of the Son of God which He demonstrated to the Father in His human nature *in death, even death on a cross.*[31]

769. This obedience of Christ is called *the cause of the righteousness of the sinner,*[32] or *emphatically*[33] *the righteousness of God,*[34] or *righteousness which is from God.*[35] For it is given to the sinner from God. There should be no hesitation to distinguish here between the active and passive.[36]

---

26. τῆς ἀσθένειας τῆς σαρκὸς. Romans 8:3. *Doctrina,* 16.26.
27. *Doctrina,* 16.27.
28. For notes on the Socinians and Remonstrants, see §355 and §687, respectively.
29. *Doctrina,* 16.28.
30. δικαίωμα.
31. Cf. Philippians 2:8. *Doctrina,* 16.29.
32. δικαίωμα, δικαιωσύνη.
33. κατ᾽ ἔμπηασιν.
34. δικαιοσύνη τοῦ Θεοῦ.
35. ἡ ἐκ Θεοῦ δικαιοσύνη.
36. *Doctrina,* 16.30–31.

770. These rights of which were spoken before are imputed to us by the surety. For in the law and prophets the future was foreshadowed and promised.[37]

771. Because the sinner must receive the gift of divine grace alone, so it is evident that to be justified is a *gift of grace*.[38] The sinner certainly does not have this from himself.

772. But this *imputation* of the obedience of Christ might not seem to be just enough for the just judgment of God unless the sinner approach it, seek it, thirst for it, and in a certain sense be able to be one with Christ. Thus, the righteousness of Christ can be understood as pertaining to him in this way.[39]

773. Now this comes to pass when the Holy Spirit excites faith in the soul of the sinner. We discussed this in the preceding chapter.[40] These acts are to hunger, to thirst, to seek, and to desire Christ as the cause of righteousness and life and to be united with Him in this pact.[41]

774. So we are said to be justified by faith (commonly said by *faith alone*), and that faith is said to be imputed to us unto righteousness.[42]

775. But this idea ought to be carefully held against the Papists and the Remonstrants. The former assert that man is appointed to justification by faith, that is, according to their opinion, to sanctification. The latter consider faith as an act of man, which they make the foundation of justification.[43]

776. For faith is purely regarded as an instrument and means by

---

37. *Doctrina*, 16.32.
38. δωρεάν.
39. Cf. *Doctrina*, 16.34, 40.
40. See esp. §734–45.
41. *Doctrina*, 16.35.
42. *Doctrina*, 16.36.
43. *Doctrina*, 16.37.

which we are *united* to Christ. But we do not for this reason separate the *actus fidei*[44] from all the acts of faith. For dead faith does not justify.[45]

777. So finally, we conclude that the ways of Jehovah are right and full of infinite wisdom.[46]

778. Justification of all the elect has certainly been accomplished on the basis of the special righteousness of Christ since He has acted as surety and satisfaction for the elect. But the justification of the elect sinner is said to come about chiefly when he believes, since the condition is finally present (it is valid to speak in this sense) which is required for the heirs of the goods of the testament.[47]

779. Now besides this justification of the sinner which has its place in the first conversion of the sinner to God and which is renewed so long as he repents (for the faithful life is the continual exercise of faith), he is also given a justification of the just which is by works, which James discusses.[48]

780. By this we understand the declaration of God with respect to the accusation of Satan, since in the regenerated sinner are true, colored, and indubitable signs and proofs of true faith which are pleasing to Him, and which are required among the heirs of the goods of grace.

781. This *second justification* is necessarily connected with the first (it is necessary to distinguish this from the variation of the Papists) so that it cannot be separated from it for any reason.[49]

---

44. For note on *actus fidei*, see §420.
45. *Doctrina*, 16.38.
46. *Doctrina*, 16.39.
47. Cf. *Doctrina*, 16.42.
48. Cf. *Doctrina*, 16.44.
49. Roman Catholics taught that one is justified by faith working through love, incorporating good works into the process. Vitringa is clarifying that his use of "second justification" no way undermines the Reformed principle of justification by faith alone. Instead, it refers to a second use of the term "to justify" in James 2:21, where good works

Reconciliation or Peace

782. The fruit of justification is *peace* which we described well enough when we treated the goods of the testament of grace. See §520.[50]

783. This is opposite in kind to accusations and hostilities which have their origin in sin.[51]

784. The relational act by which God transfers us from the state of hostility, accusation, and fear into a state of friendship, peace, and abundance of all goods is called *reconciliation*.[52]

Adoption and Liberty

785. Now since the Holy Spirit wishes distinctly to teach us that the justified have the full and certain right of approaching and possessing all goods which belong to God, so He says that those who believe are *adopted*. John calls this *the right to become children of God*.[53]

786. Additionally, they are represented as the *riches*[54] of adoption, since when the elect were born as *sons of wrath*[55] by nature they belonged to another family which is of the devil.[56]

787. And from this family they are transferred by pure grace into the family of God, which is communion with God and Christ and with the angels and all the saints, both in heaven and on earth.[57]

---

vindicate genuine faith against charges of hypocrisy and unbelief. In *Doctrina* 16.45, Vitringa abandons the term "second justification" and says that a believer's justification is "ratified" (*ratihabebitur*) in this way.

50. Cf. *Doctrina*, 16.46.

51. *Doctrina*, 16.47.

52. *Doctrina*, 16.48.

53. ἐξουσίαν τέκνα θεοῦ γενέσθαι. John 1:12. *Doctrina*, 16.49.

54. χρῆμα.

55. υἱοι ὀργῆς. Ephesians 2:3.

56. Cf. *Doctrina*, 16.50, 52.

57. Cf. *Doctrina*, 16.53.

788. The transition from one family to the other is the exciting of faith in them by the Holy Spirit, and the rousing of them in continual power toward such acts which are fitting for sons of God and heirs of His goods.[58]

789. The Spirit who does this is therefore called the *Spirit of adoption*[59] or the *noble Spirit.*[60]

790. The special working of this Spirit is liberty. *Where the Spirit of the Lord is, there is liberty.*[61]

791. By this whole kind of liberty we mean what is described and explained as the *goods of the New Testament*. See §518–19.[62]

792. Now since the kinds of liberty are more notable in the state of the church after the death of Christ, so adoption, the Spirit of adoption, and liberty are attributed *emphatically*[63] in the Scriptures to the faithful in the time of the New Testament.[64]

793. To this liberty also pertains the kind which concerns indifferent things. Nevertheless, this liberty ought to be exercised in such a way that, insofar as it is within our own power, we do not give any occasion for scandal to a brother.[65]

794. The rule according to which our actions ought to be founded is charity.[66]

---

58. *Doctrina*, 16.54.

59. τὸ Πνεῦμα τῆς υἱοθεσίας. Romans 8:15.

60. רוח נדבה. Psalm 51:12. *Doctrina*, 16.55.

61. οὗ τὸ πνεῦμά τοῦ Κυριοῦ, ἐκεῖ ἐλευθερία. Cf. 2 Corinthians 3:17. *Doctrina*, 16.56.

62. Cf. *Doctrina*, 16.57. See also §399–401, §512–17.

63. κατ̓ ἔμπηασιν.

64. *Doctrina*, 16.58.

65. Cf. Romans 14. *Doctrina*, 16.59.

66. *Doctrina*, 16.60.

795. But chiefly to this liberty pertains that *confidence*[67] and *full certitude of faith*[68] through which we are permitted to draw near to the throne of the grace of God, and to address God as our Father in the manner of a full family member and with full right.[69]

796. For as many as are sons of God have the right of attaining the inheritance with highest confidence without fear.[70]

797. Now the Spirit will testify whether the faithful are in such a state (that is, their conscience) by most certain proofs in which, if applied, cannot be deceived or deceive itself.[71]

798. And they certainly know this by that same Spirit of God who not only is the author (by which the soul of man attends to *things known*,[72] compares his state with them, and then forms a conclusion) but who also is so able to and often does affect the mind with an immediate sense of His grace such that he does not have need of extended argumentation. This we chiefly comprehend under the term *testimony of the Spirit with our spirit*.[73]

---

67. πεποίθησις.
68. πληροφορία τῆς πίστεως. Hebrews 10:22.
69. *Doctrina*, 16.61.
70. *Doctrina*, 16.62.
71. *Doctrina*, 16.63.
72. γνωρίσματα.
73. Romans 8:16. *Doctrina*, 16.64.

CHAPTER 22

Sanctification, Good Works, and Perseverance of the Saints

Sanctification and Good Works

799. Faith, which we have said is communicated to us in regeneration is not only the means by which we are justified, but also the foundation of our sanctification, since all true faith *works through love*,[1] that is, it has most certain fruits of good works.[2]

800. The word *sanctification* is often used loosely in Scripture for all the benefits presented to us by Christ, and it not only includes justification, but even glorification. This ought to be carefully observed.[3]

801. But when it is distinguished from justification, it denotes that most powerful act of the Holy Spirit by which the regenerate and the justified are purged from the stain of sin (or *guilt* with respect to justification) and all ugliness more and more each day such that they are conformed to the image of God more and more and are excited toward producing good works from the principle of faith which has been poured into them.[4]

802. From this it is also evident how sanctification can be considered distinct from calling, regeneration, and repentance, though it is

---

1. ἐνεργουμένη δἰ ἀγαπης.
2. *Doctrina*, 17.1.
3. *Doctrina*, 17.3.
4. *Doctrina*, 17.4.

hardly distinguished from these in the *expressions*[5] in Scripture. For the term *regeneration* describes the infusion of a *new life principle*, which is faith. But by the term *sanctification* the continual *producing of acts* from those habits is described, which is by the power of God in us.[6]

803. Now, that sanctification is commonly used in this sense is sufficiently evident from the description of *holiness*[7] which was given in §88. The word *chesed*[8] denotes a zeal for seeking, loving, and glorifying God. The word *holiness*[9] means the constitution of the soul and body of man, that they might be consecrated to God and His glory. The meaning can be deduced from the likeness of corporeal things which are improperly called *holy*. The Greeks use the words *sacred*,[10] *holiness*,[11] *holy*.[12]

804. Now this sanctification of man pertains to the *whole*[13] man, mind, soul, and body. But the seat of the working of the Holy Spirit is in the mind, which is considered as the light which illumines the whole man.[14]

805. So sanctification is described by the *putting off of the old* and the *putting on of the new man*, which has been noted before.[15]

806. In other places, Scripture usually describes it as *renewal*, or *transformation which is by the renewal of the mind*,[16] *washing of the body of sin, transformation into the image of the glory of God in*

---

5. φράσιν.
6. *Doctrina*, 17.5.
7. קדושה, חסד.
8. חסד.
9. קדושה.
10. ὁσιότης.
11. ἁγιότης, ἁγιότητος.
12. ἁγιασμοῦ. Cf. *Doctrina*, 17.7.
13. ὁλοτελῆ.
14. *Doctrina*, 17.9.
15. See §748. *Doctrina*, 17.10.
16. μεταμόρφοσιν τῇ ανακαινώσι τοῦ νοὸς. Romans 12:2.

Christ, crucifying and dying to the body of sin. All these particular phrases are worthy of attention.[17]

807. The author of the sanctification of the faithful *economically*[18] is the Holy Spirit. The meritorious cause is the obedience of Christ, from which flows every power and efficacy of the sanctifying of the sinner. For this reason, it is compared with *pure water.*[19]

808. This sanctification is therefore necessary in those who have been justified, so that we are not able to think that God would justify someone whom He does not will to *sanctify.*[20]

809. This sanctification manifests itself in good works, which are its fruit.[21]

810. By these [good works] we understand all the acts of the regenerate which are done in faith and love in accordance with the precept of the divine law for the glory of God in Christ.[22]

811. Therefore, it is evident that the works of the gentiles, of whatever kind they are, are not good, but rather are done from the concupiscence of the flesh which is the fount of all works of the unregenerate. A good work must be done by the Spirit inhabiting us with the power of the obedience of Christ. The sinner is not able to seek the glory of God.[23]

812. The apostle explains what it means to do good deeds by *temperately* (that is, *prudently*),[24] *justly*,[25] *living piously, seeking God*,[26]

---

17. *Doctrina*, 17.12.
18. κατ᾽ οἰκονομίαν.
19. Ezekiel 36:25–26. *Doctrina*, 17.13.
20. Cf. *Doctrina*, 17.15.
21. *Doctrina*, 17.16.
22. *Doctrina*, 17.17.
23. *Doctrina*, 17.18.
24. τὸ σωφρόνως.
25. καί δικαίως.
26. *Deum quaerere*, καί εὐσεβῶς ζῆν.

walking with Him, etc. Elsewhere it is called *glorifying the Father in heaven, loving one's brothers, keeping a good conscience.*[27]

813. These are utterly necessary for sanctification. For they are the sure signs and proofs of the grace of God in us on the part of God. And they are most clear testimonies by us of our grateful soul toward God. Additionally, they are symbols of our glorification. They are the beginning of glorification. They are the way through which communion with God ought to be sought in this life, the highest grade of this communion in the future.[28]

814. Thus, there is no greater difficulty in responding to the question, *Why must the regenerate perform good works*, than the question, *Why must the angels and the blessed ones of the Spirit glorify God?* For God cannot be sought or glorified except by the one who is like Him. But no one can be like God except the one who is holy. No one is holy, except he who presents himself as such by his works.[29]

815. Therefore, it stands that good works can be of highest necessity, although they are not considered as the *meritorious cause* of salvation, as the Papists and all the Pelagians[30] claim.[31]

816. Their opinions ought to be diligently judged and refuted as suppressing the arrogance of the flesh.[32]

817. It does not help them that the Holy Spirit calls the eternal way a *payment* because this obviously refers to the gracious dispensation of God, by which His goods, which are the goods of the Testament, have been offered to us by the pact under a condition.[33]

---

27. *Doctrina*, 17.19.
28. *Doctrina*, 17.20–21.
29. *Doctrina*, 17.22.
30. For note on the Pelagians, see §355.
31. *Doctrina*, 17.23.
32. *Doctrina*, 17.24.
33. *Doctrina*, 17.25.

818. This sanctification is not yet completed by the Holy Spirit but consists in various parts on account of most firm reasons which are everywhere found in the Scriptures. Likewise, it ought to be observed that this is against the Pelagianizers.[34]

819. For even if the sincere regeneration of the mind belongs to a zeal for glorifying God (which is why the faithful are called *perfect*,[35] and even if that zeal is continuously excited by the Holy Spirit (sometimes more and sometimes less), yet it is incomplete for those of the flesh and concupiscence by which they are attacked, provoked, and often completely seduced. *Whoever says that he has no sin, deceives himself.*[36]

820. Because of this concupiscence, which is born in the mind from the flesh, it is necessary that from the principle of life implanted in them they are illuminated, and they fight as long as they live to expel and debilitate it through the grace of the Holy Spirit.[37]

821. It is usually understood that the lament of the flesh and spirit which is mentioned in Scripture ought to be distinguished from the laments of the flesh and of the conscience of the unregenerate man. By the term *flesh*, we mean our mind as it subsists in the flesh and as it wills to serve its concupiscence. But by the term *spirit*, we understand our mind insofar as our thoughts are excited in it by the Holy Spirit, by which thoughts it resists the concupiscence of the flesh.[38]

822. The armor by which the faithful must be instructed against the flesh and against the devil who provokes us by it are rightly described somewhere by the apostle, and ought never to be neglected, lest we fall into paralysis and carnal security.[39]

---

34. *Doctrina*, 17.26.
35. תמימים, τέλειοι.
36. 1 John 1:8. *Doctrina*, 17.27.
37. *Doctrina*, 17.28.
38. *Doctrina*, 17.29.
39. Ephesians 6:14–16. *Doctrina*, 17.30.

823. Now we ought very much to pay attention to this, lest we satisfy our flesh too much with food and drink toward concupiscence which Paul calls *making provision for the flesh to gratify its desires*.[40]

824. Likewise, if we slip into a most serious fall, we might continually repent and humbly flee to the grace of God in Christ. We reject the indulgences, satisfactions, penitence, and confessions of the Papists.[41]

825. They accept fasting and prayers done in faith by which one resists *the evil one*.[42] The more man is corrupted *on the outside*[43] the more the *man on the inside*[44] comes forth.[45]

826. Now this ought chiefly to be done so that, by depending on the judgment of our mind for glorying God and constant zeal, we may conquer the affections of our flesh.[46]

827. But because the regenerate neglect this, God often sends upon them afflictions which He uses for their benefit to extinguish those affections, to summon charity, to excite faith and hope, etc.[47]

Perseverance of the Saints

828. Now, even if it often happens that God sends temptations upon the faithful, and even if the Holy Spirit sometimes works less in them during such a sad time (for most righteous reasons) in which they were overcome by the flesh and its concupiscence, nevertheless it is never the case that those who have been chosen and who had been regenerated to glory and to the hope of eternal life would simply be deserted by God, handed over to

---

40. σαρκὸς πρόνοιαν ποιεῖν εἰς ἐπιθυμία. Romans 13:14. *Doctrina*, 17.31.
41. Cf. *Doctrina*, 17.32.
42. τῷ πονηρῷ.
43. ὁ ἔξω ἄνθρωπος.
44. ὁ ἔσω ἄνθρωπος.
45. *Doctrina*, 17.33.
46. *Doctrina*, 17.34.
47. *Doctrina*, 17.35.

the devil, and become His new possession afresh, as if the habits communicated to them in regeneration were destroyed. This ought to be observed against the Remonstrants.[48]

829. The power of this perseverance ought not to be sought in the faithful themselves, who are extremely prone to fall and are surrounded by worldly allurements, sinners, and the devil, but it ought only to be ascribed to divine power and grace.[49]

830. Indeed, that the regenerate faithful so surely persevere by divine grace in that state in which they are should be proved from most certain testimonies of Scripture in which faith, which is the principle of the new life, is clearly and plainly said to have the necessary fruit of eternal life. *The water, which I will give to him, will become in him a spring of water flowing into eternal life.*[50]

831. Next, this truth ought to be demonstrated from the nature of the eternal testament which was explained before[51] and also set up as a covenant, the good of which is undoubtedly perseverance.[52]

832. Further, it ought to be explained that the whole *dispensation*[53] of the Father, Son, and Holy Spirit, insofar as it is manifested in the work of grace, also necessarily demands it.[54]

833. To the dispensation of the Father is certainly ascribed election and the giving of an inheritance to the Son. So justification and adoption have a necessary connection with salvation.[55]

---

48. *Doctrina*, 17.36.
49. *Doctrina*, 17.37.
50. John 4:14.
51. §426.
52. *Doctrina*, 17.38.
53. οἰκονομίαν.
54. Cf. *Doctrina*, 17.39.
55. *Doctrina*, 17.40.

834. Now to the Son is ascribed redemption, preservation of a redemptive seed, and intercession, which in turn accomplish most certain salvation for the faithful.[56]

835. And to the Holy Spirit is ascribed sealing and confirming of the faithful. From these arguments we rightly conclude the certitude of the salvation of the faithful without a doubt. Here we must also explain what the terms *anointing*, *down payment*, *seal*, *stamp*, *testimony*, and *firstfruits* mean in Scripture, all of which are foretold by the Holy Spirit.[57]

836. Objections which have been made against this most clear and everywhere-confirmed truth are not of very great weight.[58]

837. But this certain salvation of the regenerate is not only of God, but the faithful are able to be partakers of this certitude because the singular proof among them is of *hope, which does not put to shame*.[59]

838. This doctrine ought never to become the mother of [carnal] security among the faithful, since the Holy Spirit who confirms them is the perpetual author among them of humility and of holy solicitude and of good works.[60]

839. There is no greater doctrine than this which can supply proofs of the glorifying of God and of denying oneself (which is true piety).[61]

840. But if there is someone who persuades himself that he has become a partaker of divine grace and is also disgracefully

---

56. *Doctrina*, 17.41.
57. *Doctrina*, 17.42
58. Cf. *Doctrina*, 17.44.
59. Romans 5:5. *Doctrina*, 17.45.
60. *Doctrina*, 17.46.
61. *Doctrina*, 17.47.

squandering it, he has a reason for most legitimate doubting of whether he was ever a recipient of true grace, and whether or not he has thus most wickedly fooled himself. *Whoever has this hope laid up for himself, he keeps himself pure as he is pure.*[62]

---

62. 1 John 3:3. *Doctrina*, 17.48.

CHAPTER 23

Glorification

841. The sanctification of the sinner is so connected with his glorification that it is the very beginning of glorification.

842. The glory of the rational creature consists in this, that he possesses those virtues on account of which he ought to be judged from a whole conscience, and in which it is able to submit and rejoice.[1]

843. These virtues are knowledge and holiness, or rather uprightness of man, which is called the *image of God* in the Scriptures. For the image of God in man is that which made man more excellent than the beasts and sinners, and what makes him so that he can be valued by others and to delight in it.[2]

844. This glory of the rational creature is opposite to the ugliness and worthlessness of the sinner, which makes it so that the sinner is condemned by others, and that he is agitated by his own self.

845. But these virtues (as we call them) are considered as the foundation of peace and happiness in the rational creature. This state of the creature is specifically called *blessedness*.[3]

---

1. Cf. *Doctrina*, 18.2.
2. Cf. *Doctrina*, 18.4.
3. Cf. *Doctrina*, 18.4.

846. For to be called *blessed* is not only to be upright and holy, but to believe, to be happy, and to submit with the highest pleasure of the conscience in that state in which he is.[4]

847. Now two things pertain to glorification: first, that God adorns the creature with such virtues which are fitting for him so that he may be most free from shame and contempt of conscience and worthy of communion with God and with the saints; second, that God excites the pleasure of the conscience and indescribable happiness in the minds of the creatures.[5]

848. This state of the rational creature is usually called *glorified* and *blessed* and, *even more emphatically*,[6] *eternal life*.[7] Elsewhere it is described as *to be satisfied with the face of God, to see Him as He is, to know the Father and Christ, to know God, insofar as we are known*, etc.[8]

849. Now since the regenerate in this life *know* God, and *love* Him, they are participants of His holy and divine image; they are admitted to familial relation with God; and God excites in their minds indescribable happiness from the possession of rewards and the certain hope of future goods. So it follows that they have now *in this life* been made participants of divine glory and the heavenly life.[9]

850. But since laments of the flesh, afflictions, shame, ignorance, sin, sadness, and misery remain in this life, it is abundantly clear that their life, glory, and happiness have not been consummated in this world, but will be further consummated *after this life*, since they will be admitted to the most intimate familial relation

---

4. *Doctrina*, 18.5.

5. Cf. *Doctrina*, 18.6.

6. μάλα ἐμφατικῶς.

7. ζωή αἰώνιος.

8. Cf. *Doctrina*, 18.10.

9. *Doctrina*, 18.11.

with God; since knowledge and holiness will be made perfect in them; since they will enjoy highest and perpetual happiness of the conscience; since every shame, sadness, trouble, affliction, and the cause of all these sins will be removed; since God will be glorified in His saints and will reveal such things as will be sufficient for the blessedness of the creature. No language can express it. *We will be what has not yet appeared.*[10]

851. The consummation of the glory of the faithful will be first in the soul when it is separated from the body. For the death of the body is the effect of the death of Christ, or the benefit, which is applied to us by the power of the death of Christ, and the means by which we attain the consummation of our life and glory.[11]

852. Now that souls after the death of the body do not cease to exist and to operate (which was denied long ago by the Sadducees and today by the Socinians) is not only clearly proved from the nature of the soul, but it is also plainly demonstrated from the Scriptures.[12]

853. This applies not only to the souls of the faithful, but even to those of the unfaithful, even though the state after death may be entirely different. For heaven is attributed to the former, but hell to the later. For just as there are two different ways, so there are two most different ends for them. Besides heaven, there is no mention in Scripture of another place or state with respect to the faithful who have died. The limbo of the Fathers, limbo of infants, and purgatory have been invented by the Papists.[13]

854. Against the invention of purgatory, even if formerly among the heathen and the church there were various foundations for this

---

10. οὔπω ἐφανερώθη τί ἐσόμεθα. 1 John 3:2. *Doctrina,* 18.12.
11. *Doctrina,* 18.13.
12. *Doctrina,* 18.14.
13. *Doctrina,* 18.15–16.

opinion, it has been constructed on terrible errors which were *discovered*[14] by carnal wisdom, and it is directly contrary to the hope which is for the faithful.[15]

855. But since God is not only God of the soul but of the whole man, it is fitting that the body of the faithful would at some point arise from the dust, and that His grace would also furnish the body in a most glorious way.[16]

856. Likewise, since God is the just Judge, it is fitting that sin, which has been committed in the whole man, would be punished not only in the soul but also in the body. It follows that it is fitting that even the bodies of the impious would be joined with their souls anew.

857. The truth, goodness, and righteousness of God demand a future resurrection of this kind, of both the *just and the unjust*[17] even if there are those among the Jews who deny any resurrection, and others who deny only the latter part of this (namely, the resurrection of the impious) as the Socinians insist today.[18]

858. This opinion, which is contrary to both Scripture and reason, can only be devised of the devil and the flesh for the flattering of the flesh and the fashioning of a scam and horror which even muffles what the knowledge of the severity of God does to men.[19]

859. The bodies of all who have died will be raised by the highest power of Christ who shall come as Judge on the clouds of

---

14. ἔυρημα.
15. *Doctrina*, 18.17.
16. *Doctrina*, 18.20.
17. δικαίων τέ καί ἀδίκων.
18. *Doctrina*, 18.22.
19. *Doctrina*, 18.23.

heaven. This name of Christ is described by *command*,[20] *voice of an Archangel*,[21] *trumpet of God*,[22] etc.[23]

860. The same bodies which have fallen will be raised but transformed into such a condition which will be appropriate either for glory or for eternal punishment, but not purely *animal*[24] which are sustained by food and drink.[25]

861. Those men who have not yet died *will suddenly be changed*.[26]

862. With regard to being raised and changed, all shall at once be raptured to Christ, the Judge of the living and the dead on the clouds of heaven, with indubitable and evident signs of His Majesty which are raised by the angels who accompany Christ. Then, after their deeds have been revealed to the conscience of their own soul, they receive a sentence from the Judge which is most worthy of their deeds.[27]

863. Now since the time of Christ and the apostles, even if they usually express these acts of judgment quite ornately with sufficient clarity and simplicity, we ought to do some work so that we may prudently ponder the limits of this judgment.[28]

864. This judgment follows a twofold state of *eternal life* and of *death* in its whole degree. It is certainly glorious for the pious, and horrendous for the impious. We treated the former at the beginning of this chapter, and the latter at §288 and §348.[29]

---

20. κέλευσμα.
21. φωνὴν ἀρχαγγέλου.
22. σάλπιγξ τοῦ Θεοῦ.
23. 1 Thessalonians 4:16. *Doctrina*, 18.26.
24. *animalia.*
25. *Doctrina*, 18.27.
26. Cf. 1 Corinthians 15:52. Cf. *Doctrina*, 18.28.
27. *Doctrina*, 18.29.
28. *Doctrina*, 18.31.
29. *Doctrina*, 18.32.

865. Now just as the penalties will be of various degrees, so even the glories.[30]

866. The place in which the blessed will rejoice in their felicity is heaven. The place in which the impious will wail and dread is usually called *hell*, which is certainly distinct from the idea of the Socinians.[31]

867. It will be pleasing to God at this final time to introduce into the whole world a new phase by fire. This appearance on the earth, a decree for the good of the creatures and of everything else, is unknown to us. Scripture calls it the *consummation of the ages* even though this *expression*[32] also has a wide meaning. We know this, that every creature will be freed from the vanity to which he is now a slave.[33]

---

30. *Doctrina*, 18.33.
31. Cf. *Doctrina*, 18.34. The Socinians believed in the annihilation of the wicked.
32. φρὰσις.
33. *Doctrina*, 18.35.

CHAPTER 24

Sacraments of the New Covenant

868. The completion of these very great and illustrious benefits which the faithful eagerly await is by the one author and cause of these benefits not only exhibited to the faithful in the word of the gospel, which is perpetually enjoyed in the church, but they are even represented and sealed to believers through certain external symbols annexed to the new covenant by God. These are called *sacraments*.[1]

869. Indeed, the word *sacrament* has been ascribed to these symbols by the Latin church to translate the Greek word *mystery*[2] which the Eastern churches usually use. But we should hardly believe that the Latins considered it as the genuine meaning of this word in their own language when they named the sacred symbols in this way.[3]

870. Now the word *mystery*[4] hardly seems to be used in this sense in the Scriptures, and for this reason it should be wholly withheld from this, since we have learned in subsequent ages that both the former and the latter words for *sacrament* have given occasion for most serious errors.[5]

---

1. *Doctrina*, 24.1.
2. μυστήριον.
3. *Doctrina*, 24.2.
4. μυστηριοῦ.
5. *Doctrina*, 24.3.

871. The terms that Scripture uses are these: *sign,*[6] *seal,*[7] *pattern,*[8] *antitype,*[9] etc.[10]

872. Now the requirements for this kind of sacred symbol are these: first, they are visible things; second, they are instituted by God; third, grace is signified, which is offered to us by Christ in the word of the gospel and conferred through the Spirit, and which ought ever to be conferred in the highest grade, and finally, grace is sealed.[11]

873. Because it is most fitting, it pleased God according to His wisdom, to thus ordain that there would be a correspondence[12] between the things which signify and the thing signified. This is the reason why they are called *sacraments*, as they say.[13]

874. It ought to be held against the Socinians[14] that the power of sealing and signifying belongs equally to the sacraments. But it ought to be denied against the Papists that in them divine grace is conferred *by the working of the work*[15] and whatever else they understand. This is an invention of the flesh from which carelessness and idleness is born. Indeed, it perverts the character of the new covenant.[16]

875. Under the covenant of grace in every age of the church, the *thing signified* in all the signs is *Christ*, the author of the goods of grace which are given to the faithful by Him. But of the signs of the new covenant, Christ is now consummated by His sufferings in

---

6. אות, σημεῖον.
7. σφραγίς.
8. ὑπόδειγμα.
9. ἀντίτυπος.
10. *Doctrina*, 24.4.
11. *Doctrina*, 24.5.
12. *insignis*, ἀναλογία.
13. *Doctrina*, 24.6.
14. For note on the Socinians, see §355.
15. *ad opus operatum.*
16. *Doctrina*, 24.7.

accordance with the promises made to the Fathers, and by Him eternal righteousness has been acquired with all its goods which flow forth.[17]

876. Therefore, it is clear that the sacraments of the new covenant are more excellent than those which were instituted long ago by reason of their meaning. Likewise, they differ from the old signs of grace by clarity and levity. No sacrament is now able to be part of a yoke, as long ago.[18]

877. For this reason, it is evident to us why Christ instituted new symbols and abrogated the old ones.[19]

878. Now He has instituted only two: *baptism* and the *Holy Supper*. For there are five others which the Papists add—confirmation, penance, extreme unction, ordination, and marriage—from the rites of the ancient church which afterward were changed and corrupted. But they ought not to be called sacraments, but rather this should be treated as a figment of the human skull.[20]

879. Everyone who has been appointed by the church is qualified to administer the sacraments. For grace does not depend on the minister, but on God.[21]

880. Their necessity is certainly not absolute, since the faithful may be deprived of the opportunity, although cases of this kind are rare. But they cannot be neglected without the neglect of grace since the occasion of using them is given.[22]

---

17. *Doctrina*, 24.8.
18. *Doctrina*, 24.9.
19. *Doctrina*, 24.10.
20. *Doctrina*, 24.11.
21. *Doctrina*, 24.12.
22. *Doctrina*, 24.13.

Baptism

881. The first sign of the new covenant is *baptism*[23] which means *immersion* or *sprinkling with water*, through which justification, sanctification, and resurrection to eternal life is signified and sealed to believers by the power of the righteousness of Christ.[24]

882. This word is used *metaphorically*[25] in Scripture for the pouring out of the Holy Spirit or for afflictions and death, but it is hardly ever used for the doctrine distinct from *immersion*.[26]

883. The element (the material of the sign) is in this place common and pure water. Christ and the apostles tell us so. In the early church, other *symbols*[27] were also joined to the water.[28]

884. The administration of the element, which is called the *ceremony*, is the immersion of the faithful into the water. This is observed by the force of the term. So it was done in this way by Christ and the apostles.[29]

885. Nevertheless, it has been changed for a most important reason to *sprinkling*[30] which Scripture calls to mind by the term *washing*. It is most certain in Scripture that the terms *immersion* and *washing* are of equal force in their meanings.[31]

886. As often as the faithful are sprinkled, they are initiated. Likewise, what formula of words ought precisely to be pronounced by the minister should be left to the determination of the church. But it is enough to adhere to the words of Christ, who

---

23. ἀπό τοῦ βαπτεῖν, βαπτίζειν.
24. *Doctrina*, 24.14.
25. μεταφορικῶς.
26. Cf. *Doctrina*, 24.15.
27. σύμβολα.
28. *Doctrina*, 24.16.
29. *Doctrina*, 24.17.
30. ῥαντισμός.
31. *Doctrina*, 24.18.

commanded that they *be baptized into the name of the Father, Son, and Holy Spirit.*[32]

887. This symbol of baptism instituted by Christ could not have been seen as strange by the Jews, and in addition they were subjected to legal purifications and baptisms of proselytes, and even the baptism of John. Though it ought especially to be noted that the baptism instituted by Christ was more excellent to them because of its meaning.[33]

888. But it ought not to be believed at all that the baptism of John was a different thing than that of Christ, as the Papists wish us to believe.[34]

889. The thing, which is signified in baptism, can best be known if we understand what water signifies in Scripture. For immersion or sprinkling is communion with water.[35]

890. Now it is a *symbol*[36] of obedience and of the Spirit of the sanctification of Christ, from which it follows that communion with water signifies participation in His death and obedience, and of the spirit of Christ, by the power of the sanctification of His obedience.[37]

891. Let us speak more clearly: to be immersed into water and to be under water denotes our old man dying and being buried by the power of the death of Christ. To be washed with water denotes being justified and sanctified. To again emerge from the water denotes to be saved from death by the power of the death of

---

32. Matthew 28:19. *Doctrina*, 24.19.
33. *Doctrina*, 24.20.
34. *Doctrina*, 24.21.
35. *Doctrina*, 24.22.
36. σύμβολον.
37. *Doctrina*, 24.23.

Christ, to be regenerated unto a living hope, and to be raised to new live which will never cease.[38]

892. Here it is evident what Peter says, that *baptism*[39] is a *request unto God for a good conscience through the resurrection of Christ*.[40]

893. Likewise, it is plain that what is taught in the word of the gospel is signified through baptism. Namely, that which was long ago prefigured through the flood and circumcision. But it ought not to be concluded from this that circumcision should remain under the New Testament.[41]

894. These benefits which have been signified are also sealed by baptism, which is plain from the force of the expressions of Holy Scripture.[42]

895. The use of baptism strongly obligates us to a sufficient and lofty duty which is to call upon the name of the Father, Son, and Holy Spirit.[43]

896. Now, not only ought adults who profess that they believe in Christ to be baptized, but even infants, concerning whom it is legitimate to hope that they have gained the inheritance of Christ by the Holy Spirit and in their own time will be raised to the glory of Christ. Firm arguments are not lacking from which this is demonstrated. It is ludicrous and Jewish to baptize *lifeless*[44] things.[45]

---

38. *Doctrina*, 24.24.

39. βάπτισμα.

40. συνειδήσεως ἀγαθῆς ἐπερώτημα εἰς θεόν δἰ ἀναστάσεως Ἰησοῦ Χριστου. 1 Peter 3:21. The translation of this verse comes from *Doctrina*, 24.25.

41. *Doctrina*, 24.26.

42. *Doctrina*, 24.27.

43. *Doctrina*, 24.28.

44. *inanimatas*.

45. Cf. *Doctrina*, 24.29–31.

897. But the necessity of baptism (which the Socinians completely subvert) is not as the Papists propose, as if divine grace were dependent on the water of baptism.[46]

898. Therefore, there is no need to permit the administration of baptism to any ministers besides those appointed and ordained.

899. Likewise, the one who has been baptized does not need to be rebaptized if he falls, since the seed of God remains in him.

Lord's Supper

900. The other sign of the new covenant is the *Lord's Supper*.[47] By using bread and wine in communing together, our union together with Christ and with the faithful is signified and sealed to us. Now it is called *the supper* because it was celebrated in the evening. It was called *the Lord's* because it was instituted by the Lord and celebrated in His presence and instituted in His memory. Many other names of this sacrament are found in Scripture and in the writings of the ancient church.[48]

901. This supper consists in the use of bread and wine in a most common way. These symbols were instituted by Christ during this meal by His own hands at the Passover Feast.[49]

902. Now a change in the form of the bread has been introduced here (unleavened and thus circular). These disagreements usually move on to the wine and ought to be regarded as vain superstitions of the human skull.[50]

903. It ought to be observed here that the most legitimate reason for this discussion of why Christ instituted this sign is by way of a most

---

46. Cf. *Doctrina*, 24.32.

47. Δεῖπνον κυριακὸν.

48. *Doctrina*, 24.35.

49. *Doctrina*, 24.36.

50. *Doctrina*, 24.37. Vitringa may here be referring to the ongoing debate in his day concerning whether or not the wine in the Lord's Supper should include water.

simple, necessary, and easy comparison, and a bloodless kind of food which is not from the bloody meat of animals.[51]

904. The actions concerning these elements of bread and wine are either of the Lord, whom ministers now imitate, or of the disciples, which the communicants imitate.[52]

905. Now the actions of the Lord are these: to receive, bless, break, and give them to the disciples. These ought to be explained chiefly from the rites of the Jews in the celebration of the Passover in the usual breaking of bread.[53]

906. But the Lord (who is now the minister) also *explained*[54] what lies hidden under the symbols.[55]

907. The actions of the communicants (which belonged to the disciples) are to receive, eat, and drink.[56]

908. Christ pronounced what is signified and what is sealed to the faithful by this kind of use of bread and wine when He spoke concerning the bread: *This is my body*. And concerning the wine: *This is the New Testament in my blood*, etc.[57]

909. For in the most corrupted ages when superstition and innovation dominated, these statements were taken as literal and not as sacramental. This ought to be credited to the ignorance and cunning of men. Indeed, this has not been done without the singular and just judgment of God on the church.[58]

---

51. *Doctrina*, 24.38.
52. *Doctrina*, 24.39.
53. *Doctrina*, 24.40.
54. ἐξηγήσατο.
55. *Doctrina*, 24.41.
56. *Doctrina*, 24.42.
57. Luke 22:19–20 *Doctrina*, 24.43.
58. *Doctrina*, 24.44.

910. Therefore, let us hold that the bread signifies the bloodless body of Christ and His death by hanging on a cross. And the wine poured into the cup signifies the blood of Christ poured out. The comparisons between these signs and the things signified are for this reason so easy and obvious that they can be discovered without much effort or trouble.[59]

911. Now the body and blood of Christ ought to be understood insofar as Christ satisfied divine justice in His death in pouring out of blood and presented His highest obedience and love for the church to the Father.[60]

912. Since this death of Christ is understood as satisfying the failure and requirement of the sinner and the troublesome accusations of the conscience, so the bread is said to nourish, and the wine to gladden.[61]

913. This symbol did not seem to be foreign to the disciples of Christ since this same grace of Christ was foreshadowed long before in the same way. But this picture speaks chiefly to the atoning sacrifices by which sin was proclaimed long ago.[62]

914. What the *taking, blessing, breaking,* and *distribution* of the bread and *pouring of the wine* signify is easily able to be deduced from the words.[63]

915. To receive, to eat the bread, and to drink the wine denotes the *actus fidei*[64] through which we have communion with the death and obedience of Christ. And likewise, we have communion with one another.[65]

---

59. *Doctrina,* 24.45.
60. *Doctrina,* 24.46.
61. *Doctrina,* 24.47.
62. Cf. *Doctrina,* 24.48.
63. Cf. *Doctrina,* 24.49.
64. See note on §420.
65. *Doctrina,* 24.50.

916. Now these holy symbols are not only signs, but also seals, and this is evident from the *emphatic*[66] ways of speaking by which Christ, our highest teacher, explains their mystery.[67]

917. For when He said, *This is my body* and *This is my blood*, what else did He mean than His own self at the time of His body (which the disciples certainly saw with their own eyes at His crucifixion, but the subsequent church does not see), and that in place of the blood poured out it would substitute, hand down, and remain as a pledge *and seal*,[68] and finally, that they would regard it as entirely certain that His body suffered and His blood was poured out. And, likewise, that they would be participants in the effects of His body through faith and His spirit, as if they could see His suffering with their own eyes, and as if they were able to see with their eyes that union of our body with His body. And we equally discern the union of our members with it, or those things which we eat and drink for the nourishment and happiness which we perceive to be mingled with our own flesh.[69]

918. Since we have rightly understood these things, it is not necessary to labor any more regarding where this figure of speech ought to be understood in the syntax, whether it is in the subject or in the predicate, or in both.[70]

919. All believing adults have the right of using these symbols after diligently examining themselves before God *without hypocrisy*,[71] which should never be neglected by the people. Infants cannot be given this right, as has been practiced of old.[72]

---

66. ἐμφατικοτάτοις.

67. Cf. *Doctrina*, 24.51.

68. ἐνέχυρον.

69. Cf. *Doctrina*, 24.52.

70. Cf. *Doctrina*, 24.53. In *Doctrina*, Vitringa says that the figure of speech ought to be sought in the predicate.

71. ἄνευ ὑποκρίσεως.

72. *Doctrina*, 24.54.

920. Now both the *symbols*[73] of wine and bread should be given to all the faithful. It is a most crafty error of the Papists when they claim that the blood of Christ is included under His body and under this pretext deny the cup to the people. Certainly, the body of Christ is represented as bloodless.[74]

921. It is much more suitable that this communion be administered more frequently than more rarely. Idleness and neglect of the duties of piety are the sole cause why the faithful do not desire to stir up their faith more frequently through these symbols.[75]

Transubstantiation and the Mass

922. Opposite to this holy and faithful use of the bread in the Lord's Supper is the plainly contrary idolatrous use of the bread among the Papists, which they call *transubstantiation*, into the whole Christ (only the accidents[76] of the bread and wine remain). For the pronunciation of these five words, *For this is my body*, having been announced by the priest, are for that intended end. This astounding and inhuman error has crept into the church, when men ceased *to love the truth*,[77] when God turned them over to the *power of error*,[78] *so that men believed a lie*.[79]

923. It is greatly beneficial that we lay out the origins of this error which has progressed in the history of the church (which ought to be sought in the eighth century in the famous debate

---

73. σύμβολα.

74. *Doctrina*, 24.55.

75. *Doctrina*, 24.56.

76. An *accident* (*accidens*) is a nonessential property of a *substance*, or something that can be removed from a substance without a genuine essential alteration. In the Roman Catholic doctrine of *transubstantiation*, the accidental properties of the bread and wine remain, but the substance is changed ("transubstantiated") into Christ. See Muller, *Dictionary*, s.vv. "accidens," "substantia."

77. ἀγαπᾶν τὴν ἀλήθειαν.

78. ἐνέργειαν πλάνης.

79. 2 Thessalonians 2:10–11. *Doctrina*, 24.57.

concerning *iconolatry*[80]) so that the mystery of this iniquity might be uncovered.[81]

924. The best way to shatter this view of transubstantiation is to begin with the deconstruction of the foundation of the error, which is the corrupt explanation of the words, *This is my body*.[82]

925. It is legitimate (besides the explanation of sacramental ways of speaking) if we compare with these words the words of Christ concerning the cup, or the blood—*This is the new covenant in my blood*[83]—and the words of Paul—*The cup of blessing is a communion with the blood of Christ; the bread, which we break, is a communion with the body of Christ*.[84] Like the preceding ones, these statements cannot be understood without *a way*[85] of understanding them.

926. Now it is evident that the Papists who interpret these words do not interpret them as they are. Additionally, many other reasons are collected which militate against that fictitious local presence of Christ in the supper which are collected from the first institution of the supper[86] and from the word of Christ with John,[87] and in the epistle to the Corinthians, in which the bread is called that which is eaten in the supper after the blessing,[88] and also from the most certain analogy of faith, from the ancient professions of the church, from the nature of the sacraments, from

---

80. *Iconolatry* is the worship of icons or images in religious worship. Vitringa here refers to the great controversy in the eighth century between the iconolaters and the iconoclasts, who were against the use of images. The debate reached its end in 787 AD when the Second Council of Nicaea declared that the use of icons was legitimate for moderate use (*iconodulia*) but that they should not be worshiped in a strict sense.

81. *Doctrina*, 24.58.

82. *Doctrina*, 24.59.

83. Luke 22:20.

84. 1 Corinthians 10:16.

85. τρόπῳ. Cf. *Doctrina*, 24.60.

86. Matthew 26:29.

87. John 6:54.

88. 1 Corinthians 10:16.

reason, from the senses, from most absurd hypotheses and contradictions without which this opinion cannot be defended.[89]

927. Many of these arguments also work against *consubstantiation* which the Lutherans defend. This was the first fruit of strife[90] among brothers. If only it had never been raised! But it ought to be well understood that this opinion should not be compared to that of the Papists, since the Lutherans reject that most absurd consequence which the Papists defend.[91]

928. Impious is the consequence of the offering of this bread for the living and the dead which is in the Mass, and its adoration and exhibition of adoring by certain priests who are appointed to do this. Anyone who does not believe this was proclaimed as anathema in the Council of Trent.[92]

929. Against this it ought to be demonstrated that at no time of the church did sacrifices, altars, or priests ever have power for the remission of sins, and these things pervert the once-for-all sacrifice of Christ which cannot be repeated.[93]

930. Now it ought to be advanced cautiously when we argue from the nature of the sacraments and from the nature of this sacrament, as is usually done. For it ought not to be denied that the bread represents the sacrifice of Christ, or that one and the same thing is able to be a sacrifice and a sacrament. For both of these are true. But this point ought to be refuted from the institution of the Holy Supper because the Lord Christ offered bread to His Father in the supper, etc.[94]

---

89. *Doctrina*, 24.61.
90. ἔριδος.
91. *Doctrina*, 24.62.
92. *Doctrina*, 24.63. See also Session 22 of the Council of Trent.
93. Cf. Hebrews 9:26; 10:1–18. *Doctrina*, 24.64.
94. *Doctrina*, 24.65.

931. It ought also to be demonstrated from antiquity that the Roman Catholic Church, with innocent notions, disgracefully abused the useful instruments of the Holy Supper (which were made for it) in the ancient church, and built over them this horrendous error with skill and deceit.[95]

932. Therefore, we acknowledge the only presence of Christ in the supper to be that which the Lord Christ was accustomed to manifest by His singular grace to those who rightly and duly use these symbols. From this sense of divine grace, the most efficacious teachings are learned among both ancient and more recent theologians.[96]

---

95. *Doctrina,* 24.66.
96. *Doctrina,* 24.67.

CHAPTER 25

&

The Church[1]

933. The people in the world who have been made participants of the goods of the testament of grace and who have their faith and mutual communion with Christ and bear witness among themselves and before the world through the *ministry of the Word* and *partake of the sacraments* are called the *church,*[2] *the called assembly.*[3]

934. The reason for this term plainly refers to an effectually called gathering of the heirs of the goods of the testament of grace by the voice of Christ in the gospel, corresponding to the eternal purpose of grace which we have treated before.[4]

935. Now by the term *church* we understand all those who have been chosen and called, true believers, dispersed throughout the whole world, who profess with heart and mouth Christ and His grace without fundamental error, the various parts of which are called *particular churches.* The Hebrews use for the term *church*[5] the

---

1. References to *Doctrina* in this chapter are to the fourth edition of 1702.
2. ἐκκλησία.
3. ἀπό τοῦ εκκαλεῖν. *Doctrina,* 25.1.
4. See §711–33. *Doctrina,* 25.2.
5. ἐκκλησία.

words *assembly*[6] and *congregation*.[7] The Greeks used *synagogue*,[8] which was, however, rarely used by Christian assemblies.[9]

936. It is evident from this definition that all do not belong to the church who have been called externally and can be called *hypocrites*. The church does not consist of any except the saints. Under the New Testament, there is no *external covenant* as there was of old. This ought to be well held if we understand the nature of the church under the New Testament. To this pertains the very best testimonies of Holy Scripture.[10]

Attributes of the Church

937. It is also evident from this definition that the church is *one* and *catholic*. Yet beware of attributing connections to any particular assembly.[11]

938. And also, that the church is *infallible*, which nevertheless ought not to be affirmed of any particular church nor of any particular person, but of the elect whom God preserves, lest they reject the foundation of truth.[12]

939. And also, that the church is *invisible*, since the principle of faith resides in the mind, and it is not able to be known by man except through profession of the mouth and a constant exercise of full piety.[13]

940. An assembly of this kind, or a multitude of the faithful, was always on the earth, and is now and *always will be*, even if it

---

6. קהל.

7. עדה.

8. συναγωγή.

9. *Doctrina*, 25.3. In his day, Vitringa was an expert on the synagogue. See his *De Synagoga Vetere Libri Tres*.

10. Cf. *Doctrina*, 25.5–8. In *Doctrina*, Vitringa distinguishes between the *external* and *internal* church, or what other theologians would call the *visible* and *invisible* churches.

11. Cf. *Doctrina*, 25.9.

12. *Doctrina*, 25.10.

13. *Doctrina*, 25.11.

is often varied and changed in appearance and is of greater or smaller number.[14]

941. If we examine the matter carefully, there was no time in the world in which it was not able to be discerned where those who professed God in truth and righteousness were, that is, where the true church was. Indeed, the church was always *visible* in this manner. But there were times, and there will be without a doubt most troublesome times later, when truth and piety were not very much suppressed and oppressed, at which times the church did not raise its head in the world. In this way, it can be said that the church ceased to be visible.[15]

Marks of the Church

942. Whether one assembly or another belongs to the *true church* ought to be discerned from the purity of the preaching of the Word and the administration of the sacraments and discipline in accordance with the institution of Christ. These are the marks of the true church.[16]

943. We also ought not to omit attending to the fruit of the preaching of the gospel, not only as to whether it is important or not (even if that also merits careful attention and can also vary according to divine dispensation), but also what is its fruit and what kind of fruit is there in all those who have been called. This is *charity*.

944. Yet the consideration of the doctrine ought to be treated, since an outward charity can often be born out of an impure heart.

945. Among the marks of the church which Bellarmine[17] proposes are certain goods and certain evils. But the goods are not able to be applied to the Roman Catholic Church.

---

14. *Doctrina*, 25.13.
15. *Doctrina*, 25.12.
16. *Doctrina*, 25.14.
17. Robert Bellarmine (1542–1621) was the premiere Roman Catholic theologian

946. The question, *Whether and at what time there was a church before the Lutherans and Calvinists* should be resolved in this: whether and at what time there were those who professed the same doctrine of truth and lived a life in accordance with the truth. For there is an easy response to this. For there were in that same multitude some who called themselves *of the Roman Catholic Church* who separated themselves afterward from that multitude.

947. Nevertheless, it cannot be concluded that the multitude of men which call themselves of the Roman Catholic Church are of the *true* church.

948. This question ought to be prudently considered, *How long ought we to tolerate the corruption which invades the church, whether in doctrine or in discipline and morals, before we separate ourselves from it?* Now we can confidently say that the corruption of the Roman Catholic Church was and is such that our Fathers left its communion with highest justice, and after the revealing of its idolatry no one without injury of the conscience and highest peril of his salvation would be able to persevere in the Roman Catholic Church.[18]

Head of the Church

949. The church is excellently compared to a *body* since it regards the supreme ruler to be the Lord on whom it depends and with whom it is united, and since it is evident from various members which attend to various functions for one another for the good of the whole communion.[19]

950. The Supreme Ruler and Lord of the church is the *Son of God,* the Lord Christ, who gathers it and defends it, from whom it receives the law, who alone builds it up, who alone gives to it His [Holy] Spirit. And for this reason, He is called *the*

---

during the latter part of the Reformation. The Reformed scholastics spilled much ink refuting Bellarmine's arguments which promoted Roman theology.

18. Cf. *Doctrina,* 25.22.

19. *Doctrina,* 25.23.

head of the body, and elsewhere the *surety* and *husband* of the church. Let the blasphemy that the Roman Pontiff can be the head of the church be done away with, in whatever way it is constructed.[20]

951. Therefore, no dogmatics or precepts can now be set forth to be believed or to be done by man which cannot be demonstrated to flow forth from those which Christ taught and commanded. Those which pertain necessarily to *good order*,[21] Christ Himself has decreed to order. The rest of those things which are ordered are not able to be without the consent of the whole communion.[22]

952. The members or the parts of the body are twofold. Some are *ministers*, which are compared with the hands and feet, etc., and, like Paul, administer the ministry to *others*. Now this is by divine wisdom, which shines forth exceedingly in the arrangement of the church.[23]

Divisions of the Ministers of the Church

953. Everyone regards the *divisions of the ministers*[24] which perform the work of ministry in the public assembly of the faithful as, first, extraordinary, such as the prophets, John the Baptist, and in the beginning of the instituted church of the New Testament, apostles, Evangelists, and prophets, etc.[25]

954. The *apostles* were twelve teachers specially chosen by Christ so that they would be witnesses of the things which He did, and they were immediately sent with authority and power to testify concerning Christ and His works among the Jews and gentiles, so that by them they would build a church for Christ. Their

---

20. *Doctrina*, 25.24.
21. ἐυταξίαν.
22. *Doctrina*, 25.25.
23. *Doctrina*, 25.26.
24. By "ministers" (*ministrantes*), Vitringa means *church officers*.
25. *Doctrina*, 25.27.

infallibility ought not to be denied, but prudently explained. The church had to be built on their doctrines.[26]

955. From these there were not more than seventy *evangelists*, except that they all were not always with Christ, and for this reason their ministry was not constant and perpetual.[27]

956. Also, the *prophets* ought not to be neglected, who were excited by the Spirit in the early church to explaining prophecy or foretelling future things.[28]

957. The rest of these gifts were the extraordinary knowledge of languages (among which Hebrew should not be ignored) and healings, etc., which Paul describes.[29]

958. In the founding of the church, the necessity of this extraordinary working of the Holy Spirit was highest among these men because of the general quietness which was commonly found among those who rejoiced at the ordinary gifts of the Spirit. But this necessity, after the foundation was laid, has now ceased. But observe that God never leads His church into the world to a more perfect state than through the extraordinary working of His Spirit in them.[30]

959. The *ordinary* ministers of the church under promise were the heads of the families, but under the law were the priests and Levites, and now the *elders*[31] and *deacons*.[32] Elders are also called *teachers*[33] and *pastors*.[34]

---

26. *Doctrina,* 25.28.
27. *Doctrina,* 25.29.
28. *Doctrina,* 25.30.
29. 1 Corinthians 12:28. Cf. *Doctrina,* 25.31.
30. *Doctrina,* 25.32.
31. πρεσβύτεροι.
32. διάκονοι.
33. ἐπίσκοποι, διδάσκαλοι.
34. ποιμένες. *Doctrina,* 25.33.

960. *Elders* have been appointed to the church (which are divided into many assemblies) for *teaching* and *ruling*. If they are less apt for teaching, they can receive a good man who is skilled in teaching and learning, or to choose such a one from their assembly. So it seems that this was conveniently done in the early church in the arrangements of the Hebrews in their synagogue.[35]

961. All these elders were part of the institution and office in this way. Nevertheless, it is doubtful that one of them should have elevated himself above the rest under the name *bishop*. But this happened shortly after the time of the apostles.[36]

962. All the elders, who ought to live with *serious morals*, *piety of life*, and *knowledge of divine things*, and *prudence for others* are by the church chosen, called, confirmed, and preserved. Today it ought chiefly to be observed with respect to the minister of the church that he is the first of the elders.[37]

963. This right belongs to the church. If, however, other customs have been introduced in some place by the magistrates, it is not necessary to resist these supreme powers too rashly.[38]

964. The *deacons* are ministers of the elders, and of the whole church for the carrying out of those duties which seem to be mixed with labor and work. Such things are understood now as the *collection of alms*. They can also be *readers*, *singers*, and *doorkeepers*.[39]

965. Whoever removes the necessity of these ministries, whoever desires to neglect a study of the literature on them, and whoever

---

35. *Doctrina*, 25.34. See Vitringa, *De Synagoga Vetere*, prolegomena, cap. 2.

36. Cf. *Doctrina*, 25.35. Vitringa argues, against the Roman Catholics and Anglicans of his day, that the office of "elder" and "bishop" are two names for the same office. See Vitringa, *Hypotyposis Historiae*, 266.

37. *Doctrina*, 25.36.

38. *Doctrina*, 25.37.

39. *Doctrina*, 25.38.

denies provision for ministers and teachers ought to be regarded as the authors of the worst confusion.[40]

Body of the Church, Which Is Its Ministry

966. The multitude of the faithful to which this ministry is administered, having been *equally*[41] made participants of dear and precious faith, ought neither to be denied nor oppressed nor governed with authority, since they are by this right dwelling in the house of God. This multitude He furnishes to be a distinct *portion*[42] and *people*.[43] Yet they are to respect their *superiors*.[44]

Functions of the Ministers of the Church

967. The functions which fall on the part of the ministers are provided in their descriptions. But let us repeat them distinctly. They are those things which pertain to the *public assembly*, and they are those things which pertain to other *ecclesiastical gatherings*.[45]

968. To the public assembly pertains the *reading of the Word of God, singing of Psalms, sermons, catechization*, and *administration of the sacraments*, all of which can be ordered variously according to the habits and character of the people, etc.[46]

969. But great care ought to be employed, lest these appointed functions are altered into *ceremonies* and tied up too much with certain procedures. This is most opposite to the most free operations of the Holy Spirit under the New Testament.[47]

970. Also, to the public assembly pertains the *excommunication* of those who withdraw from the truth and simplicity of the gospel

---

40. *Doctrina*, 25.39.
41. ἰσοτίμου.
42. κλήρου.
43. λαοῦ.
44. τοὺς προεστῶτας. *Doctrina*, 25.40.
45. *Doctrina*, 25.41.
46. *Doctrina*, 25.42.
47. *Doctrina*, 25.43.

in doctrine or morals. Now since this cannot occur without an examination of life and morals which may be more fitting in and by large assemblies, this is entrusted to the *ecclesiastical gathering of the elders*.[48]

971. The stages of excommunication were long ago among the Hebrews *reproof*,[49] *separation*,[50] and *anathematizing*,[51] which are equally observed and taught by Christ and the apostles with clarity and plainness in the church regarding those who sin publicly and who do not wish to make confession for their crime by *public penitence*.[52]

972. This power is usually described as *binding* and *loosing*, and also by the term *keys of the kingdom of heaven*, and certainly not unfittingly. But it ought to be noted by this *expression*[53] that when it was used by Christ, it admits a particular explanation which does not vary too much from the ordinary.[54]

973. In the exercise of excommunication and in the admission of penitence, it must be most prudently analyzed. It ought chiefly to be probed carefully, lest too much *favoritism*[55] appear which cannot originate anywhere else than an affection which should be far removed.[56]

974. This excommunication—insofar as it is called a bare declaration of the church that some member is unworthy of its communion and ought to be regarded as such by the brothers so that he may be ashamed and might come to his senses—pertains to the whole church, and it follows ecclesiastical gatherings which

---

48. Cf. *Doctrina*, 25.44–45.
49. נזיפה.
50. נדוי.
51. חרם.
52. Matthew 18:15–20. *Doctrina*, 25.46.
53. φρασεις.
54. *Doctrina*, 25.47.
55. προσωπολημψία.
56. *Doctrina*, 25.48.

have been appointed by the church, the sole purpose of which is and can be to give this declaration.[57]

975. But it is the duty of pious *magistrates*, who are nourished by the church, to care for its authority, and to cherish it in every way, lest this discipline be denied and become worthless.[58]

976. There are also many other duties and obligations concerning holy matters regarding how far the *church* relates to the *state*, and how those things conducted in the church pertain to the public security of every city whose care has been entrusted to them. This singular rule of judging must be employed in various cases: *what* and *how much* power in the church is conceded to the magistrates.[59]

977. To the brotherhood and communion of various assemblies developed among themselves pertains *classes* and *synods*, which are provincial, national, and ecumenical. In these a matter is conducted, and in this way their advantage is sufficiently evident.[60]

978. Gatherings of this kind are most useful and are very necessary for preserving the purity of doctrine. But one thing ought to be observed, that a matter be not conducted there by *authority* but by *arguments* without prejudice, taken from the word of Christ and the apostles. The authority of the church is nothing without Christ.[61]

Various States of the Church in the World: Afflictions, Its Corruption, and Antichrist

979. This church, or the multitude of the faithful, dispersed throughout the whole world on which it has lived thus far, will not always continue in this same state in the world, but it is experiencing

---

57. *Doctrina*, 25.49.
58. *Doctrina*, 25.50.
59. *Doctrina*, 25.51.
60. *Doctrina*, 25.52.
61. *Doctrina*, 25.53.

various changes and undertaking diverse appearances of which the first and last are most glorious and most beautiful.[62]

980. For it was *clearly*[63] foretold by the Holy Spirit that the church would sustain many afflictions, and next, that eminent corruption of *doctrine* and *morals* would arise in the church, which is plainly against the institution of Christ.[64]

981. The multitude, which constitutes the corrupt church along with its rulers, is described as *a twofold beast*, the highest ruler as the *image of a beast, the adversary*,[65] and *antichrist*,[66] even if this last term was meant more generally. Elsewhere, the *rulers* are depicted as another multitude by the *unfaithful woman of the beast* which had *seven heads* and *ten horns, Babylon, Sodom*, and as *spiritual Egypt*.[67]

982. Whoever does not clearly see that the multitude represented by these symbols is that which calls itself the *Roman Catholic Church* as it is now and was before this present age with its rulers and its highest ruler, the Roman pope, is either ignorant of the Scriptures or has been blinded by divine judgment. Let us hold fast to this confession.[68]

983. The characteristics of this multitude in the Scriptures are for this reason described and depicted so that no one who pays attention to them is able to avoid them: corruption of doctrine, idolatry, intolerable pride, confusion of languages, raising of a name, a great multitude dispersed throughout the whole world, captivity of the people of God (which is why it is called Babylon), grave tyranny, affliction, and enemies from which the faithful

---

62. *Doctrina*, 25.54.
63. ῥητῶς.
64. *Doctrina*, 25.55.
65. ἀντικέιμενον.
66. ἀντίκριστον. 2 Thessalonians 1:8–10; 1 John 4:3; Revelation 13:1, 11, 14.
67. Revelation 11:8; 17:3–5. *Doctrina*, 25.56.
68. Cf. *Doctrina*, 25.57.

ought to be freed through various plagues (which is why it is compared with Egypt), the highest corruption of morals, which is why it is compared with Sodom.[69]

984. The kingdom of this beast endures for 1,260 days, or 42 months, but when these are supposed to begin is uncertain. It deserves the serious consideration whether the greater part of these years (which some believe to have already passed) yet remains.[70]

985. Those who desire to drag out prophecies elsewhere, from themselves and the Holy Scriptures which pertain to this, thrust onto themselves a manifest power as has been known in the world. No wisdom of the flesh prevails against God.[71]

986. This corruption of the church—this affliction and persecution of the church from within, which must be regarded among the chief efforts of Satan—has occurred in various stages, through long periods, through crafty arts and *schemes*[72] in which the wisdom of the flesh, which has the devil as its author, is clearly seen by the eye.[73]

987. To this point, they have made distinctions between the *bishops* and the *elders*, and then between bishops, archbishops, and patriarchs, when the church began to be formed according to the form and direction of the state. They have crafted heresies on account of which synods had to be convened, on which occasion disputes arose *about the seat of authority*.[74] They have made quarrels about the primacy of the Roman and Constantinopolitan patriarchs. They have made confession of the name of the universal bishop, made good by the seal of the emperor. They have made various changes which the West put to test. They have

---

69. *Doctrina*, 25.58.
70. *Doctrina*, 25.59.
71. *Doctrina*, 25.60.
72. μεθοδείας.
73. *Doctrina*, 25.61.
74. περί τῆς πρωτοκαθεδρίας.

made gifts to the emperors, chiefly to Charlemagne the Great.[75] Eminent ignorance and superstition through the monks, priests, and frequent ravaging maintained among the people. They have made insatiable flattery and greed of the popes joined with carnal desire. They have created a fictitious infallibility and power for the pope, and many other things.[76]

988. Such heaps have been built up upon most false principles: first, that Peter was the Roman bishop; second, that he was the head and primate of the apostles and of the whole church; finally, that the Roman popes are his successors by the same power and authority. All three of these are most false.[77]

989. Now, even if the first two are true (though they are not), the third consequence is most false—that the Roman popes succeed Peter with the same authority and power.[78]

990. Indeed, it is far more probable that Peter was never in Rome.[79]

991. Now, just as this whole edifice was not built up without the providence of the Lord Christ, so it is not able to be built up except according to the singular demonstration of His power and righteousness.[80]

992. Therefore, it is certain for our consolation (even if there is no doubt that the church must for a long while undergo even greater persecutions than it has experienced thus far) that Rome and the Roman Catholic Church will perish, and that the Roman pope will be deprived of his authority and power and become exposed

---

75. Charlemagne (748–814) was an emperor of the Holy Roman Empire. The "gift" of which Vitringa here speaks is the crowning of Charlemagne as emperor by Pope Leo III in 800 AD.

76. *Doctrina,* 25.62.

77. *Doctrina,* 25.63–64.

78. *Doctrina,* 25.65.

79. Cf. *Doctrina,* 25.66.

80. *Doctrina,* 25.67.

to the hissing of all. This is clearly foretold and foreshadowed by Babylon, Sodom, Egypt, and Antiochus Epiphanes.[81]

993. There are two reasons for this: first, the Word of God and the clear preaching of the truth; second, the extraordinary judgments which are administered through the Eastern kings, and through those kings who thus far have placed their own necks under a yoke. These things are clearly in Scripture.[82]

994. When the glory of our King will be manifested, *the fullness of the gentiles shall come* without a doubt, and *all of Israel will be saved.*[83] How happy shall the eyes be which see it![84]

995. And the rest of the enemies of the church will be so conquered that the course of the gospel will not perish. And the *flash of lightning*[85] shall certainly not be able to be stopped.[86]

996. Who doubts that at this time the Spirit of God in the church will be the author of the most abundant knowledge and holiness?[87]

997. Whether the Jews shall return to their own land and there be constituted as a national state is doubtful. We surely believe so because: first, the land of Canaan at that time will be *accursed*[88] as it has been up till now and inhabited in this way; second, it shall not be *more holy* than the other parts of the earth; and finally, neither can inhabitance and possession of the land of Canaan be understood as a privilege of the Jews in light of the gentiles.[89]

---

81. *Doctrina*, 25.68. Vitringa here refers to Antiochus IV who reigned from 175 to 164 BC, as well as Daniel 11:21–35 as a prophecy of Antiochus's actions.

82. *Doctrina*, 25.69.

83. Romans 11:25–26.

84. *Doctrina*, 25.70.

85. Matthew 24:27.

86. *Doctrina*, 25.71.

87. *Doctrina*, 25.72.

88. ἀνάθεμα.

89. *Doctrina*, 25.73.

998. Now it seems doubtful that the church, after it has existed long enough, shall be taken over by idleness and carnal security, and it is also doubtful that there will be new enemies. Then indeed the end will burst open when our Lord and King Jesus will be revealed on the clouds of heaven! Blessed is he to whom it is granted by his King and Judge to meet Him with a good conscience![90]

999. What follows this? Eternal happiness, and eternal punishment of which kind has not been specifically revealed. *Who shall live when He ordains it?*[91]

1000. This is the application: *by denying impiety and worldly lusts, let us live temperately, justly, and piously in the present age, expecting that blessed hope and that brilliant advent of the glory of our great God and Savior, Jesus Christ.*[92]

Αὐτῷ δόξα
To Him be the Glory

---

90. *Doctrina*, 25.74.
91. מי יחיה משומו. Numbers 24:23. *Doctrina*, 25.75.
92. Titus 2:12–13. *Doctrina*, 25.76. Vitringa's translation.

Bibliography

Primary Sources

Ames, William. *The Marrow of Theology: Translated from Latin with an Introduction by John Dykstra Eusden*. Translated by John D. Eusden. Grand Rapids: Baker Books, 1997.

———. *Medulla S. S. Theologiae, ex Sacris Literis, earumque, Interpretibus, Extracta, & Methodice Disposita*. 3rd ed. London: Robertus Allattus, 1629.

Cloppenburg, Johannes. *Exercitationes super Locos Communes Theologicos: Quibus Praecipui Religionis Christianae Articuli Lucide Explicantur, ac ab Adversariorum Corruptelis Nervose Vindicantur*. Franeker: Idzardus Balck, 1563.

Cocceius, Johannes. "Aphorismi per Universam Theologiam Breviores." Vol. 7 of *Opera*. Amsterdam: P. & J. Blaev, 1701.

———. "Commentarius in Epistolas Pauli ad Romanos, Corinthios, Galatas, Ephesios & Philippenses." Vol. 5 of *Opera*. Amsterdam: P. & J. Blaev, 1701.

———. "Disputatio IV: De Origine Boni." Vol. 7 of *Opera*. Amsterdam: P. & J. Blaev, 1701.

———. *The Doctrine of the Covenant and Testament of God*. Translated by Casey Carmichael. Classic Reformed Theology, Volume 3. Grand Rapids: Reformation Heritage Books, 2016.

———. *Philosophia S. Scripturae Interpres: Exercitatio Paradoxa, in qua, Veram Philosophiam Infallibilem S. Literas Interpretandi Normam esse, Apodictice Demonstratur*. Eleutheropoli, 1666.

———. *Summa Theologiae Ex Scripturis Repetita*. Amsterdam: Joannes Ravesteinius, 1665.

Maccovius, Johannes. *Loci Communes Theologici*. Edited by Nicolaus Arnoldi. Amsterdam: Daniel Elsevirius, 1658.

Marckius, Johannes. *Compendium Theologiae Christianae Didactico Elencticum: Immixtis Problematibus Plurimis & Quaestionibus Recentioribus Adauctum*. Amsterdam: Borstius, 1690.

Polanus, Amandus. *Syntagma Theologiae Christianae ab Amando Polano a Polandsdorf iuxta Leges Ordinis Methodici Conformatum atque in Libros Decem Tributum*. 10 vols. Hanau: Johannes Aubrius, 1609.

Röell, Herman Alexander. *Commentarius in Principium Epistolae ad Ephesios. Quibus etiam Continetur Demonstratio Divinitatis Scriptorum Pauli*. Amsterdam: Jacobus Orstius, 1715.

———. *Dissertatio de Religione Rationali*. 4th ed. Franeker: Johannes Gyselaar, 1700.

———. *Dissertationes Philosophicae de Theologia Naturali II. De Ideis Innatis Una*. Franeker: Johannes Georgius Böttiger, 1729.

———. *Dissertationes Philosophicae de Theologia Naturali II: De Ideis Innatis Una, Cl. Gerardi de Vries, Diatribae Opposita*. Frankfurt and Leipzig: Georgius Böttiger, 1729.

———. *Dissertatio Theologica Altera de Generatione Filii, et Morte Fidelium Temporali, Opposita Epilogo Clarissimi Viri Campegii Vitringa*. Franeker: Johannes Gyselaar, 1690.

———. *Dissertatio Theologica de Generatione Filii, et Morte Fidelium Temporali, qua Suas de iis Theses Plenius Explicat, & contra Clarissimi Viri Campegii Vitringa Objectiones Defendit*. Franeker: Johannes Gyselaar, 1689.

———. *Explicatio Catecheseos Heidelbergensis: Opus Postumum*. 4th ed. Utrecht: Gysbertus van Paddenburg, 1728.

———. *Kort en Eenvoudig Berigt van het Verschil over de Geboorte des Soons, en Tydelicke Dood der Geloovige*. Amsterdam: Gerardus Borstius, 1691.

Ursinus, Zacharias. *The Commentary of Dr. Zacharias Ursinus on the Heidelberg Catechism*. Translated by Rev. G. W. Williard. 2nd ed. Columbus: Scott and Bascom, 1852.

van Mastricht, Peter. *Theoretical-Practical Theology*. Translated by Todd Rester, 4 vols. Grand Rapids: Reformation Heritage Books, 2018–2023.

———. *Theoretico-practica theologia: qua, per capita theologica, pars dogmatica, elenchtica et practica, perpetua sumbibasei conjugantur; præcedunt in usum operis, paraleipomena, seu sceleton de optima concionandi methodo.* 2 vols. Amsterdam: Henricus et Vidua Theodorus Boom, 1682–87.

Vitringa, Campegius. *Anakrisis Apocalypsios Joannis Apostoli qua in Veras Interpretandae ejus Hypotheses Diligenter Inquiritur; & ex iisdem Interpretatio Facta, Certis Historiarum Monumentis Confirmatur atque Illustratur.* Amsterdam: Henricus Strickius, 1719.

———. *Animadversiones ad Methodum Holiliarum Ecclesiasticarum rite Instituendarm.* Franeker: Henricus Halma, 1721.

———. *Aphorismi, Quibus Fundamenta Sanctae Theologiae Comprehenduntur.* Franeker: Johannes Gyselaar, 1688.

———. "Appendix 1. De Scriptura Sancta, Altero Theologiae Principio." In *Wrestling with Isaiah: The Exegetical Methodology of Campegius Vitringa (1659–1722)*, translated by Charles K. Telfer, 229–37. Göttingen: Vandenhoeck & Ruprecht, 2016.

———. *Commentarii ad Librum Prophetiarum Zechariae, Quae Supersunt cum Prolegomenis, Cura et Sudio Campegii Vitringa.* Edited by Herman Venema. Leeuwarden: Tobias van Dessel, 1734.

———. *Commentarius ad Canticum Mosis Deut. XXXII. Cum Prolegomenis Cura et Sudio Campegii Vitringa.* Edited by Herman Venema. Harlingen: Folkert Jansz van der Plaats, 1734.

———. *Commentarius in Jesaiam, Quo Sensus Orationis ejus sedulo Investigatur; in Veras Visorum Interpretandorum Hypotheses Inquiritur, & ex iisdem Facta Interpretatio Antiquae Historiae Monumentis Confirmatur Atque Illustratur: Cum Prolegomenis.* Editio Nova. Vol. 1. Basel: Joannes Rodolph, 1732.

———. *Commentarius in Jesaiam, Quo Sensus Orationis ejus sedulo Investigatur; in Veras Visorum Interpretandorum Hypotheses Inquiritur, & ex iisdem Facta Interpretatio Antiquae Historiae Monumentis Confirmatur Atque Illustratur: Cum Prolegomenis.* Vol. 2. Herborn: Johan. Nicolai Andreae, 1722.

————. *De Synagoga Vetere Libri Tres: Quibus tum De Nominibus, Structura, Origine, Praefectis, Ministris, & Sacris Synagogarum, Agitur; tum Praecipue, Formam Regiminis & Ministerii Earum in Ecclesiam Christianam Translatam esse, Demonstratur: Cum Prolegomenis.* Franeker: Johannes Gyzelaar, 1696.

————. *De Theologia Symbolica Liber Posthumus: Accedit Index Omnium Lacorum S. Scripturae, Quae in Hoc Opusculo Explicantur.* Guilielmus Croon., 1726.

————. *Disputatio Theologica de Argumento Psalmi Secundi, Secunda.* Leiden: Johannes Elsevirius, 1679.

————. *Disputatio Theologica Inauguralis de Genuino Sensus Versu VII Psalmi Secundi.* Leiden: Johannes Elsevirius, 1679.

————. *Doctrina Christianae Religionis: Per Aphorismos Summatim Descripta.* Edited by Martin Vitringa. 6th ed. 9 vols. Arnhem: Joannes Henricus Möelemann, 1761–1786.

————. *Epilogus Disputationis, Non Ita Pridem a Se Habitae, De Generatione Filii, et Morte Fidelium Temporali; In Quo Fidem Ecclesiae de His Articulis Porro Adstruit ex Verbo Dei, eandemque Tuetur contra Dissertationem, Illi Novissime Oppositam.* Franeker: Johannes Gyselaar, 1689.

————. *Hypotyposis Historiae et Chronologiae Sacrae.* Bovardia: Joh. Bernhard. Hartung., 1722.

————. *Hypotyposis Theologiae Elencticae, Graviores Exhibens Controversias, Quae Super Christianae Religionis Doctrina Ecclesiae Reformatae cum Diversis ejusdem Sectis Intercedunt.* Franeker: Franciscus Halama, 1702.

————. *Korte Schets van de Christelyke Zeden-Leere Ofte van het Geestelyk Leven Ende Desselfs Eigenschappen.* 1st ed. n.p.: n.p., 1696.

————. *Korte Schets van de Christelyke Zeden-Leere Ofte van het Geestelyk Leven Ende Desselfs Eigenschappen.* 3rd ed. Amsterdam: Hendrik Strik, 1717.

————. *Korte Stellingen, in Welke Vervat Worden de Grondstukken van de Christelyke Leere.* 5th ed. Rotterdam: Jan Daniel Beman, 1736.

————. "On the Interpretation of Prophecy." *The Interpreter* 4 (1835): 153–76.

————. *Oratio de Amore Veritatis Dicta in Templo Academico.* Franeker: Johannes Gyselaar, 1683.

————. *Oratio de Synodis, earumque Utilitate, Necessitate, Auctoritate.* Franeker: Franciscus Halama, 1706.

————. *Oratio Funebris in Memoriam Henr. Philiponei de Hautecour.* Franeker, 1716.

————. *Oratio Funebris, Recitata in Exsequiis Amplissimi et Gravissimi Viri, Ulrichi Huber, Supremae Frisiorum Curiae Ex-Senatoris, Jurisconsulti Eruditissimi ac Celeberrimi.* Franeker: Leondardus Strickius, 1700.

————. *Rechte Verstant van den Tempel Ezechiels Verdeedigt en Bevestigt.* Haarlem, 1693.

————. *Sacrarum Observationum.* 6 vols. Franeker: Johannes Gyselaar; Wibius Bleck, 1689–1708.

————. *The Spiritual Life.* Translated by Charles K. Telfer. Grand Rapids: Reformation Heritage Books, 2018.

————. *The Synagogue and the Church, Being an Attempt to Show, That the Government, Ministers, and Services of the Church, Were Derived from Those of the Synagogue, Condensed from the Original Latin Work of Vitringa.* Translated by Joshua L. Bernard. London: B. Fellowes, 1842.

————. *Typus Doctrinae Propheticae.* Bovardia: Joh. Bernhard. Hartung., 1722.

————. *Typus Theologiae Practicae sive de Vita Spirituali, ejusque Affectionibus, Commentatio.* Franeker: Wibius Bleck, 1716.

————. *Verklaringe en Heilige Bedenkingen over de Verborgene Sin der Miraculen van Jesus Christus.* Edited by Herman Venema. Franeker: Wibius Bleck, 1725.

————. *Verklaringe Over de Agt Eerste Capittelen van de Brief Pauli aan de Romeinen, Voormaals Opgegeven in de Latijnsche Tale aan de Voedsterlingen van de Academie tot Franeker, Door den Hoogwaardigen en Zeer Vermaarden Heer Campegius Vitringa, In Leven Hoogleeraar in de Heilige Godgeleertheit en Kerkelijke Gechiedenissen, en nu in het Nederduitsch Vertaalt.* Franeker: Wibius Bleck, 1729.

Vitringa, Campegius, and Wilhelmus Stamhorst. *Theses Controversae super Doctrina Christianae Religionis Pars I. Quam, Ope Divinae Gratiae, sub Praesidio Campegii Vitringa.* Franeker: Franciscus Halma, 1701.

Witsius, Herman. *De Oeconomia Foederum Dei cum Hominibus Libri Quatuor.* Leeuwarden: Jacob Hagenaar, 1677.

————. *The Economy of the Covenants between God and Man.* Translated by William Crookshank. 2 vols. Edinburgh: Thomas Turnbull, 1803. Reprint, Grand Rapids: Reformation Heritage Books, 2010.

————. *An Essay on the Use and Abuse of Reason in Matters of Religion.* Translated by John Carter. Norwich: Crouse, Stevenson, and Matchett, 1795.

————. *Exercitationes Sacrae in Symbolum Quod Apostolorum Dicitur.* 3rd ed. Amsterdam: Joannes Wolters, 1697.

————. "Exercitatio XVII: Usu et Abusu Rationis circa Mysteria Fidei." In *Miscellaneorum Sacrorum,* 582–98. Herborn: Johannes Nicolai Andreae, 1712.

————. *Sacred Dissertations: On What Is Commonly Called the Apostles' Creed.* Translated by Donald Fraser. Vol. 1. Edinburgh: A. Fullerton, 1823.

Secondary Sources

Alexander, Joseph A. *The Prophecies of Isaiah.* New and Revised. 2 vols. New York: Charles Scribner & Co., 1870.

Allen, Michael, and Scott Swain, eds. *The Oxford Handbook of Reformed Theology.* Oxford: Oxford University Press, 2020.

Bauch, Herman. *Die Lehre vom Wirken des Heiligen Geistes im Frühpietismus.* Hamburg-Bergstedt: Herbert Reich, 1974.

Baugus, Bruce P. "Covenant Theology in the Dutch Reformed Tradition." In *Covenant Theology: Biblical, Theological, and Historical Perspectives,* edited by Guy Prentiss Waters, J. Nicholas Reid, and John R. Muether, 379–400. Wheaton, IL: Crossway, 2020.

Bavinck, Herman. *Reformed Dogmatics.* Edited by John Bolt. Translated by John Vriend. 4 vols. Grand Rapids: Baker Academic, 2003.

Boeles, W. B. S. *Frieslands Hoogeschool en het Rijks Athenaeum te Franeker.* 2 vols. Leeuwarden: H. Kuipers, 1878.

Bolt, John. "The Bavinck Recipe for Theological Cake." *Calvin Theological Journal* 45, no. 1 (April 2010): 11–17.

Büsching, M. Anton Friedrich. "The Life and Work of Campegius Vitringa Sr. (1659–1722)." *The Spiritual Life.* Translated by Charles K. Telfer. Grand Rapids: Reformation Heritage Books, 2019.

Buß, Harro. "Johannes Wübbena." In *Biographisches Lexikon für Ostfriesland*, edited by Martin Tielke, 3:441–43. Aurich: Ostfriesische Landschaft, 2001.

Childs, Brevard S. "Hermeneutical Reflections on Campegius Vitringa, Eighteenth-Century Interpreter of Isaiah." In *In Search of True Wisdom: Essays in Old Testament Interpretation in Honour of Ronald E. Clements*, edited by Edward Ball, 89–98. U.K.: Sheffield Academic Press, 1999.

Diestel, Ludwig. *Geschichte des Alten Testamentes in der Christlichen Kirche*. Jena: Mauke, 1869.

Dunkel, Johann Gottlob Wilhelm. "Campegius Vitringa." Vol. 2 of *Historisch-Kritische Nachrichten von Verstorbenen Gelehrten und deren Schriften*. Hildesheim: Georg Olms, 1968.

Ellis, Brannon. *Calvin, Classical Trinitarianism, and the Aseity of the Son*. Oxford: Oxford University Press, 2012.

Fensham, F. C. "Johannes Coccejus en Campegius Viringa Se Beginsels Vir die Uitleg van Jesaja en die Kaap." *Skrif en Kerk* 8.2 (1987): 170–81.

Fesko, J. V. *Adam and the Covenant of Works*. Ross-shire: Christian Focus Publications, 2021.

———. *The Covenant of Works: The Origins, Development, and Reception of the Doctrine*. Oxford Studies in Historical Theology. New York: Oxford University Press, 2020.

———. "The Doctrine of Scripture in Reformed Orthodoxy." In *A Companion to Reformed Orthodoxy*. Brill's Companions to the Christian Tradition 40, edited by Herman J. Selderhuis, 429–64. Leiden: Brill, 2013.

Gesenius, Wilhelm. *Commentar über Jesaia*. Vol. 1. Leipzig: F. C. W. Vogel, 1821.

Gill, John. *An Exposition of the Old Testament*. 4 vols. London: W. Clowes, 1810.

Israel, Jonathan I. *The Dutch Republic: Its Rise, Greatness, and Fall: 1477–1806*. The Oxford History of Early Modern Europe. Oxford: Clarendon Press, 1998.

———. *Radical Enlightenment: Philosophy and the Making of Modernity, 1650–1750*. Oxford: Oxford University Press, 2001.

Kautsch, Emil Friedrich. "Vitringa, Campegius." In *The New Schaff-Herzog Encyclopedia of Religious Knowledge*, edited by Samuel Macauley Jackson. Vol. 12. New York: Funk and Wagnalls, 1912.

Keil, Carl Friedrich, and Franz Delitzsch. *Isaiah*. Biblical Commentary on the Old Testament 26. London: T&T Clark, 1892.

Lee, Brian J. "The Covenant Terminology of Johannes Cocceius: The Use of Foedus, Pactum, and Testamentum in a Mature Federal Theologian." *Mid-America Journal of Theology* 14 (2003): 11–36.

———. *Johannes Cocceius and the Exegetical Roots of Federal Theology: Reformation Developments in the Interpretation of Hebrews 7–10*. Reformed Historical Theology 7. Göttingen: Vandenhoeck & Ruprecht, 2009.

Lehner, Ulrich L., Richard A. Muller, and A. C. Roeber, eds. *The Oxford Handbook of Early Modern Theology, 1600–1800*. New York: Oxford University Press, 2016.

Muller, Richard A. *After Calvin: Studies in the Development of a Theological Tradition*. Oxford Studies in Historical Theology. Oxford: Oxford University Press, 2003.

———. *Dictionary of Latin and Greek Theological Terms: Drawn Principally from Protestant Scholastic Theology*. 2nd ed. Grand Rapids: Baker Academic, 2017.

———. Foreword to *The Spiritual Life*, by Campegius Vitringa, xi–xiv. Translated by Charles K. Telfer. Grand Rapids: Reformation Heritage Books, 2019.

———. *Post-Reformation Reformed Dogmatics: The Rise and Development of Reformed Orthodoxy, ca. 1520–1725*. 2nd ed. 4 vols. Grand Rapids: Baker Academic, 2003.

Nimmo, Paul T., and David Fergusson, eds. *The Cambridge Companion to Reformed Theology*. Cambridge Companions to Religion. Cambridge: Cambridge University Press, 2016.

Ortlund Jr., Raymond C. "John Gill as Interpreter of the Old Testament." In *The Life and Thought of John Gill (1697–1771): A Tercentennial Appreciation*, edited by Michael A. G. Haykin, 93–111. Studies in the History of Christian Thought 77. Leiden: Brill, 1997.

Postma, Ferenc. "Campegius Vitringa Professzor." *Könyv és Könyvtár* 20 (1998): 151–61.

Rosenmüller, Ernst Friedrich Karl. *Scholia in Vetus Testamentum*. 16 vols. Leipzig: Joh. Ambros. Barthius, 1808.

Schrenk, G. *Gottesreich und Bund im Alteren Protestantismus, Vornehmlich bei Johannes Cocceius*. Gütersloh, 1923.

Selderhuis, H. J., ed. *A Companion to Reformed Orthodoxy*. Brill's Companions to the Christian Tradition 40. Boston: Brill, 2013.

———, ed. *Handbook of Dutch Church History*. Göttingen: Vandenhoeck & Ruprecht, 2014.

Singer, Isiodore. "Campegius Vitringa, the Elder." Vol. 12 of *The Jewish Encyclopedia*. New York: Funk and Wagnalls, 1906.

Strehle, Stephen. *Calvinism, Federalism, and Scholasticism: A Study of the Reformed Doctrine of Covenant*. Bern: P. Lang, 1988.

Telfer, Charles K. "Campegius Vitringa (1659–1722): A Biblical Theologian at the Turn of the Eighteenth Century." In *Biblical Theology: Past, Present, and Future*, edited by Carey Walsh and Mark W. Elliot, 18–30. Eugene, OR: Cascade, 2016.

———. "Campegius Vitringa, Sr. Praefatio ad Lectorem and De Interpretatione Prophetiarum." In *Handbuch der Bibelhermeneutiken*, 433–48. Boston: Walter de Gruyter GmbH, 2016.

———. "'The Holy Exercises of Piety' in the Canons of Dort and in Campegius Vitringa (1659–1722)." In *The Synod of Dort: Historical, Theological, and Experiential Perspectives*, edited by Joel R. Beeke and Martin I. Klauber, 163–84. Göttingen: Vandenhoeck & Ruprecht, 2020.

———. *Wrestling with Isaiah: The Exegetical Methodology of Campegius Vitringa (1659–1722)*. Reformed Historical Theology 38. Göttingen: Vandenhoeck & Ruprecht, 2016.

van Asselt, Willem J. "Expromissio or Fideiussio?: A Seventeenth-Century Theological Debate between Voetians and Cocceians about the Nature of Christ's Suretyship in Salvation History." *Mid-America Journal of Theology* 14 (2003): 37–57.

———. *The Federal Theology of Johannes Cocceius (1603–1669)*. Studies in the History of Christian Thought 100. Leiden: Brill, 2001.

———. *Introduction to Reformed Scholasticism*. Translated by Albert Gootjes. Reformed Historical-Theological Studies. Grand Rapids: Reformation Heritage Books, 2011.

———. "Structural Elements in the Eschatology of Johannes Cocceius." *Calvin Theological Journal* 35.1 (2000): 76–104.

van den Belt, Henk. *The Authority of Scripture in Reformed Theology: Truth and Trust.* Studies in Reformed Theology 17. Leiden: Brill, 2008.

———. "Theology in Franeker and Leiden in the Eighteenth Century." In *Religious Currents and Cross-Currents: Essays on Early Modern Protestantism and the Protestant Enlightenment.* Studies in the History of Christian Thought 45, edited by Heiko A. Oberman, 253–67. Leiden: Brill, 1999.

van der Sleen, J. J. "Johannes Coccejus en Campegius Vitringa: Een Vergelijking van hun Theologie op Hoofdpunten." MA Thesis, University of Utrecht, 2001.

van der Wall, Ernestine. "Between Grotius and Cocceius: The 'Theologia Prophetica' of Campegius Vitringa (1659–1722)." In *Hugo Grotius, Theologian*, edited by G. H. M. Meyjes, Henk J. M. Nellen, and Edwin Rabbie, 195–215. Leiden: Brill, 1994.

van Heel, Willem Frederik Caspar Johannes. "Campegius Vitringa Sr. als Godgeleerde beschouwd." PhD Diss., 1865.

van Hoorn, H. J. E. *Disquisitio Historico-Dogmatica exponens Röelli Litem de Aeterna Generatione Filii Dei a Patre.* Utrecht: Uiterweer & Soc., 1856.

van Sluis, Jacob. "Campegius Vitringa (1659–1722)." In *Encyclopedie Nadere Reformatie: II: Biografieën L–Z.* Edited by W. J. op 't Hof, 462–65. Kampen: Groot Goudriaan, Uitgeverij, 2016.

———. *Herman Alexander Röell.* Leeuwarden: Fryske Akad., 1988.

———. *The Library of Franeker University in Context, 1585–1843.* Library of the Written Word 81. Leiden: Brill, 2020.

Vos, Antonie. "Reformed Orthodoxy in the Netherlands." In *A Companion to Reformed Orthodoxy.* Brill's Companions to the Christian Tradition 40, edited by Herman J. Selderhuis, 121–76. Leiden: Brill, 2013.

Witteveen, Klaas Marten. "Campegius Vitringa und die Prophetische Theologie." *Zwingliana* 19.2 (1993): 343–59.